J03

Concepts and the
Structure of Memory

SYMPOSIUM ON COGNITION, 2nd,
c.
Carnegie Institute of Technology, 1966

Concepts and the
Structure of Memory

Editor
BENJAMIN KLEINMUNTZ
Department of Psychology
Carnegie Institute of Technology
Pittsburgh, Pennsylvania

Contributors for this Volume

LYLE E. BOURNE, University of Colorado
CHARLES N. COFER, The Pennsylvania State University
LEE W. GREGG, Carnegie Institute of Technology
JAMES G. HOLLAND, University of Pittsburgh
EARL B. HUNT, University of Washington
EDWIN MARTIN, The University of Michigan
ARTHUR W. MELTON, The University of Michigan
BENNET B. MURDOCK, Jr., University of Toronto
ALLEN NEWELL, Carnegie Institute of Technology
CALVIN F. NODINE, Carnegie Institute of Technology
LLOYD R. PETERSON, Indiana University
HERBERT A. SIMON, Carnegie Institute of Technology

*The Second of an annual series of symposia in the
area of cognition under the sponsorship of
Carnegie Institute of Technology*

JOHN WILEY & SONS, INC.
New York · London · Sydney

Dedicated in Fond Memory of
Gordon Ierardi

Preface

The papers presented at the Second Annual Symposium on Cognition, held at the Carnegie Institute of Technology on April 7 and 8, 1966, comprise the major portion of this volume. The remainder of the book consists of specially prepared chapters and added materials to enhance its format. In keeping with the principle that each annual symposium for the next several years concentrate on an area conveniently subsumed under "cognition," this year's announced topic was concept attainment and the structure of memory. The choice of this timely area enabled us to attract outstanding contributors. The reception given these scientists and their papers was indeed impressive.

The format and subject matter of the symposium presentations were as follows: On the morning of April 7, Lyle E. Bourne and Edwin Martin presented their papers, and these were discussed by James G. Holland. Bourne's presentation (Chapter 1), which was data-oriented rather than theoretical, contained a summary of a set of five studies. The rationale for conducting these experiments came largely from Earl B. Hunt's (1962) cogent analysis of concept learning. The research reported by Bourne concentrated mainly on attempts to investigate how humans learn and use conceptual rules. Accordingly he varied both the physical dimensions of concepts to be learned and the rules governing their interrelationships. His findings, somewhat tempered by the modesty of this energetic but humble investigator, provide a reasonable beginning and a basis from which a more general, scientific understanding of the complex process of thought and behavior that are involved in concept attainment can be achieved.

In contrast to Bourne's almost atheoretic approach, Edwin

Martin's presentation (Chapter 2), which was highly critical of existing formulations of concept attainment, was cast almost entirely within the Hullian hypothetico-deductive framework. Martin's analysis of the origins of conceptual behavior relies heavily on inhibition as an explanatory construct. His was a closely-reasoned paper, which began with the assumption that all behavior is caused (e.g., "every response has a stimulus") and in stepwise fashion proceeded to the point where he defined "concept" as "a set of mutually induced response tendencies."

James G. Holland's critical comments (Chapter 3), not surprising in view of his well-documented association with B. F. Skinner, suggested that neither Bourne nor Martin is on the right track. He believes that both papers leave us without an adequate systematic development for the area of concept formation. His preference was for Martin's approach, since it is closer to a learning theory formulation of concept attainment. However, Holland went to some pains to show Martin's theory to be wrong, and he rested his argument mainly on experiments which demonstrated that discriminations can be readily formed without Martin's central construct—inhibition.

The afternoon of April 7, began with a paper by Earl B. Hunt; this was followed by Lee W. Gregg's presentation and a discussion by Bennet B. Murdock. The first of these papers (Chapter 4) reported a series of studies in which several computer programs for concept learning were tested on five problems of varying complexity. Because these experiments were conducted within the framework of the study of rational thinking (e.g., versus the simulation of actual thinking), they are perhaps of greater importance for the field of artificial intelligence than for human concept learning. Hunt's position constitutes a shift in emphasis from the viewpoint he expressed in his earlier publications (Hunt, 1962), which essentially placed the human in the central role. However, Hunt did extrapolate from his data, and speculated about their implications for human concept learning.

Gregg's work reflected considerably greater concern with the human concept learner (Chapter 5). After describing a series of experiments in which he carefully controlled the subjects' antecedent concept learning histories and devised techniques for forcing these subjects to explicate their concept utilization rules, Gregg stipulated that concepts are nothing more than names for cohesive sequences of information processing. The implications of his findings for short-term memory center mainly around the notion that memory serves the function of providing "place-keepers"in human concept formation. An interesting implication of this assumption is that the number of place-keepers necessary for any concept learning task can set an upper limit on efficiency of performance.

Some of the background literature on concept learning is reviewed briefly in Bennet B. Murdock's discussion paper (Chapter 6). Readers who are not familiar with this literature may find that review helpful. Murdock's discussion of Gregg's and Hunt's papers was especially notable because he skillfully managed to intertwine their efforts within the context of existing literature in the field. He was less impressed by Gregg's presentation than by Hunt's, and found little rationale for introducing the computer as a model of the way subjects in an experiment *say* they learn concepts. Although cognizant that some results of artificial intelligence work has found support in experimental literature, Murdock nevertheless was led to the conclusion that the computer has not stimulated any new and insightful experiments and therefore that computer simulation has been largely unproductive. This view of the limited role of the computer, admittedly not original with Murdock and often expressed by proponents of the more traditional approaches to concept learning, was counterbalanced by Newell and Simon's comments in this volume's concluding chapter (Chapter 11; see especially the section called "Representation of Concepts in Memory").

On the morning of April 8, Lloyd R. Peterson and Charles N. Cofer delivered their presentations which were discussed by Arthur W. Melton. The first paper (Chapter 7), by a psychologist who is firmly associated in most minds with traditional work in short-term memory, was refreshingly surprising for its open-minded view of the information-processing approach. According to Peterson, "there is considerable evidence from the long history of verbal learning research that supports such an approach." Even more surprising, at least to me, was Peterson's efforts at computer simulation of the human search process in paired-associates learning. Unfortunately he was not completely successful in his attempts. Again the reader is referred to Newell and

Simon's concluding comments regarding the reasons why Peterson's computer program may have failed.

The topic of Cofer's scholarly paper concerned the influence of conceptual organization on the extent of retention in free recall (Chapter 8). He summarized a set of five experiments which he considered evidence consistent with the following views: (a) interitem associations are important as factors influencing amount recalled; (b) there is a link between list length and the serial position effect; and (c) contextual or conceptual factors are unimportant in recall of correct items.

Apparently Lloyd Peterson's paper touched a sensitive spot in Arthur W. Melton's associationist super structure, because Melton spent the better part of an hour (Chapter 9) examining Peterson's model. He commented rather favorably on Cofer's contribution, and then took issue with Peterson's need to invoke the "magic of cognitive organization" to account for storage and retrieval. More specifically, Melton pointed out that while Peterson has a great deal to say about the way in which the decision process operates on the store of available responses in memory, he has very little to say about what determines stimulus coding or how the variations in stimulus coding and response availability influence the decision process.

The conference was concluded on the afternoon of April 8 when the participants and our faculty and graduate students had an opportunity to communicate with one another. This session, which lasted three hours, added the informal but problem-oriented interaction so necessary for the conduct of symposia such as the present one. Although this post-conference session served a valuable educational function for both faculty and students, it became increasingly apparent that wide communication channels must be laid down between the traditional and information-processing approaches (see concluding comments in Murdock's chapter).

To provide readers of this volume with an integrated overview of the areas of concept attainment and memory, Allen Newell and Herbert A. Simon, both of whom were present at the symposium, have jointly written the concluding review chapter. It appears as Chapter 11 in this book and predictably it favors an information-processing approach to the study of such complex behavior as concept formation and

attainment. Their chapter, which reflects a thorough understanding of the methodological issues that must be resolved
prior to formulating a theory of concept formation, is completely enjoyable reading.

One chapter (Chapter 10) has been added to this book
which touches upon a facet of concept acquisition not covered
during the conference—namely, the role of temporal variables
in concept learning. This chapter by Calvin F. Nodine,
should be of special interest to readers who are concerned
with the finer points of some of the methodological issues that
arise in laboratory experiments on verbal learning.

The publication of this volume has been made possible by
grants from the Carnegie Corporation and the National
Science Foundation. Some of the time I spent in organizing the
symposium and editing this volume was supported in part by
a Public Health Service grant (GM 11734-03). Equally important, and fully as responsible for the success of the symposium
and the publication of this book, are the tangible and intangible
contributions of all the active participants of the conference
and my department colleagues. To these foundations and
persons I am duly grateful.

Thanks are also due to the Administration of Carnegie
Institute of Technology, especially to Dean Richard M. Cyert
whose cooperation in this venture has been unstinting. For her
part in handling administrative and secretarial details as well
as the many annoyances of conducting a symposium, Mrs.
Betty H. Boal deserves special mention. And to my wife
Dalia, I am as usual indebted for showing more than just a
wifely interest in my work.

In dedicating this book to the memory of Gordon Ierardi,
whose untimely death last year deprived psychology of a close
friend, I acknowledge the support and friendship he had so
enthusiastically given me at the outset of the first annual
symposium. His wisdom and warmth invariably left their
marks on all who were associated with him.

Benjamin Kleinmuntz,
Pittsburgh, Pennsylvania

Contents

CHAPTER 1

Lyle E. Bourne, Jr.
University of Colorado

LEARNING AND UTILIZATION
OF CONCEPTUAL RULES*

I shall begin with a banal observation: Real concepts take on a wide variety of forms. Real concepts differ both in their defining or relevant stimulus properties and, perhaps more generally, in the rules which specify relations between or among defining properties. While I doubt that many would disagree with these statements, they are not completely harmless. When one surveys the literature, he might get the impression that psychologists have a fairly narrow definition of concepts—most concepts seem to be nominal and nonprobabilistic classes of stimuli, usually geometrical designs, which are fully determined by one or at most two common (conjunctively-related) relevant attributes. Occasionally, something called the "verbal concept" is studied, but this too is defined typically on a single relevant and invariant feature such as a common associate or meaning of a set of words. The rich variety and full complexity of natural concepts and conceptual processes seem scarcely touched by contemporary research, including, I should hastily add, most experiments for which I have had some responsibility. Therefore, it is doubtless true that some interesting aspects of conceptual behavior have rarely, if ever, been studied and analyzed.

This paper is Publication No. 89 of the Institute of Behavioral Science, University of Colorado. Its preparation and much of the research herein reported was facilitated by grants MH-08315 from the National Institute of Mental Health, U. S. Public Health Service, and GB-3404 from the National Science Foundation.

The author is indebted to David Dodd, Donald Guy, and Nancy Wadsworth, who conducted Experiments III and IV, to R. C. Haygood, who supplied the raw data for Experiment V, and to Dodd, Guy, Haygood, Peder Johnson and Keith Davis for their critical comments on an earlier version of the manuscript.

1

While the limitations of our present research enterprise are readily apparent, the proper approach to expansion and breadth are not. I have no revolutionary methodology—one which removes the usual constraints yet preserves the accustomed rigor—to propose. However, out of an awareness and some concern for the problem, I have recently attempted to modify the more or less standard procedures for the study of seemingly neglected aspects of concept attainment. My aim in this paper is to report the results of this exploratory work.

GENERAL CONSIDERATIONS

Much of the rationale for these experiments comes from Hunt's (1962) analysis of concepts and human conceptual processes. Particularly important is his description of the rules or logical operators which define certain types or classes of concepts and the essential independence of the rule and the relevant stimulus properties of any particular concept. With respect to the latter point, we may note that the distinction between any two types of concepts, for example, conjunctive and disjunctive concepts, is totally indifferent to specific stimulus attributes and dependent only on how two (or more) attributes, x and y, are related. This analysis immediately raises questions about how human beings learn concepts based on various rules, to what extent the rules themselves are learned as generic principles, and the manner in which newly acquired rules are used to solve different conceptual problems.

Conceptual Rules

There are many rules for combining stimulus attributes and for forming classes of objects. Our work thus far has been limited to rules (described in detail by Hunt [1962] and by Neisser and Weene [1962]) for constructing nominal groups with, at most, two relevant attributes. To illustrate these rules, we consider first a well-defined, multi-dimensional stimulus population, such as a set of geometrical designs characterized by variations in color, shape, and perhaps several other dimensions. Suppose two attributes, each from a different dimension, say, redness and squareness, are arbitrarily designated as relevant attributes. A concept is realized whenever some specifiable relationship between these attributes results in a two-group partition of the entire stimulus population. Thus, a conjunctive relationship or rule produces a two-group partition consisting, on the one hand, of those stimuli which are both red and square (positive instances) and, on the other hand, of those which lack either one or both of these attributes (negative instances). A disjunctive rule yields positive instances which are red, square, or red and square and negative instances which are neither red nor square.

TABLE 1.1 Conceptual Rules Describing Binary Partitions of a Stimulus Population

	Basic Rule			Complementary Rule	
Name	Symbolic Description*	Verbal Description	Name	Symbolic Description	Verbal Description
Affirmation	R	All red patterns are examples of the concept	Negation	$\bar{R}$	All patterns which are not red are examples
Conjunction	$R \cap S$	All patterns which are red and square are examples	Alternative denial	$R\|S$ $[\bar{R}\cup\bar{S}]$	All patterns which are either not red or not square are examples
Inclusive disjunction	$R \cup S$	All patterns which are red or square or both are examples	Joint denial	$R\downarrow S$ $[\bar{R}\cap\bar{S}]$	All patterns which are neither red nor square are examples
Condition	$R \rightarrow S$ $[\bar{R}\cup S]$	If a pattern is red then it must be square to be an example	Exclusion	$R \cap \bar{S}$	All patterns which are red and not square are examples
Bicondition	$R \leftarrow S$ $[(R\cap S) \cup(\bar{R}\cap\bar{S})]$	Red patterns are examples if and only if they are squares	Exclusive disjunction	$R\overline{\cup} S$ $[(R\cap\bar{S}) \cup(\bar{R}\cap S)]$	All patterns which are red or square but not both are examples

*R and S stand for red and square (relevant attributes), respectively. Symbolic descriptions using only three basic operations, $\cap$, $\cup$, and negation, are given in brackets.

Of the 16 possible binary partitions of a stimulus population based on, at most, two relevant attributes, it may be shown
(Haygood and Bourne, 1965) that only 10 are unique and non-
trivial. Further, the remaining 10 fall into 5 pairs having the
property that any instance which is positive under one member
of a pair is negative under its complement. Each of the 10
partitions is determined by a rule for relating relevant attributes. Table 1.1 presents a verbal and symbolic description of
these complementary pairs.

Conceptual Tasks and Conceptual Behaviors

Attribute identification. Most studies of human conceptual
behavior, particularly the concept identification experiments
(e.g., Archer, Bourne, and Brown, 1955), have used tasks or
problems in which the primary requirement for the subject is
to discover and identify one or more relevant stimulus attributes. Typically, the experimental problem is preceded by
elaborate instructions and pretraining designed to familiarize
the subject with the general form of solution (rule) to be used.
Furthermore, the solution is usually based on a familiar conjunctive relationship of stimulus attributes. In this work, then,
the rule more or less constitutes a "given condition" of the
problem.   Once the unknown relevant attributes have been
identified, the problem is solved.

Attribute identification problems are, of course, not
necessarily limited to conjunctive solutions. In principle, if a
subject can in some sense be "given" an understanding of any
rule, it should be possible to study how he goes about identifying
the particular stimulus features which it relates.

Rule learning and rule utilization. Instead of describing
the rule which defines a concept and asking the subject to find
the attributes, suppose we name the attributes and require that
he determine how they are related. Here the subject's problem is to discover the appropriate rule. To the extent that
the rule is unfamiliar or is poorly understood, the task may
require original learning. Potentially, some evidence on rule
learning may be derived from an experimental paradigm
wherein the subject solves a series of problems each involving
a different, but "given" pair of relevant attributes and the

same rule. The necessary criterion of rule learning is fairly obvious. Once the subject solves a problem or a series of successive problems without error, that is, without misclassifying a single stimulus pattern, he has for present purposes mastered the rule. Since the attributes are known through instructions, errorless performance depends only on an understanding of how these attributes are related to each other and to the binary response system.

If a subject can master two or more rules, interesting questions arise about his ability to use them in new ways. To study these questions, we have constructed a rule-utilization task which requires the subject to discover which of several known rules defines the solution to a problem. The task is an obvious complement to attribute identification, the two differing only with respect to which problem element—rule or attribute— is unknown.

EXPERIMENTS

In the research to be reported, we have attempted to study how human beings learn and use conceptual rules. The experiments are admittedly primitive and exploratory. Further, they have a rather simple purpose—to determine whether there are any important characteristics of behavior uniquely associated with different types of conceptual problems, and, if so, to describe them. The results, however, are neither simple nor easily understood. While some of the observations seem quite natural, others resist an easy interpretation. In the main these experiments show, as the layman would surely expect, that human conceptual processes are a matter of considerable complexity.

The first two studies have been reported in detail elsewhere (Haygood and Bourne, 1965). Because they establish the validity of experimental procedures, however, the results will be reviewed briefly.

Experiment I

The first experiment dealt with some questions, arising from earlier research, about the difficulty of various rules for forming concepts. Neisser and Weene (1962), Hunt and Kreuter (1962), and others have shown that speed or efficiency of concept attainment depends heavily on the rule which defines solution. It may be noted that rules are arranged from top to bottom in Table 1 in ascending order of difficulty. A number of interpretations of these findings have been proposed. Neisser and Weene, for example, showed that rules differ in structural complexity and argued that the difficulty of any concept is related to the length of its symbolic description in terms of the primitive operators, conjunction, disjunction, and negation. It may be seen in Table 1.1 that rule difficulty does increase with the complexity of these expressions. Another possibility is contained in Hunt and Kreuter's demonstration that varying rule difficulties may result from subject use of a general problem-solving strategy. They assume that the subject begins each problem by trying a conjunction of attributes; when a nonconjunctive solution holds, he encounters subproblems which require special treatment. In a sense, then, the number and difficulty of subproblems determine overall performance on the problem. Finally, Haygood and Bourne (1965) noted that uncertainty in the stimulus-to-category assignments also varies with the rule and suggested that difficulty might be a function of the different informational requirements of these problems.

The proper interpretation of data is unclear for at least two reasons. First, all available studies used problems in which the subject knew neither the relevant attributes nor the conceptual rule. In the sense of our earlier analysis, each problem had two unknowns. Observed performance differences might have resulted from (a) some inherent complexity factor within rules, a possibility similar to that suggested by Neisser and Weene, (b) differences among rules in the strategies they require for identifying relevant attributes, a possibility more closely related to the Hunt-Kreuter proposal, or (c) both. Thus, it seemed appropriate to make performance comparisons in tasks for which only the rule or the relevant attributes, but not both, were unknown to the subject. In this way, we hoped to gain a better understanding of the source(s) of rule difficulty.

A second question concerned the stability of the observed ordering of difficulty. While a naive subject might find disjunctive and biconditional concepts harder to attain than conjunctions, sufficient experience and familiarity could bring him to a point of equal competence with all rules. The results of Wells (1963), showing that an initial preference for conjunctive, as opposed to disjunctive, concepts can be changed markedly with training, suggest this possibility. Thus, we decided to present subjects with a series of problems based on the same rule with the intent of observing any significant changes in performance.

Method. Four different rules and three instructional conditions were combined factorially in the design of the study. The rules—conjunctive, inclusive disjunctive, joint denial, and conditional—were arbitrarily selected to represent comparable levels of complexity in the sense of Neisser and Weene and one pair of complements. Subjects solved a series of five problems, each based on the same rule, but differing with respect to the particular pair of attributes chosen to be relevant. The instructional conditions were labeled *AI* (attribute identification), *RL* (rule learning), and *CL* (complete learning). For subjects in Condition *AI*, the rule for solving all problems was defined, described, and illustrated and practice in using it to categorize sample stimulus patterns was given. To solve an experimental problem, the subject presumably had only to discover a pair of relevant attributes. In Condition *RL*, the relevant attributes were named at the beginning of each problem but no instructions or explanation concerning the rule were given. Condition *CL*, in which neither the rule nor the relevant attributes were described, was included to provide both continuity with the procedures of earlier experiments and a baseline for comparing the effectiveness of *AI* and *RL* instructions.

The stimulus patterns in this and all subsequent experiments were geometric designs, varying in four dimensions—size, color, form, and number of figures each with three levels. The 81 designs were described in detail and illustrated for all subjects. Subjects were told that stimulus patterns would be presented one at a time, and that these were to be assigned to one of two categories, examples and nonexamples of the (initially-unknown) concept. Subjects were permitted to take as much time as necessary to respond to a pattern and each response was followed by immediate corrective informative feedback. The order of stimuli was essentially random. However, because the proportion of positive instances within the basic population of 81 designs differed markedly with the rule, some duplicate patterns were included so that, over any given series of 40 trials, roughly equal numbers of positive and negative instances were shown. The criterion of problem solution was 16 consecutively-correct category responses. When each problem was completed, the subject was reminded that the next would involve the same rule, but a new pair of relevant attributes.

Results. The numbers of trials to last error in each problem are presented in Fig. 1.1. The trends are fairly clear. First, there are significant differences, even on Problem 1, among the three instructional conditions. Subjects solved both *AI* and *RL* problems in fewer trials than *CL* problems, demonstrating some contribution of preliminary knowledge about the rule or the relevant attributes to performance in conceptual tasks. Second, rules differ in difficulty, at least on the initial problems; the ordering is exactly the same as that reported by Hunt and Kreuter.

These initial differences within instructional conditions and across rules change significantly with practice. In Condi-

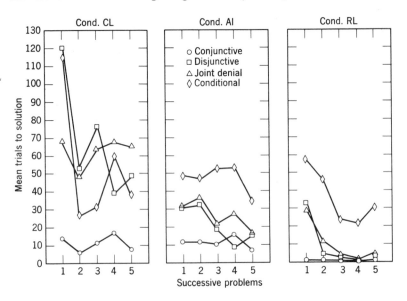

Fig.   1.1   Mean trial to solution of problems based on 4 different rules. Experiment I.

tion RL. subjects made virtually no errors on conjunctive concepts, indicating an initial familiarity with or expectation of the rule. While performance was inefficient at the outset, the same degree of mastery was attained for joint-denial and disjunctive rules over the course of three RL problems. The fact that some subjects continued to make errors on conditional concepts might reflect either the need for a longer training series or some special source of difficulty inherent in this rule. Subsequent experiments provide more direct evidence on that point.

Once the subject has learned the appropriate rule, it is possible for him to categorize patterns without error in Condition RL. On the other hand, to identify the relevant attributes of a problem, the subject must observe the category assignments of a certain minimal number of instances. As described in the original report of this experiment (Haygood and Bourne, 1965), detailed analyses suggest that on the fifth problem most subjects are able to identify the relevant attributes of a conjunctive, disjunctive, or joint-denial concept with minimal information. As in Condition RL, performance on conditional concepts is still relatively inefficient after five problems.

In summary, the results demonstrate that rules differ in difficulty for the naive subject. These differences obtain in problems which require attribute identification, rule learning, or both. They are, however, strongly affected by practice. Adult human subjects (college students) can probably learn to use with equal facility all rules of the sort considered here. Further, they seem to develop the appropriate response tendencies or strategies for identifying the relevant attributes of any type of nominal concept. Given these results, we planned a second experiment with the intent of training subjects on several rules. We were concerned with their ability to use more than one rule and with the collection of additional evidence on the difficulty of conditional concepts.

Experiment II

The primary purpose of this experiment was to study the utilization of known rules in a task analogous to attribute identification. Subjects were first trained to sort patterns on the basis of four different rules. These subjects were then asked to identify which of the rules determined the solutions in two final problems. *RI* (rule identification), like attribute identification, can be accomplished in a computable minimal number of trials depending on the alternative possible solutions. It should be clear that the amount of information required to determine the correct rule is the same for all alternatives. Therefore, assuming prior complete mastery, no performance difference among rules in *RI* problems would be expected.

Procedure. The experiment consisted of two parts. In the first, the *RL* phase, subjects solved a series of problems based on three different rules, disjunctive, conditional, and biconditional. All possible sequences of rules were used for different subjects. The routine was essentially the same as, though more informal than, that of Experiment I. The purpose was to train subjects to a reasonable level of facility with these three conceptual rules, plus a fourth, conjunctive, which was explained in detail and illustrated during preliminary instructions.

In the *RI* phase, all subjects solved two problems, each based on a different one of the four rules. In accord with a balanced incomplete blocks design, all possible pairs of rules were used for an equal number of subjects. For each of these problems, the relevant attributes were named, and subjects were instructed only that one of the four previously learned rules was relevant to the solution.

Other details of experimental procedure were essentially the same as those in Experiment I.

Results. Two aspects of the data obtained in the *RL* phase are particularly noteworthy. First, the three rules—disjunctive, conditional, and biconditional—differ in difficulty, especially on the first problem. Mean trials to last error were: Disjunctive - 19.5, conditional - 24.4, and biconditional - 65.6, which is precisely the order observed by Hunt and Kreuter and Neisser and Weene. Second, these differences were reduced, though not entirely eliminated with successive problems. Improvement across problems in this experiment is attributable to interrule transfer rather than, as in Experiment I, a specific process of learning how to solve problems based on the same rule.

Performance on problems given during the *RI* phase

requires a more detailed examination. Recall that the subject attempts to determine the correct one of four rules (and to categorize stimulus patterns accordingly) in each problem. Certain stimulus patterns and their category assignments are critical to this determination, as can be seen from Table 1.2.

TABLE 1.2 Category Assignment, Positive or Negative, of Each Combination of Attributes from Two Dimensions (here, Color and Form) Known to be Relevant to a Concept

Stimulus Patterns	Rule			
	Conjunctive	Disjunctive	Conditional	Biconditional
Red squares	+	+	+	+
Red triangles	-	+	-	-
Red circles	-	+	-	-
Green squares	-	+	+	-
Green triangles	-	-	+	+
Green circles	- ·	-	+	+
Blue squares	-	+	+	-
Blue triangles	-	-	+	+
Blue circles	-	-	+	+

Rules uniquely assign the various stimulus patterns, represented in Table 1.2 as the possible combinations of values on the two known relevant dimensions, to the response categories. For the particular rules used, stimulus patterns which display both relevant attributes are identically assigned and are therefore noncritical instances, that is, they provide the subject with no information relevant to distinguishing among rules. The remaining patterns, however, are critical to the distinction between at least some pairs of rules. In a sense, then, if the subject understands these rules, he should make at most one error in classifying each of these attribute contingencies and, once he has observed the proper category assignment for one example of each, should attain criterion to an *RI* problem. Thus, to solve these problems, subjects might require as many trials as are necessary to present the different attribute combinations.

An analysis of the stimulus sequences observed by subjects in these problems indicates that they perform considerably more efficiently than this description would imply. On the average more than 19 trials were needed to present examples of each of these stimulus combinations. Except for biconditional problems, mean trials to solution, shown in Table 1.3, were well below this figure.

TABLE 1.3 Mean Numbers of Trials (T) and Errors (E) to Solution and Numbers of Trials Necessary to Present at Least One Instance of Each Stimulus Class (TP) in Rule Identification Problems. Experiment II.

| | Problem | | | | | |
| | 1 | | | 2 | | |
Rule	E	T	TP	E	T	TP
Conjunctive	1.8	8.0	8	3.2	5.8	5
Disjunctive	1.5	4.2	5	2.3	7.2	5
Conditional	3.5	8.8	7	6.8	16.3	6
Biconditional	8.5	30.2	9	6.2	27.8	5

An inspection of individual protocols suggested that subjects were able somehow to reduce the effective complexity of the stimulus population by a preliminary assignment of stimuli to subsets. To illustrate, after responding to and learning the appropriate response for a green triangle (given red and square as the relevant attributes), a subject was quite likely to place green circles, blue triangles, and blue circles in the same category. Or, upon learning the proper placement of red triangles, a subject would respond similarly to red circles. In other words, many subjects appeared to behave (properly and correctly) as if green triangles, green circles, blue triangles, and blue circles were members of the same set of patterns, to be treated identically under any possible rule. Similarly, red triangles and red circles, with all their variations on other irrelevant dimensions, formed for the subject a subset to be assigned as a whole to one of the two conceptual categories. The first class contains those patterns which display neither relevant attribute (not red—not square) while patterns in the second class contain one relevant attribute but not the other (red—not square).

The foregoing observations indicate a different type of data analysis. There are four subsets of patterns which we shall call stimulus classes and designate: TT (the class containing patterns with both relevant attributes), TF and FT (two classes with one attribute but not the other, and *FF* (the class of patterns which display neither relevant attribute). These classes are recognizable as the four rows of a two-dimensional truth table. As shown in Table 1.4, the stimulus classes are uniquely assigned to responses for the rules used in this experiment and for all rules described in Table 1.1. In fact, the uniqueness of these assignments is one basis for distinguishing among the rules. If subjects somehow acquire the necessary knowledge to reduce the stimulus population to the classes, then an *RI* problem is soluble in as few trials as may be necessary to present one example of each class.

TABLE 1.4 Assignments of Stimulus Classes to Response Categories (+ and -) under the Four Rules used in Exp. II.

Stimulus Class	General Notation	Stimulus Set*	Conjunctive $(R \cap S)$	Disjunctive $(R \cup S)$	Conditional $(R \to S)$	Biconditional $(R \leftrightarrow S)$
RS	TT	RS	+	+	+	+
$R\overline{S}$	TF	RTr, RC	-	+	-	-
$\overline{R}S$	FT	GS, BS	-	+	+	-
$\overline{RS}$	FF	GTr, GC, BTr, BC	-	-	+	+

*The following abbreviations are used: *T*, true (or present); *F*, false (or absent); *R*, red; *G*, green; *B*, blue; *S*, square; *Tr*, triangle, *C*, circle.

The number of trials necessary to present at least one example of each class for the various *RI* problems is shown in Table 1.3. Except for the second conditional and both biconditionals, observed mean trials to last error are respectably close to these values. The percentage of *RI* problems solved with minimal information, that is, with at most one example of the 4 classes was 75% for conjunctives, 83% for disjunctives, 33% for conditionals and 25% for biconditionals. We shall return to these percentages.

Note from Table 1.3 that the ratios of errors (incorrect category responses) to trials to last error are appreciably less than .5. If subjects use the scheme for collapsing the stimulus population to classes, this error rate could be the product of identifying certain class-to-category assignments earlier than others. To explore this possibility, the following statistics were calculated for each problem: *TI* (the number of examples of each class prior to last error on the problem), *LI* (the number of examples of each class prior to last error on an instance of that class), *E* (the number of errors made on examples of each class), and *E/LI* (the ratio of errors to trials to last error on each class). Table 1.5 presents the combined results for *RI* problems. Note first that the error rate within each class is close to .5 (actually, .56 for *RL* problems and .53 for *RI* problems). Thus, it would appear that patterns in each class were assigned to categories with roughly chance probability of being correct until the assignment of that class was learned.

TABLE 1.5   Mean Number of Total Examples (*TI*), Examples to Last Error (*LI*), Errors (*E*) and Ratio of Errors to Examples (*E/LI*) for the Four Stimulus Class in Rule Identification Problems. Experiment II.

Stimulus Classes	Conjunctive				Disjunctive			
	TI	*LI*	*E*	*E/LI*	*TI*	*LI*	*E*	*E/LI*
TT	3.0	.6	.4	.67	1.0	0	0	-
TF	1.3	1.2	.9	.75	1.0	.9	.5	.56
FT	1.1	.9	.6	.67	1.4	1.3	.8	.61
FF	1.5	1.5	.6	.40	2.3	1.7	.6	.35

Stimulus Classes	Conditional				Biconditional			
	TI	*LI*	*E*	*E/LI*	*TI*	*LI*	*E*	*E/LI*
TT	1.4	.3	.3	1.00	3.7	.7	.3	.43
TF	6.0	4.0	1.8	.45	5.7	5.2	2.4	.46
FT	1.5	1.2	.9	.75	7.9	3.8	2.1	.55
FF	3.7	3.4	2.2	.65	11.7	5.0	2.5	.50

Variations among stimulus classes in trials to last error reveal some sources of rule difficulty. Particularly noteworthy is the inefficient performance on *TF* (negative instances) and *FF* (positive instances) classes for conditional problems and on *TF*, *FT* (both negative) and *FF* (positive) classes for biconditional problems. Much the same alignment of class difficulty within rules was observed in *RL* problems although the differences were considerably larger. In all probability the difficulty of certain class assignments is a product of their "unnaturalness." Most subjects expect instances assigned to the same class, particularly the positive class, to embody some common attributes. Strategies for attribute identification, as Hunt (1962) and Bruner, Goodnow, and Austin (1956) have noted, are typically based on a search for common attributes. Thus, any rule which assigns both *TT* and *FF* instances to the positive class is likely to present difficulties. Similarly, there appears to be a tendency to assign *TF* and *FT* classes to the same category. Subjects often ignore the distinction between these classes, treating them as a single more inclusive group characterized by one, but not both, relevant attributes. A rule which requires a distinction between these classes, such as the conditional, presents peculiar difficulties which show up mainly in a delineation of the negative category.

The data reported in Table 1.5 imply that most subjects performed with maximal efficiency on *RI* problems with conjunctive and disjunctive solutions. Only on 21% of these problems did subjects use more than the minimal number of trials. The evidence suggests that most subjects acquired (a) the technique of reducing the stimulus population to classes, and (b) the assignment of classes to response categories identified with these rules. The same conclusion does not hold for conditional and biconditional rules. While there is evidence of improvement in performance during the *RL* phase, 71% of *RI* problems based on these rules required more than the minimal number of trials. It is important to note, however, that 86% of the subjects who did perform optimally on either a conditional or a biconditional also solved their other *RI* problem in minimal trials. Therefore, it is likely that most subjects mastered the scheme for collapsing the stimulus population, and that the difficulty of conditional and biconditional problems stems primarily from a failure to learn completely the assignment of classes to responses required by these rules.

Comment. There is an admitted element of naivete in our approach in the first two experiments. We did not anticipate finding evidence on the attainment and use of the strategy by subjects—called forthwith the "truth-table" strategy—documented in Experiment II. In retrospect, however, the result seems both reasonable and natural, even though the behavioral end-product is slightly more complex than is usually reported in psychological studies of learning.

Assured, however, of the reliability of this behavior and of the adequacy of our procedures to elicit and measure it, we attempted next a series of experiments designed to influence the use of the truth-table approach to conceptual tasks.

Experiment III

The third study derived both from the limitations of Experiment I and from a desire to explore further the ability of subjects to use the truth-table strategy. Experiment I was partially replicated with slight changes of procedure. The primary purpose was to show once and for all that subjects can, with sufficient practice, master the conditional and biconditional rules. Therefore, we extended the length of training from 5 to 9 problems. Secondly, in an attempt to gain additional information on the acquisition and use of a truth-table strategy, subjects were provided with sample patterns illustrating the proper response assignment of each of the 4 stimulus classes. The effect of these samples is particularly interesting in attribute identification problems. If the subject understands the rule, described and demonstrated during preliminary instructions, and if the subject has acquired the notion of stimulus classes and, finally, if the 4 sample patterns are properly chosen, sufficient information is available at the outset to identify the two relevant attributes of the concept. Therefore, under these conditions, subjects can solve both attribute identification and rule learning problems without error. To attain this level of performance, however, it is critical that subjects recognize the relationship among patterns within the same class.

Procedure. Subjects were assigned to 8 experimental conditions formed by the factorial combination of 4 rules—conjunctive, inclusive disjunctive, conditional, and biconditional—with 2 instructional or task procedures—attribute identification and rule learning. Each subject solved successive problems utilizing the same rule within the same instructional condition until 2 were solved without error or until 9 problems in all had been solved. Each problem, of course, was based on a different pair of relevant attributes.

In most respects the procedures were identical to those of the preceding studies. There were, however, two notable changes. First, rather than equating the numbers of positive and negative instances for all problems, stimuli were selected to equate, within each set of 40 trials, the numbers of TT, TF, FT and FF instances. Stimulus patterns were arranged randomly within this limitation, with the further restriction that no more than 3 positive or 3 negative instances could appear successively.

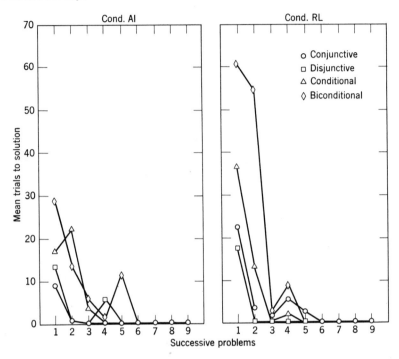

Fig. 1.2 Mean trials to solution of rule learning and attribute identification problems based on 4 different rules. Experiment III.

The second change, noted above, was to provide the subject with sample patterns throughout each problem. These samples were displayed in racks labeled "yes" and "no" next to similarly-designated response buttons used by the subject. Four patterns, one representing each of the 4 stimulus classes, were displayed for the duration of each problem. Each group of 4 patterns was selected so that subjects could determine the relevant attributes and/or the rule without responding to any of the stimuli presented in the problem. The fact that sample patterns provided sufficient information to solve the problem was indicated without explanation to all subjects.

Results. The important trends are represented in Fig. 1.2, in which mean trials to last error on each problem are plotted. First of all, on Problem 1, rules differed reliably in difficulty; the conditional and biconditional rules required more trials for solution than the conjunctive and disjunctive. The availability of sample patterns was not sufficient to overcome rule differences, although it is clear that, in general, performance was superior to that observed in Experiment I. Also, in contrast to the results of Experiment I, there was no statistically significant difference between performance in the rule learning and the attribute identification tasks. It would appear that the major effect of making these samples available was to reduce the difficulty of the attribute identification aspect of concept attainment. Finally, performance on all rules within both instructional conditions improved significantly with practice, such that, after Problem 5, no errors were made by any subject.

An analysis of responses to instances representing each of the 4 stimulus classes revealed an additional result of some interest. One example of each class was available to the subject throughout the problem. Within the trial series, some of the patterns presented contained the same values on the two relevant dimensions as these examples, while others took on different values. Specifically, about one-half of the *TF* and *FT* instances and one-fourth of the *FF* instances presented to the subject embodied the same values as their respective samples. In the first attribute identification problem, subjects made errors with nearly equal probability on stimulus patterns which were the same as or different from the samples, reflecting either some failure to attend to or an inability to utilize given information. On the next three problems, category errors occurred with reliably higher probability on patterns not represented in the samples. This, it would seem, is indicative of a tendency to use the samples but a failure to understand the implications of each sample for other instances of the same class. Performance later in the problem series (after Problem 5), of course, implied both the proper utilization of samples and the ability to make inferences from one to other members of each stimulus class. We take this as evidence of the acquisition of a truth-table strategy, in this case for attribute identification tasks, in much the same form as that shown in Experiment II.

Experiment IV

Recall that the results of Experiment II showed some evidence of a positive interrule transfer effect. Number of trials required to solve the problems decreased with successive problems given during the rule-learning phase of that study. Here, in contrast to Experiments I and III, no rule preceded itself in the training series so that improved performance was the result of some more general process. Data obtained in the rule-identification phase suggest that the facilitative effect might in part be a consequence of the stimulus coding component of the truth-table strategy. If subjects learn to reduce the relatively large amount of stimulus variation to 4 classes, problems which require the identification of a known rule or the learning of a new one are converted to a four-to-two paired-associates task.

Experiment II, of course, was not directly concerned with nor was it properly designed to study interrule transfer. To confront this question, subjects in Experiment IV were given a series of 6 training problems followed by a transfer task based on a new rule. Two variables seemed likely to affect degree of transfer on intuititive grounds. First, the distinctions among stimulus classes, and therefore the stimulus coding strategy, should depend on familiarity with a variety of rules making differing assignments of classes to response categories. Therefore, transfer effects might be expected to increase directly with variety of rule-learning experience. Second, some class-to-category assignments are the same for almost any pair of rules. To the extent that these identical S-R pairings are transferable, the particular selection of training rules should be a variable of some consequence.

Procedure. With the exceptions noted below, all problems were conducted under the rule-learning procedure described for Experiment III. There were 4 basic training conditions. In 3 of these, RL-1, RL-2, and RL-3, 6 practice problems preceded the transfer task. In a fourth, control (C) condition, only the transfer task was given. For subjects in RL-1, all 6 training problems were based on the same rule. For an equal number of subjects (4) the rule was conjunctive, inclusive disjunctive, or conditional. In RL-2, the subject solved 3 problems based on each of 2 rules. For different subgroups ($N = 4$), the 3 possible combinations of 2 rules (selected from those mentioned above) defined the solution. In RL-3, subjects solved 2 problems based on each of the 3 rules. The arrangement for Conditions RL-2, and RL-3, was such that all possible rule orders were represented for an equal number of subjects. The transfer task consisted of two successive problems both based on the biconditional rule.

Before each problem was begun, the experimenter named the relevant attributes, and indicated whether the rule was the same as or different from that of the preceding problem. No sample patterns illustrating the positive and negative response classes were shown.

Results. The experiment provides for a variety of analyses, only a few of which can be summarized in the space available.

Stage 1 *performance.* As we have come to expect, rules differed significantly in difficulty. Summing over all conditions, mean trials to last error on Problem 1 are: Conjunctive—4.1, disjunctive—24.9, conditional—51.8 and Biconditional (Condition C)—65.4. A comparison of these scores with data obtained under similar conditions in Experiment III may be taken as evidence of a mild facilitative effect of the availability of sample cards on rule-learning performance.

The initial differences among rules are in part associated with their unique assignments of stimulus classes to response categories. Table 1.6 shows for each rule the mean number of examples of each class presented prior to the subject's last error on that class for Problem 1 only. Whereas the values

TABLE 1.6 Mean Numbers of Examples of Each Stimulus Class Prior to Last Error on that Class. Problem 1 only, Experiment IV

Stimulus Class	Rule			
	Conjunctive	Disjunctive	Conditional	Biconditional
TT	.50	.25	3.00	3.25
TF	.67	4.25	12.00	10.33
FT	.92	6.17	5.58	9.92
FF	.27	3.75	12.75	15.42

are relatively homogeneous for the conjunction, there is considerable variability among classes for the other rules. Particularly noteworthy are Class *FF* for the conditional and biconditional problems and Classes *TF* and *FT* for the conditional. Precisely as was found in Experiment II, the response assignments of these stimuli require more trials to learn than any of the others. Assigning an *FF* instance to the positive category, as required by both rules, probably prompts considerable interference from common sense and past experience. The asymmetry of the conditional rule produces a unique difficulty in handling *TF* and *FT* instances. As before, however, the positive instances, *FT*, are learned with fewer trials than the negative, *TF*.

Over 6 problems of training on the same rule, differences among the rules and among stimulus classes within rules were eliminated. On Problem 6 of training, all subjects except one in a conditional problem solved without error. Although there was clear evidence of improvement in *RL*-2 and *RL*-3, trends were much less regular. Still all subjects, for whom the sixth problem was a conjunction or a disjunction of attributes, solved without error.

Stage 2 performance. Because the rule (biconditional) for the transfer task was new, of which all subjects were forewarned, the first response to any stimulus class must be a guess. The probability of guessing correctly is, of course, .5. Once informed, and assuming accurate memory, no further errors should be made on trials which display a member of that class. Thus, if the subject had attained the truth-table strategy for solving new *RL* problems, he could complete Problem 7, the first biconditional, within 7 trials, for this was the number necessary to present at least one instance of each of the 4 stimulus classes. Mean numbers of trials to solution on the first transfer problem were 65.4, 37.0, 31.8, and 20.6, for groups *C*, *RL*-1, *RL*-2, and *RL*-3, respectively. Thus, it is clear that maximally efficient performance was not, on the average, achieved in any condition. An inspection of individual protocols, however, revealed that 9 subjects, of the 48 serving in the experiment, did attain solution with minimally sufficient information. That is, these subjects made at most one error on instances of all 4 stimulus classes. All 9 were trained in one of the *RL* conditions. Not one control subject even approximated this level of performance. The outcome is highly unlikely to have occurred by chance. Thus, not unexpectedly, prior rule learning contributes to the acquisition and use of the truth-table strategy. But somewhat more penetrating questions remained to be answered.

What kind of rule experience results in the acquisition of the strategy? First, the majority of efficient solvers served in Conditions RL-2 and RL-3. The numbers were so small, however, that it is difficult to detect a trend. More dramatic were the data based on trials to solution. Here there were reliable differences among groups, with performance on the first biconditional problem improving directly and significantly with the number of different rules (0-3) practiced. Thus, it would appear that variety of experience contributes importantly to the formation of an efficient strategy.

But even these data fail to reflect the real state of affairs. All 9 subjects who solved the first biconditional in minimal trials were trained on the conditional rule; 7 of the 9 solved 2 or more conditional problems immediately preceding the transfer task. Additional evidence on the facilitative effects of conditional training is found in separate analyses of variance on the three RL conditions. For RL-1 and RL-2, those subgroups who solved conditional problems were significantly better on Problem 7 than were comparable subgroups trained exclusively on conjunctions, disjunctions, or both. There was no overall difference among the subgroups of RL-3.

Earlier, evidence that the major difficulty of the biconditional rule is associated with instances of the FF stimulus class was reported. Inspection of the present data shows that only rule learning experience with the conditional rule reduces the relative difficulty of these instances. Table 1.7 shows the mean number of instances of each class presented before the last error on that class for the first biconditional transfer problem after training in Condition RL-1. Practice on the conditional rule results in dramatic improvement on all stimulus classes, but most noteworthy for present purposes is its effect on FF instances.

In summary, this experiment demonstrates that positive interrule transfer effects do exist and provides some insight into the source of these effects. No facilitation of performance on biconditional problems obtains from training based exclusively on conjunctions and very little is added by experience with disjunctions. Given that subjects are in all likelihood familiar with conjunctions from pre-experimental experience, such training probably serves at best to provide a warm-up task. Maximal transfer obtains from training on the conditional rule which (a) enforces strict attention to the distinction between *TF* and *FT* instances and thereby promotes the utilization of stimulus classes, and (b) requires, as does the biconditional rule, an assignment of *FF* instances to the positive response category. We take the data to suggest that interrule transfer stems first from the acquisition of a scheme for simplifying the stimulus population. This scheme is more likely to be realized from training with rules, like the conditional, which impose unusual, unnatural, or difficult assignments of stimulus classes to categories. Given this scheme, any problem, even one based on a new or unfamiliar rule, becomes an almost trivial paired-associates task requiring only a few trials to master.

TABLE 1.7 Mean Numbers of Examples of Each Stimulus Class Prior to Last Error on that Class After Training on Different Rules in Condition *RL*-1. First Biconditional Problem, Experiment IV.

Stimulus Class	Rule		
	Conjunctive	Disjunctive	Conditional
TT	9.50	2.50	0.50
TF	12.50	4.75	2.25
FT	12.75	5.25	2.00
FF	14.25	8.75	1.50

Experiment V

We have come to think of conceptual rule learning as a two-stage process in which subjects (a) learn to encode stimulus patterns into a contingency matrix equivalent to the truth-table of Formal Logic, and (b) learn the proper assignments of these stimulus classes to response categories. While there may be peculiar difficulties with certain classes (analogous to the familiar item difficulty phenomenon in verbal paired-associates learning), rule learning and rule identification problems should become quite simple once the subject has mastered the stimulus encoding scheme. From several of the preceding experiments, we have evidence of this effect. However, in none of the studies was any direct attempt made to teach subjects about the truth-table arrangement or the equivalence of instances within each of the stimulus classes. Rather the strategy was allowed to evolve naturally over the course of solving several conceptual problems. In the next experiment, conducted by Haygood and Kiehlbauch (1965), some subjects were given preliminary training designed to familiarize them with the 4-fold classification of stimulus patterns based on any pair of attributes. This experience was expected to facilitate subsequent performance in tasks which require learning a novel or difficult rule. Indeed, mastery of the stimulus coding scheme could entirely eliminate the differences in difficulty among rules.

Procedure. Subjects were assigned randomly to two groups, *PT* and *NPT*. Those in Group *PT* were given 3 pretraining problems which consisted of learning to sort a series of stimulus patterns into the 4 categories defined by the presence or absence of 2 named relevant attributes (*TT*, *TF*, *FT*, and *FF*). The criterion of success in each pretraining problem was 16 consecutively-correct classifications. The population of stimulus patterns was shown and described to subjects in Group *NPT* but no pretraining on the stimulus classes was given.

Subsequently all subjects solved a conceptual problem under exactly the same procedure used in the *RL* conditions of preceding experiments. For an equal number of subjects within each pretraining group, the rule for solution was conjunctive, inclusive disjunctive, conditional, or biconditional. (Parenthetically we may note that the complements of each of these rules were also represented orthogonally in the design of the study. Since no reliable performance difference obtained for any pair of complements, we may treat each pair as a single rule.)

Results. Trials to last error for each of the 8 rule and training conditions are shown in Fig. 1.3. Overall, rules differ reliably in their difficulty—the order is consistent with earlier findings. Pretraining on the assignment of patterns to

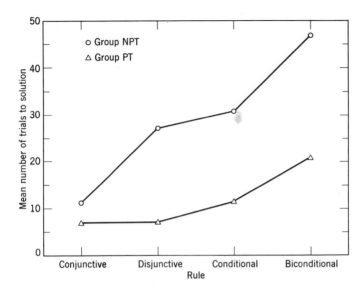

Fig. 1.3   Trial to last error on problems given in Experiment V.

the 4 stimulus classes clearly facilitated performance on all rules.   The effect, however, was more noticeable on the initially more difficult rules; the rules by pretraining interaction was   highly   significant.   The   trend   is   toward   a   reduction in differences in rule difficulty with prior training on stimulus classes.   In these problems it took an average of 6 trials to present at least one instance of each class. With pretraining, conjunctive and disjunctive problems were solved in almost precisely 6 trials, strongly suggesting that subjects did utilize the stimulus coding method.   The fact that, even with pretraining, more than the theoretical minimal number of trials was required on conditional and biconditional problems is once again largely attributable to the difficulty of learning to assign certain classes to their proper categories. The FF instances, in biconditional problems, and the FF and the TF instances, in conditional   problems,   were   miscategorized   with   reliably greater frequency than members of any other class.

   This study demonstrates conclusively that familiarity with and a working understanding of the principle for coding the stimulus population facilitates the solution of conceptual problems in which the rule is an unknown.   These problems become relatively simple paired-associates tasks for the subject who has acquired the principle. The remaining difficulty associated with any rule is primarily a function of its mapping of classes onto the response system, a task which, while not trivial in the case of some rules, is far less imposing than that which faces the naive subject.

OTHER STUDIES

Research summarized heretofore has had the primary aim of elucidating some characteristics of performance in a variety of conceptual problems. While the data by no means describe completely the structure of conceptual behavior, they do provide an empirical base from which more detailed studies of important independent variables can be attempted. We are just beginning to undertake this work so that, at best, we can supply only a faint suggestion of outcomes and implications. It might, however, be of some value to mention briefly two of our current efforts.

The Role of Positive and Negative Instances

A fair amount of empirical research has been invested in the study of positive and negative instances as sources of solution-relevant information in conceptual problems. The general effect, most clearly documented by Hovland and Weiss (1953), is that negative instances are more difficult to use (to make proper inferences from) than positive, even when the two types are equated logically for informational content. The generalizability of this conclusion is brought into question by the analyses of conceptual problems provided by Bruner, Goodnow, and Austin (1956), Hunt (1962), and the results of the experiments reported here. Most of the data on positive and negative instances have been obtained from attribute iden-tification problems based on a conjunctive solution. The re-sults may in part be an artifact of task conditions and of the manner in which the conjunctive rule partitions a stimulus population. We may note that when the number of levels on a relevant dimension is three or greater, the class of positive instances in a conjunction (TT instances only) is smaller and less variable than its counterpart (or complement) under any other rule. Both Bruner *et al.*, and Hunt have remarked on the appropriateness and efficiency of a "natural" positive focusing strategy for solving conjunctive problems. The question that arises is whether positive instances provide a more efficient base psychologically for solving conceptual problems when the rule is not conjunctive and/or when the task necessitates rule learning. In general, it seems more reasonable to expect the relative usefulness of positive and negative instances to be some function of the distribution of stimulus classes into response categories under any given rule, particularly if subjects adopted the truth-table approach to such problems.

To explore this possibility, the following experiment was undertaken. Subjects were assigned to the 18 conditions of a factorial design which combined three rules, conjunctive, inclusive disjunctive, and conditional; three training sequences, positive only, negative only, and a mixture of positive and negative instances; and two types of task, attribute identification and rule learning. All subjects were given much the same pretraining on stimulus classes as was used in Experiment V, after which they solved one experimental problem.

The procedures were somewhat different from those described earlier. At first, 8 stimulus patterns, all positive, all negative, or a mixture, were presented. Each pattern, presented individually, was appropriately designated as an example or nonexample of the concept by the experimenter. Each training series of 8 stimuli provided enough information to solve the problem logically. After this, 4 test patterns, 1 from each of the 4 stimulus classes, were shown and the subject had to make a category response to each. Informative feedback was withheld on test trials. Next a different series of 8 patterns was presented and identified, followed by 4 more test trials. This alternation between training and test trials continued until 12 successive test stimuli were identified correctly. In order to attain this criterion, subjects had either to identify 2 relevant attributes or to use the proper rule as usual in *AI* and *RL* tasks.

The data are complex. Analyses are still in progress and we do not claim to understand the outcome completely. However, the general trends seem clear. First of all, it is comforting to report that the data compare favorably with Hovland and Weiss (1953). Subjects take most trials on conjunctive *AI* problems when the training instances are all negative and least when they are all positive. For the corresponding *RL* problems, however, there is little difference among the training series with a slight tendency for the mixture of positives and negatives to produce best performance. When the rule is disjunctive, the trend is the same for both *AI* and *RL* tasks: All negatives just slightly worse than all positives and a mixture affording best performance. In conditional problems, solutions are attained in fewer trials with all negatives than with all positives, with the mixture being better than both. It is significant to note that when only negative instances are presented relevant attributes are identified more quickly and with fewer errors for disjunctions and conditionals than for conjunctions.

Without considering the more detailed analyses, it is clear that the relative values of positive and negative instances depend on both the conceptual rule defining a solution and the task conditions under which it must be solved. For rule-learning tasks a mixture of instances leads to the most rapid concept attainment. Actually, there is little difference between positives only and negatives only for all rules. When the problem requires attribute identification, however, the difference among rules becomes quite dramatic. For disjunctive and conditional concepts, the negative class (*FF*—disjunction and *TF*—conditional) is both smaller and more homogeneous than the positive class, while for conjunctions, just the opposite is true. With this in mind, the data lead naturally to the conclusion that the degree of stimulus variation within the positive and negative categories determines in part the usability of these two sources of information. The result also suggests, though weakly, that once the truth-table scheme for collapsing the stimulus population is known, the subject might be better able to adopt a negative focusing orientation toward the task of attribute identification.

Differences with Chronological Age

There are even fewer data to report of the effect of age on differences in rule learning and rule utilization. Those we do have, however, show clearly the need for a detailed investigation. (Some of these results have been described by

King, 1964.) Children between the ages of 6 and 12 years and young adults were trained on conjunctive and disjunctive *RL* problems. Subsequently, they were given a task which required identification of one of the two rules. Note that the distinction between these rules rests only on the assignment of *TF* and *FT* instances to response categories. For the conjunction, both are negative and, for the disjunction, both are positive. Knowledge of the truth-table should permit solution as soon as the correct category for one instance of either class is indicated.

All subjects learned both rules so well that very few errors were made on the identification problem. However, those that were made present an interesting pattern. They suggest that some younger children do not respond identically to members of the same stimulus class nor do they make the proper inference from *FT* to *TF* (or vice versa) instances in the *RI* problem. Older children appear more likely to attain the class distinctions but still may err on an *FT* (or *TF*) instance even after a trial which shows the response category for *TF*s (or *FT*s). Twelve-year-olds and adults appear quite capable of making both within-class and between-class inferences.

The data are too few to support a firm conclusion or interpretation. They do suggest, however, a potentially important and interesting developmental process in inferential behavior. We have planned more intensive studies with younger children, using a greater variety of rules and systematic variation in mental age and verbal ability. If the truth-table strategy resembles, in function and structure, the mediational behavior described by Kendler and Kendler (1962) and others, we can expect these experiments to reveal important behavioral differences with age, intellect, and the like.

GENERAL DISCUSSION

While the foregoing description fails to provide a neat or complete picture of conceptual rule learning and utilization, it does represent just about all the empirical data available to work with at the moment. I have no intention of abandoning the problem, but neither can I produce any further resolution here. I shall conclude, then, with a brief résumé of results and a final attempt to make some sense of them.

First of all, an analysis of concepts discloses two critical features or components, the relevant, defining physical attributes of stimulus objects, and the rule, prescribing a relationship between them. The experiments have shown that it is feasible methodologically to distinguish these components and to construct tasks in which one or the other, but not both, defines the conceptual problem to be solved. Further, they have uncovered evidence of some unique characteristics of behavior associated with problems which require, on the one hand, an identification of relevant attributes and, on the other, the learning and/or identification of a conceptual rule.

These experiments, like their antecedents (e.g., Neisser and Weene, 1962; Hunt and Kreuter, 1962), demonstrate that conceptual rules vary in difficulty for the naive subject. But, regardless of whether these differences are a product of structural complexity within rule-governed stimulus relationships, of conformance with a natural strategy which seeks communalities among stimulus members of the class of positive instances, or of other factors, they rapidly vanish with training. Over the course of a series of rule-learning problems, the subject does acquire knowledge about how a rule assigns stimulus patterns to response categories. Rule learning proceeds regularly to a level of mastery such that, given the relevant attributes, the subject categorizes stimuli without error. The effect of sufficient practice is to eliminate all differences in rule difficulty.

It is possible to think of concept attainment, regardless of task features and the givens or the unknowns, as the acquisition—either by associational processes or an hypothesis-testing routine—of information on the assignment of all combinations of values on relevant stimulus dimensions to response categories. In the stimulus population used in the present series of experiments, this means a mapping of 9 different patterns (combinations of 3 values on each of 2 relevant dimensions) on a binary response system. We have interpreted the evidence of these studies to imply that most subjects learn and use a strategy which simplifies and facilitates this attainment process. It may be comforting to think of the strategy as a mediational link in the behavioral chain interceding between the external stimulus features of the problem and the behavior which corresponds to an acceptable solution. In any case, simplification of the problem seems to result from collapsing, in the present case, a 3 × 3 or, in general, an m × n matrix of stimulus combinations (representing the arrangement of values on relevant dimensions) to a 4-fold table, each cell of which contains a set of stimulus patterns describable in terms of the presence or absence of the 2 relevant attributes.

It has been shown that, with suitable instruction, practice on sorting patterns into stimulus classes, or training on a variety of rules the subject comes to respond identically to all instances of a given class. Further he devises what can be called an algorithm for solving problems based either on one of a number of known rules or on a totally new one whose general features are like others with which the subject is familiar. The routine is to observe the assignment of one example of each of the stimulus classes and then to classify all subsequent instances in accord with these examples. The plan reduces a potentially unlimited stimulus population to four classes, then merely maps these four on a binary response system. While we have no reason to believe that the algorithm is carried out formally—attempts by subjects to tell us in post-experimental interviews about their own problem-solving behavior are often rather unintelligible—our measures and analyses of category responses do strongly suggest the utilization of some such routine on an informal or intuitive level.

Learning to use nominal, deterministic rules of the type considered in this research can be conceived then as a 2-phased process involving (a) reductive coding of a stimulus population to a small number of classes and (b) acquisition of the associations between classes and response categories. Our data do not imply that the general coding principle is mastered in advance of class-to-category assignments. They indicate only that the performance of sophisticated subjects is distinguished by an intervening step which reduces the effective complexity of the stimulus population. Evidence from Experiments II, IV, and V, however, does suggest that some subjects use the coding principle prior to complete mastery of class-to-category assignments associated with the more difficult conditional and biconditional rules.

We have noted the obvious similarity of the subject's behavior to a truth-table. If our interpretation is correct, the data reported here imply the utilization of some informal version of this deductive method, which of course is well-known to have considerable power in logic.

Concluding Comment

The purpose of this paper has been to summarize a small, though complicated set of empirical results. The approach, while analytic in tone, has been data-oriented and strictly descriptive. Little concern for possible theoretical implications has been expressed. The reasons for this constraint are several, not the least of which is an awareness of the limits on what can be accomplished in a single paper. But, it is also pertinent to point out that no particular theoretical orientation has guided this research. The studies were not undertaken to test systematically derived hypotheses, in the usual sense. Our questions arose from what some might call "pre-theoretic" considerations—common sense, curiosity, and the results of the preceding experiment. The findings, it seems, are neither critical nor decisive for any known theory of concept attainment. Neither the data nor the interpretations, which make occasional use of such admittedly suggestive terms as rule-governed behavior and strategies, are meant to imply any strong theoretical commitment. Indeed, I am aware of no adequate theory to which to be committed. If I were, it might help make more sense of the available data.

Although the results sustain no impressive theoretical argument, they are, I think, interesting and useful. The structural analysis of concepts defines a set of problems, which taken as a whole does not impose the constraints on performance which have been characteristic of a fair amount of experimentation. Consequently, through continued studies a somewhat more realistic picture of the true complexity of human conceptual behavior can be developed without sacrificing any appreciable amount of rigor. The procedures and data of course are neither complete nor entirely sufficient to describe all facets of conceptual behavior. A fairly lengthy list of problems, extensions, and modifications could easily be recited. But, the research outlined does constitute a reasonable beginning and a basis from which a more general, scientific understanding of the complex process of thought and behavior that are involved in concept attainment can be achieved.

CHAPTER 2

Edwin Martin

University of Michigan

FORMATION OF CONCEPTS*

Concept attainment is a state conferred upon an organism by an external observer who decides that a certain sequence of responses exhibited by the organism matches, according to some arbitrary rule invented by the observer, a certain sequence of stimulus events to which the organism is sensitive. A theory of concept attainment, therefore, must be a set of statements that describe a process whereby the organism reaches this state of agreement with his observer. Various attacks on this problem have appeared in the literature; thus we have concept attainment understood as strategy selection (Restle, 1962), as cue conditioning (Bourne & Restle, 1959), and as a combination of dimension sampling and paired-associate learning (Bower and Trabasso, 1964).[1] In addition, concept attainment has been analyzed in terms of implicit mediator responses (Kendler and Kendler, 1962) and computerized information-processing programs (Hunt, 1962).

The explanative and predictive success of an extant theory or model has long been deemed the critical dimension on which evaluation should depend. While it is true that the theories now available in the concept-attainment area sometimes yield admirable "fits" in selected experimental settings, it is equally true that they tend to be of limited scope and, consequently, of little help in forming a general unified picture

Preparation of this paper was supported by the Advanced Research Projects Agency, Department of Defense, monitored by the Air Force Office of Scientific Research, under Contract No. AF 49(638)-1235 with the Human Performance Center, Department of Psychology, University of Michigan.

[1] These approaches to concept attainment have been reviewed in detail elsewhere (Martin, 1965).

of organismic behavior. Certainly small-scale models that do not interlock with other facets of psychological thought cannot be of lasting interest. This seeming parochialism manifests itself in many ways; for example, in some of the current formulations, the content terms of the postulates are well-nigh impossible to identify with real-world events or processes; in others, processes are assumed that are unconvincing in the face of current neurophysiological knowledge. But, even in addition to these reservations, there are four critical points to be made about most of the theoretical activity surrounding concept attainment.

First, there is an understandable but clearly restrictive tendency for theorists to tie their formulations too closely to the observer's particular frame of reference. We have learned from the physical sciences that laws depending for their veridicality on observations at a particular station, for example, Newton's fixed platform in space, are soon displaced in favor of laws that are free of spatial and temporal frames of reference. The clearest point of deficiency of this type in current formulations of concept attainment is the matter of dimension relevancy. New data will be presented that show how inappropriate it is to assume that just because a dimension is seen as relevant (or irrelevant) from the observer's point of view, it is also relevant (or irrelevant) from the learning organism's point of view. In other words, in the last analysis, such constructs as dimension relevancy must somehow be taken off the observer's hook and given a relativistic meaning, or dropped altogether.

Second, in most of the formulations now available to us, the process of concept attainment is seen as progress from a trial-and-error posture of some sort to a stimulus-bound state. This predicament results from a combination of being concerned only with a small segment of laboratory behavior and of adopting a task orientation rather than a process orientation, both of which tendencies favor construction of theories that are non-relativistic. No doubt, from the learning organism's point of view, his behavior appears to be stimulus-bound throughout; and certainly one can always discover a frame of reference such that, in contrast with a given theorist's frame of reference, the learning organism's observed behavior seems to disintegrate from an organized variety into a neurotic variety. The critical point to be made is that current formulations are in a sense protected from being broadly significant by making the implicit, if not explicit, assumption that conceptual behavior arises from nothing rather than something. It would seem that knowledge of the something out of which conceptual behavior arises must not only indicate the form of concept attainment theories, but also link them with many other areas of psychology.[2] This criticism does not apply to the work of Kendler and Kendler (1962).

Third, a number of the current formulations make heavy derivational use of certain distinctions that arise from the often problematic procedure of inferring processes from operations. Thus we see generalization distinguished from failure to discriminate at the process level; but invariably the argument rests on procedural and instructional distinctions at the experimental or operational level. We will return to this particular problem shortly, because its resolution is essential to the view of concept attainment to be evolved in this paper. Another example that will be treated below is the tendency to read into the learning organism a process or two by which he, the organism, can differentially categorize information that is classified as relevant or irrelevant from the observer's precarious point of view. The most magnificent example of an operations-to-processes argument, however, is the verbal bridge built in the late 1930s by Skinner (1935, 1937) and Hilgard (1937), a bridge that spans from the Pavlovian-Thorndikian distinction in procedure on the operations end to the classical-instrumental distinction in type of learning on the processes end. The critical point is, these so-called inferences are no more valid than is an induced generalization:

[2]Along these lines, it is of historic interest to note that neither Thorndike nor Hull conceived of presolution behavior in trial-and-error experiments as random or chance behavior, as convincingly charged by Krechevsky (1932). "The situations and responses of a human life are obviously not haphazard. If a certain situation, call it S_1, occurs in a certain man's life, he is not equally likely to make any one of the million, or more, responses which a man can make. On the contrary, S_1 usually has well-marked tendencies to call forth some one particular response or some one of certain few responses" (Thorndike, 1931, p. 4). "The range or variety of reactions which may be evoked by a given problem situation is limited to the reactions which have become conditioned during the life of the organism to one or another stimulus components of that situation" (Hull, 1930a, p. 248).

processes do not follow logically from operations; rather they are inductions and must be recognized as such. To act as if these derived processes were analytically necessary usually serves primarily to impede progress toward a unified view of behavior.

The fourth, and final, critical point regarding current formulations of concept attainment refers to the conspicuous absence of a place for inhibitory processes. As long ago as 1876, Ferrier wrote: "The centers of inhibition...constitute the organic basis of all the higher intellectual faculties. A great profusion of remembered images, ideas, or notions, avails little for practical ends without the power of arrest or selection." Sherrington's (1906) opinion was: "If resting paths all lie open to conduction, prevention of confusion must depend not on the path excited being the only one open for conduction, but on its excitation being accompanied by inhibition of others that, did they enter into action, would detrimentally confuse the issue of events." A scholarly and up-to-date review of what is known about the intimate and pervasive involvement of inhibitory processes in all forms of behavior and thought is now available to psychologists at large (Diamond, Balvin, and Diamond, 1963). While it is generally seen as less sporting to decry a theoretical omission than a point-at-able error, one cannot help but classify as error a continued disregard of an obviously omnipresent process.

The present paper will concern itself with the origins of conceptual behavior, that is, with the continuity from generalization through discrimination learning to concept formation. As we progress, what is intended is a cumulative picture that accounts for behavior over many levels of complexity. In this analysis, inhibition will play a central role. Also intended is an integration of some of the reaction-time literature with that ordinarily referred to as the concept-identification literature. Before proceeding, three fundamental orienting statements must be made.

First, it is assumed that all behavior is caused, that is, that every response has a stimulus. If responses R_1 and R_2 are different in any way, then their causes, S_1 and S_2, are different.

An important implication of this assumption is that if an observer catalogues R_1 and R_2 as alternative responses in stimulus situation S, intending that the learning organism has a choice to make, then the observer is seen as failing to discriminate the components S_1 and S_2 of S. From this, it follows that the existence of "choice" as a descriptive term in an observer's vocabulary is an unnecessary peculiarity of the observer's frame of reference, a peculiarity due, hopefully, only to current crudities in detection techniques. Another way of saying this is: The observed probabilistic relation between S and R is descriptive of the discrepancy between frames of reference of observer and learner. This first assumption, then, serves to deny at the outset that the observer's point of view is in any way privileged and to affirm the relativistic intention that for a behavioral law to be of lasting interest, it must, at minimum, be free of any given vantage point. All this is implicit in the idea that every response R_i has a cause S_i such that if R_1 is different from R_2, then S_1 is different from S_2.

Second, it is assumed that all responses give rise to stimuli. This assumption seems reasonable at all levels of analysis. At the most molecular level, where nervous activation is the response, the unavoidable arrival of the impulse at the telodendria constitutes the natural stimulus for the next neuron. At the intermediate level, there are the facts of proprioceptive feedback and other CNS monitoring systems. At the most molar level, many responses simply reorient the organism, thereby bringing the receptor organs into contact with a different stimulus matrix. To assume that all responses give rise to stimuli is to provide for the processes that frequently come to be called "cognitive," that is, the processes that are responsible for the difficulty encountered in trying to correlate external stimuli (as detected by an observer) with overt responses (also as detected by an observer). For example, to refer to a cognitive process that will be of major importance in the present paper, the intervention of perceptual mediator responses in on-going behavior has received considerable attention from behavior theorists, beginning with Hull's (1930b) notion of the pure stimulus act (r_G) and its resulting interoceptive event (s_G) and culminating with Lawrence's (1963) impressive analysis of the relation between learning and perception in terms of stimuli-as-coded (s-a-c).

The third, and final, assumption has to do with the automaticity of learning: It is assumed that association formation between internal, response-producing representations is automatic, that the learning organism has no choice in the matter.

If the external stimulus event S is received (sensed) by the organism in the form of response r, which in turn gives rise to the representation s that causes the overt response R, and if the external events S_1 and S_2 relate to each other both physically and temporally such that representations s_1 and s_2 interact neurophysiologically, then upon subsequent occurrence of, say, S_1, a composite representation $s_{1,2}$ will be elicited, and hence a composite response $R_{1,2}$ will be caused. This process can be schematized as follows:

Independent occurrence,

$$S_1 \rightarrow r_1 \rightarrow s_1 \rightarrow R_1$$

$$S_2 \rightarrow r_2 \rightarrow s_2 \rightarrow R_2$$

Contiguous occurrence,

$$S_1 \rightarrow r_1 \rightarrow s_1 \rightarrow R_1$$
$$\updownarrow$$
$$S_2 \rightarrow r_2 \rightarrow s_2 \rightarrow R_2$$

Single occurrence,

$$S_1 \rightarrow r_1 \rightarrow S_{1,2} \rightarrow R_{1,2}$$

Implicit in this assumption is the idea that association formation "...is non-selective in nature, and it occurs for those aspects of the total stimulus which are arbitrarily wrong as well as those which are arbitrarily right" (Wickens, 1954, p. 25). As this paper will show, the antidote for this seemingly necessary assumption is the conditioning of differential inhibitory tendencies.[3]

Although more a conclusion than an assumption, one

[3] The notion of automaticity of learning and subsequent refinement of responding through acquired differential inhibition was initially systematized by Pavlov (1927) in physiology and given an enthusiastic reception by Hull (1929) in psychology. The extension of this work as represented by the present paper is, in many respects, in very close agreement with Wicken's (1954) analysis of the concept-formation process. Applications to still higher-order behavior are currently meeting with impressive success (e.g., Bandura, 1961; Wolpe, Salter, and Reyna, 1964).

additional orientational stance might be cited. The present writer sees all behavior as the net result of excitatory and inhibitory processes. It will be argued that learning and problem solving are primarily, if not entirely, a working out of what excitations shall be inhibited. As one passes along the line from generalization through discrimination learning to concept formation, an idea that insistently recurs is that the learning organism is forever learning not to do or, especially, not to see something.

PART I

In an analysis of concept attainment, a minimum restraint on the analyst is the offering of definitions of "concept" and "attainment." This will be done shortly. But first, the relationship between generalization and discrimination must be explicated; then we will argue that only certain combinations of discriminations constitute a concept, where the combination rule is that of reciprocal induction in the standard Pavlovian sense.

The first step is to come to an understanding of what is meant by "generalization" and by "discrimination" so that it is clear that in all cases, and in all circumstances, generalization is no more nor no less than a failure to discriminate. Let S be the stimulus situation, and let R_1 be the response that is caused by S. From an observer's point of view, if a similar but different situation S' also causes R_1, it is said that generalization occurs; while if S' causes a different response R_2 (which can be any not-R_1 response), it is said that generalization does not occur. From the organism's point of view, however, if R_1 is caused by S', then S and S' must be identical; whereas if R_2 is caused by S', then S and S' must be different. This is consonant with the relativist caveat that organisms never generalize and that the term "generalization" is peculiar to the vocabulary of the observer.

But the observer knows that S and S' are different; therefore, how can the organism respond as if S and S' are identical? Let $s_1, s_2, ..., s_n$ be n physical aspects of the stimulus situation S such that each is a value on one of the dimensions $D_1, D_2, ..., D_n$. Thus, specification of a single value (s_i) for each dimension (D_i) completely describes the situation S. If the observer knows S and S' differ only on dimension D_i, and if the organism makes R_1 to both S and S', it then follows that the organism, for some presumably discoverable reason, is insensitive to variations in dimension D_i, that is, he does not notice the difference between s_i and s_i'.

This is the crux of the matter—insensitivity to variations on a selected dimension. The dispute over whether or not generalization is a failure to discriminate arises when in some situations the organism appears to be insensitive to variations on dimension D_i, but in others he is obviously sensitive. As a case in point, consider the red traffic light. Under one in- structional set, the organism dutifully emits a brake-pedal response, R_1, to each of many different shades of red; under another instructional set, however, he can easily emit R_2 to one shade, R_3 to another, and so on. Thus whether or not dimen- sion D_i is a dimension to which the organism is sensitive depends upon certain other, concomitant dimensional values (since dimensional values are all that can distinguish one situation from another). The point of interest is that being sensitive to a given dimension can be, and more often than not is, conditional upon other aspects of the situation. It is not impossible to argue that such conditional sensitivity, or selec- tive orientation, makes up the bulk of what is learned over trials or what is transmitted in instructions. Being sensi- tive to dimension D_i means noticing aspect s_i of situation S, where the selection of aspect s_i is itself a conditional response of the orienting or perceptual variety (r).

In a given situation, suppose the organism has learned or has been instructed to attend to or orient toward the variable dimension D_i, and therefore toward aspects s_i of S and s_i' of S'; while in another situation, he has learned to inhibit orientation toward D_i. In the former setting, the observer says the or- ganism is sensitive to variations in D_i, that is, the organism is capable of making discriminations; but in the latter, the observer predicts that the organism cannot discriminate, that is, the organism must generalize. (In either case, of course, all is strictly an observer's game; for the organism is re- sponding only in accordance with the causal events detected by him.)

The foregoing argument has been summarized schemati- cally in Fig. 2.1. In shifting from situation S to situation S', whether or not response R_1 occurs to S' depends upon whether or not the organism orients (r_0) toward the dimension (D_3) that changes in value from S to S'.

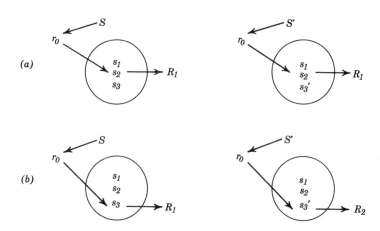

Fig. 2.1   In stimulus situations S and S', the organism makes the receptive response r_0, which produces the differential cue s_{ji}. (a) Generalization: The organism orients toward dimension D_2, thereby not detecting the change on dimension D_3 between situations S and S'. (b) Discrimination: The organism orients toward dimension D_3, thereby detecting the change on dimension D_3 between situations S and S'.

This picture is that of stimulus generalization, where the observer knows about a dimensional change not detected by the organism. Response generalization is another phenomenon peculiar to the observer's frame of reference: When the observer fails to detect a dimensional change that is detected by the organism, the resulting different response is seen by the observer as random noise or chance variability and the phenomenon is labeled "response generalization."[4]

_____

[4] The Gestalt psychologists have frequently cited the phenomenon of response generalization as particularly troublesome for S-R theorists (e.g., Koffka, 1925, p. 160). Guthrie (1952, p. 164) treats this problem by emphasizing that the critical conditonal response is not the overt response but rather the selective orientation of the organism.

Given that S causes R, generalization to S' is tested by presenting S' and observing whether or not the organism emits R. Suppose R occurs to S'; but suppose also that due to the circumstances of the situation, the relationship between S' and R is not "protected," that is, it is interfered with because subsequent responses (other than R) are allowed to occur in the presence of S'. The generalization test is then Trial 1 of discrimination learning, where the organism is to learn to make R to S but to refrain from making R to S'. The second step in this analysis of concept attainment is to explicate what happens in discrimination learning.

Why does the organism make R to both S and S'? From the account of generalization just given, it is because he is orienting toward a dimension that does not change value between S and S'. If, then, the result of discrimination learning is that the organism makes R to S but refrains from making R to S', what must occur is a reorientation toward a dimension, any dimension, that changes value between S and S'. In articulate organisms, this shift in selective attention can sometimes be accomplished by verbal instructions; in non-articulate organisms, the orienting response r_0 must be redirected by a longer sequence of tests and responses. In any case, discrimination learning involves the acquisition of a perceptual response that provides discriminant cues on which to base excitation of R in situation S and inhibition of R in situation S'. In Fig. 2.1, this would involve extinction of the receptor response r_0 of Panel A and acquisition of the receptor response r_0 of Panel B. (The R_2 of Fig. 2.1 is here interpreted as not-R, or $\bar{R}$.) Thus the positive tendency R becomes conditional upon s_3, while the negative tendency $\bar{R}$ becomes conditional upon s_3'.

We have spoken as if the only dimension mediating discriminative behavior is D_3. This is an oversimplification that should give cause for concern: The extensive literature on incidental learning indicates that organisms associate responses with a considerable array of cues, and that this association formation is automatic.[5] Thus it may often be

---

[5] Postman and Sassenrath's (1961) paper, "The automatic action of verbal rewards and punishments," is a scholarly and fascinating treatise on these matters. See also Postman (1964, pp. 184-194) on incidental learning.

naive to assert that s_3' is the only determining component in situation S'. To the extent that component s_2 is attended, even incidentally, in situation S, situation S', which does not differ from situation S on dimension D_2, will provide cause for the elicitation of R via s_2. If R occurs in situation S, and if the organism perceives component s_2 of S as he emits R, then, since s_2 is also a component of situation S', situation S' will support a tendency for R to occur. It therefore follows that, if discrimination learning is to be successful, the component s_3' of situation S' must provide *even further inhibition of R* where the additional amount of inhibition required depends directly upon the extent of incidental association formation between R and those components of S (namely, s_2 in the schema of Fig. 2.1) that remain unchanged in S'. In other words, to the extent that the organism orients toward dimensions that do not change value from S to S', the relevant component s_3' must elicit a counter-control that prevents the implied generalization.

To generalize this argument, consider stimulus situations S and S' and let each be partitioned into two components. Those aspects of S and S' belonging to dimensions that change value between S and S' will be denoted s and s', respectively; those aspects of S and S' belonging to dimensions that do not change value between S and S' will be denoted s_c, for contextual or common cues. Then if r is taken as the perceptual response congruent with the orienting response r_0 of Fig. 2.1, situation S causes response R in the following way:

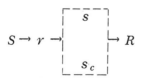

Upon a test for generalization, one has

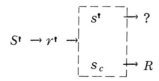

But following discrimination learning, one has

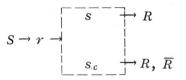

and

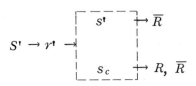

The point is, contextual components (cues common to S and S') become the cause of conflict between R and $\overline{R}$. What this implies is: (1) Situations S and S' are related not only in terms of certain physical dimensions as seen from the observer's point of view, but also in terms of what responses are mutually induced, both positively and negatively, from the organism's point of view. This implication will be spelled out in more detail shortly, for it is essentially the definition of a concept. (2) The successful discrimination of S from S' evolves only at a cost. Whereas before discrimination learning, S might have caused R without complication, after discrimination learning, certain components of S, namely s_c, produce an inhibitory tendency counter to R.

Experimental verification of the second point is available in a number of places. Consider first the work of Gynther (1957), who studied discrimination learning in the eyelid-conditioning situation. In his experiments, S and S' were small lights 2 in. apart. Learners in Group 0 were given 50 conditioning trials to S alone; that is, on each of 50 trials, first S occurred, then the unconditional stimulus; the alternative stimulus S' was never presented. Thus the situation for Group 0 was a straight, uncomplicated conditioning situation with S as the conditional stimulus. Learners in Groups 17 and 50 were treated as Group 0 except that, respectively, 17 and 50 presentations of S' were randomly intermixed with the 50 presentations of S. Presentations of S' were never followed by the unconditional stimulus. In Fig. 2.2 are shown the percent conditional responses

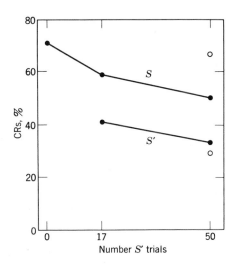

Fig. 2.2 Percent conditional responses given to S and S' for groups having 0, 17, and 50 S' trials randomly intermixed with 50 S trials. An unconditional stimulus always followed S, but never S'. The two open circles represent data from a group having 50 S' trials intermixed, except that the psychological distance between S and S' was greatly increased. (From Gynther, 1957)

given to S and S' over the last 10 trials of the experiment for Groups 0, 17, and 50. Note that as more discrimination learning was permitted, that is, as more opportunities (17, 50) were allowed for differentiating S and S', a greater response decrement to the positive conditional stimulus S accrued. Whereas for Group 0, the conditioning paradigm is simply

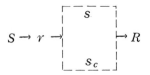

for Groups 17 and 50 it is

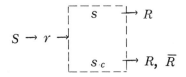

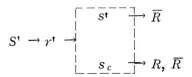

The reason for a greater conditional-response decrement for Group 50 than for Group 17 is that the former learners had 33 additional trials on which to form an association between s_c and $\overline{R}$.

The two open circles in Fig. 2.2 represent data from a group identical with Group 50 except that one of the lights was made red, thus making S and S' differ on at least two additional dimensions, hue and brightness. As argued earlier, the strength of inhibition required for discrimination depends directly upon the amount of association formation between R and those cues (s_c) that are common to S and S'. For this modified situation, then, s_c encompassed two fewer dimensions and hence was less of a mediator of the competing response tendencies R and $\overline{R}$.

Thus Gynther has shown that elaboration of a discrimination involves inhibition. The extent to which the conditional response R is reciprocally inhibited depends (a) directly upon the number of S' trials, and hence upon the strength of the $s_{,} \rightarrow \overline{R}$ association, and (b) inversely upon the number of dimensions that change value between S and S'. Related findings come from Green (1955), who varied the ratio of S to S' occurrences in a human operant conditioning experiment.

Using RT (reaction time) as her dependent variable, Gibson (1939) found that after 50 trials of responding with the syllable DUT (R) to a tactile stimulus at a certain location (S), the introduction of tactile stimuli at other locations (S') to which the learner had to refrain from saying DUT $(\overline{R})$ produced a clear decrement in RT to the original location (S). In one experimental setting, the mean RT during the first 50 trials when only S was presented was 170 msec.; but during the next 100 trials, of which 36 were of the S' variety, the mean RT to S events was 233 msec. In another experimental setting, the corresponding mean RTs were 128 and 170 msec. Thus, in order to learn not to generalize the vocal response DUT from S to S', inhibition of saying DUT to S' must have developed; this inhibition, mediated by the common elements (s_c) of S and S', impeded the vocal response DUT to S itself (by 63 and 42 msec., respectively, for the two experiments). Gibson (1939, p. 252) concludes: ". . . .reaction time increases significantly when other stimuli of the same dimension as the practiced stimulus are introduced. . . . It may be tentatively suggested that in such situations a type of inhibition is set up comparable to the inhibitory aftereffects reported by Pavlov."

It is interesting to note that in spite of very clear data from Pavlov's laboratory, Hull (1943, p. 278) took as his definition of I_R (reactive inhibition) the Mowrer-Miller hypothesis that any response leaves behind a state of negative motivation for that response[6]. Pavlovian evidence warrants a more differentiated use of "inhibition." Using the stimulus sequence {light flash, cutaneous stimulus, sound of bubbling water} as his S, and the reverse of that sequence as his S', Pavlov (1927, p. 146) found that following S with S did not impair

---

[6]Hull's definition of I_R, and hence the Mowrer-Miller hypothesis, is precisely Heidenhain's principle, first announced in 1881: every cortical excitation tends to arouse a local inhibitory process that has the function of limiting the excitation. See Diamond, Balvin, and Diamond (1963, p. 49) for a more extensive discussion.

performance on the second S, but that when S followed S', the salivation response to S was inhibited. As an example, he exhibits the following protocol, where the trials were approximately 7 min. apart:

Stimulus	S	S	S'	S	S'	S	S
No. Drops	10	11	0	7	0	5	7

The point is, inhibition induced by one response is differential in that the brunt of its effect is against the related reponse tendency rather than against the inducing response itself. Further, in agreement with the findings of Gynther (1957) discussed above, Pavlov (1927, p. 126) reports that more inhibition is involved with finer discriminations. Thus where S and S' were tones that differed by a semitone, the trial sequence S', S, S, with approximately 20 min. between trials, yielded the following numbers of drops of saliva: 0, 4, 4; but when they were tones that differed only by an eighth-tone, the corresponding numbers of drops were 0, 1.5, and 4.

In summary, we have seen that in progressing from the simple reaction paradigm to the discriminative reaction paradigm, one is well-nigh forced to infer an active inhibitory process. (Note that this inference is not task bound.) In fact, one might very well say that two different stimuli S and S' are related if and only if learning to emit R to one and $\overline{R}$ (not-R) to the other involves an inhibitory decrement of R. In addition, we have seen that the inhibition responsible for the decrement of R is mediated by aspects common to S and S'; for the more similar are S and S', the greater is the decrement of R.

PART II

We are now in a position to ask what happens when a learning organism must give R_1 to S and R_2 to S', or, to adopt a more workable notation, when the learner must simultaneously acquire the contingencies $S_1 \rightarrow R_1$ and $S_2 \rightarrow R_2$ where S_1 and S_2 are related (similar) in some way. Once this is accomplished, it is a small matter to explicate the usual concept-attainment situation where the organism must learn to make R_1 to each member of the set $\{S_{11}, S_{12}, \ldots, S_{1n}\}$

and R_2 to each member of the set $\{S_{21}, S_{22}, \ldots, S_{2m}\}$. Our task is facilitated by considering a number of choice RT (reaction-time) experiments in an integrative manner and then extracting a systematic set of conclusions. This particular gambit has been chosen because choice-RT paradigms are (a) essentially concept-attainment paradigms with the concept explained to the organism ahead of time, and (b) especially designed to reveal the interplay of excitatory and inhibitory processes.[7]

It has been known since 1885 that when an organism must respond to one of a number of equiprobable stimuli, his RT increases with the number of alternative stimuli (Merkel, 1885). Since then Hyman (1953) has shown, by varying (a) the number of equiprobable alternatives, (b) the probability distribution of the alternatives, and (c) sequential dependencies, that choice RT is a linear increasing function of the number of bits of information per stimulus presentation. Without further ado; we will assert that the reason this is so is that in experimental settings such as that of Hyman, where there is a unique response for each alternative stimulus, responding with any one response requires the simultaneous inhibition of the remaining responses; hence the more responses there are to inhibit, the more inhibition there is involved when making any one of them. This interpretation will gain support as we go along.

An experiment by Morin, Forrin, and Archer (1961) makes it clear that the amount of inhibition involved in a stimulus-response system depends not on the number of alternative stimuli, but indeed on the number of alternative responses that must be inhibited. The design of their experiment can be seen in Table 2.1. (Thus for Group III, for example, each of the four stimuli shown occurred over trials with equal frequencies; the response to S_1 and S_3 was R_1 while the response to S_2 and S_4 was R_2. The paradigm of this group is precisely that used in most concept-attainment

---

[7]The choice paradigms used in RT research are, in most respects, the same as those used in concept-attainment research, with the following contrasted features: In the former, the experimental setup is such that few errors are committed, while in the latter the instructions and procedures are such that many errors are committed; in the former, the dependent variable is RT, while in the latter the dependent variable is number or percent choice of the various alternative responses.

TABLE 2.1 Experimental Design, Paradigmatic Representation, and Resulting Mean RTs from the Morin-Forrin-Archer (1961) Experiment

Group	Stimuli				Paradigm	Est'd Mean RT for First Block of 16 Trials, msec.
	• (S_1)	■ (S_2)	•• (S_3)	■■ (S_4)		
I	R_1				$S_1 \rightarrow R_1$	135
II	R_1	R_2			$S_1 \rightarrow R_1, \bar{R}_2$	
					$S_2 \rightarrow R_2, \bar{R}_1$	460
III	R_1	R_2	R_1	R_2	$S_1, S_3 \rightarrow R_1, \bar{R}_2$	
					$S_2, S_4 \rightarrow R_2, \bar{R}_1$	460
IV	R_1	R_2	R_3	R_4	$S_1 \rightarrow R_1, \bar{R}_2, \bar{R}_3, \bar{R}_4$	
					$S_4 \rightarrow R_4, \bar{R}_1, \bar{R}_2, \bar{R}_3$	690

experiments. Note that the Group-IV paradigm is that of paired-associate learning.) When the simple $S_1 \rightarrow R_1$ paradigm was used (Group I), the mean RT was 135 msec.; but when making R_1 simultaneously involved inhibiting R_2 (Groups II and III), the mean RT was 460 msec. Note that the number of stimuli involved (two for Group II, four for Group III) was irrelevant. That it is the number of responses to be inhibited that determines RT can be further affirmed by comparing the mean RTs for Groups III and IV, where the numbers of alternative stimuli were identical but where there were two additional responses for Group IV. The mean RT for Group IV was 230 msec. longer than that for Group III.

A particularly impressive demonstration that choice performance depends upon how many responses must be inhibited in making a given response comes from an experiment by Fitts and Switzer (1962). The stimuli were numbers and the responses were saying as rapidly as possible whichever number was shown. Focusing only on RT to the number 2, the mean RT over 80 trials (Session 1) was 355 msec. when the set of numbers involved was $\{1, 2\}$, but 375 msec. when the set was $\{1, 2, \ldots, 8\}$. So far, nothing new: the more alternatives there are, the slower the response. Consider now the mean RT when the set was $\{2, 7\}$. Here there were only two stimuli, but the mean RT was almost identical with the mean RT when the set was $\{1, 2, \ldots, 8\}$. Explanation: 2 and 7 do not "go together" as do 1 and 2; hence in order to respond to 2 when 7 is its partner, all responses corresponding to the most likely set of numbers to contain 2 and 7 must be inhibited, where "the most likely set," namely, {1, 2, ..., 8}, is a product of past experience. Fitts and Switzer continued their experiment over two additional sessions of 80 trials each, and by Session 3 the mean *RT* when the set was {2, 7} had shortened to half-way between the mean *RT*s for the other two groups (whose mean *RT*s remained approximately stable), thus indicating that the subset {2, 7}, though "unnatural" at first, was being learned.

Forrin and Morin (1966), in a study of number-naming *RT*s, have shown quite clearly the role of inhibition of related alternative responses in skilled behavior. Under one condition, which we can call the choice condition, three separate groups of subjects were required to name the numbers of one of the following three sets as they (the set members) appeared singly in random order: {1, 2, ..., 8}, {2, 4, 7, 8}, or {2, 8}. Their mean *RT*s are shown as the lower curve of Fig. 2.3. As the size of the set decreases (going from right to left), mean *RT* decreases. This is the usual finding. In another condition, which we can call the inhibition condition, separate groups of subjects were required to name the same sets of

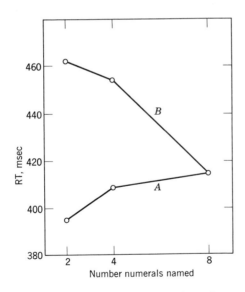

Fig. 2.3 Mean *RT*s as a function of number of numerals to be named. (a) Choice condition: Only the numerals to be named were presented. (b) Inhibition condition: All eight numerals were presented, but the size of the set to be named matched the respective size for the choice condition. (From Forrin and Morin, 1966)

numbers as in the choice condition, but the remaining numbers from the complete set of eight, which in the choice condition did not appear, here appeared but were not to be named. In other words, for all three groups under the inhibition condition, the size of the set of presented numbers remained fixed at 8, but the size of the set of numbers actually to be named matched the respective size for the choice condition. Thus in progressing from right to left on the upper curve of Fig. 2.3, there were 0, 4, and 6 presented numbers for which the naming response had to be inhibited. Accordingly, we find an appropriate increase in mean RT.

Fitts, Peterson, and Wolpe (1963) throw further light on the nature of the inhibitory processes underlying choice behavior by showing that in the choice paradigm

$$S_1 \rightarrow R_1, \bar{R}_2$$

$$S_2 \rightarrow R_2, \bar{R}_1$$

the following statement is true: $P(S_1) > P(S_2) \rightarrow RT_1 < RT_2$, which reads, "Given that the stimulus S_1 occurs more frequently than, or has a higher probability-of-occurrence than, stimulus S_2, the RT of response R_1 is shorter than the RT of response R_2." The important point is that the right-hand inequality does not hold over early trials but develops with practice, indicating a learning factor of some sort. In other words, because $P(S_1) > P(S_2)$, the organism strengthens the $S_1 \rightarrow R_1, \bar{R}_2$ association more than he strengthens the $S_2 \rightarrow R_2, \bar{R}_1$ association, which means that $\bar{R}_2$ becomes more surely associated with common or contextual cues (s_c) than does $\bar{R}_1$. This interpretation is supported by the fact that practice does not simply shorten RT_1 faster than RT_2, rather RT_2 actually gets longer over trials. Thus the Fitts, et al., study indicates that both excitatory and inhibitory tendencies are acquired and that skilled performance depends upon their resolution.

An implication of the interpretation given to the studies discussed above is that if inhibition is involved in responding to related sets of stimuli, then that inhibition should produce a decrement on the response of the next trial if the intertrial interval is short enough. Bertelson (1961) has not only shown that this is true but, in agreement with Pavlov, that there is a certain selectiveness about this transferred inhibition. Let the paradigm be the one used by Fitts, et al., in the preceding paragraph, and suppose $P(S_1) = P(S_2)$. The RT to S_1 turns out to be shorter if the preceding stimulus event was also an S_1 than if it was an S_2. In other words, RTs to repeated stimuli are shorter than RTs to "new" stimuli. Why should this be? Since the occurrence of S_2 causes the composite event R_2, $\overline{R}_1$, to the extent that these response tendencies do not dissipate immediately there will be a differential effect on the next trial. If the next stimulus is S_2 again, the aftereffects $(R_2, \overline{R}_1)$ of the first S_2 trial summate with the appropriate composite response $(R_2, \overline{R}_1)$ for that trial; but if the next stimulus is S_1, then the after-effects of the composite R_2, $\overline{R}_1$ provide direct interference for the appropriate response R_1, $\overline{R}_2$. Bertelson has also shown that this carry-over of inhibition is transitory in that lengthening the intertrial interval reduces the effect.

That the carry-over of inhibition is a genuine interference phenomenon is attested to by some of Hyman's (1953) data. He found that RT_1 gets longer as the number of other tests $(S_i \rightarrow R_i, i \neq 1)$ intervene between tests of $S_1 \rightarrow R_1$. Moreover, the more alternative responses there are, the more marked is this effect.

Still further verification comes from a study of concept identification per se: Granting that additional irrelevant dimensions give rise to additional orienting-response tendencies that must be inhibited if a solution is to be attained, Bourne, Guy, Dodd, and Justesen (1965) have shown that the optimal intertrial interval is longer when there are five irrelevant dimensions than when there is only one.

On the other hand, the inhibitory factors underlying RT data are not entirely as response-specific as they may seem from the foregoing review. It is known that the inhibition induced on a given trial will carry over and interfere with a neutral response that involves no choice of any kind. Favreau (1964) presented stimuli of various shapes and colors such that the following choice paradigm obtained:

$$S_1 \rightarrow R_1, \overline{R}_2; P(S_1) = .125$$
$$S_2{}^* \rightarrow R_2, \overline{R}_1; S_2{}^* = \{S_2, ..., S_8\}; P(S_1) = .125$$

Three seconds after a choice response was made, a ready light came on to which a separate key had to be pressed that started the next trial. Favreau found that RT to this ready signal was longer after $S_1 \to R_1$, $\bar{R}_2$ trials than after $S_2^* \to R_2$, $\bar{R}_1$ trials. The reason for this is that because the $S_2^* \to R_2$, $\bar{R}_1$ reaction occurs seven times more often than the $S_1 \to R_1$, $\bar{R}_2$ reaction, the inhibition that must be evoked by S_1 to ensure the R_1 response must be greater than that evoked by S_2 to ensure the R_2 response. Thus an S_1 event involves more inhibition than does an S_2 event. The net result is a longer RT to the neutral ready signal after an S_1 trial.

Before extracting a systematic set of conclusions, consideration of an experiment by Broadbent and Gregory (1962) is appropriate. By comparing the b- and c-reaction paradigms of Donders, with both compatible and incompatible S-R pairings, one gets a clear picture of what is added in passing from the discrimination learning paradigm, namely,

$$S_1 \to R_1 \qquad \text{(c-reaction)}$$
$$S_2 \to R_1$$

to the simplest form of the more complex paradigm of concept formation, namely,

$$S_1 \to R_1, \bar{R}_2 \qquad \text{(b-reaction)}$$
$$S_2 \to R_2, \bar{R}_1$$

Consider first their incompatible situation. Those subjects giving c-reactions had to say DECK (R_1) whenever they heard BID (S_1), and refrain from saying DECK ($\bar{R}_1$) whenever they heard DID (S_2). Those giving b-reactions had to say DECK (R_1) to BID (S_1) and DIM (R_2) to DID (S_2). This means that upon presentation of BID, those subjects giving c-reactions responded with DECK, while those giving b-reactions also responded with DECK but in addition had to inhibit the alternative response DIM.[8] The mean RTs over 120 stimulus presentations are shown as the upper curve in Fig. 2.4. The necessity of inhibiting the alternative response under the b-reaction paradigm resulted in a mean RT of 444 msec., which is 90 msec. longer than the mean RT

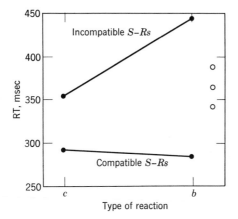

Fig. 2.4   Mean RTs for conditions where (a) the response paradigm was either a b- or a c-reaction and (b) the responses required were either compatible or incompatible with 'natural' associates. (From Broadbent and Gregory, 1962) The open circles are mean RTs for three degrees of S-R compatibility. The lowest circle represents the most compatible condition. (From Bertelson, 1963)

under the c-reaction paradigm where an alternative response was not in competition.

An associative connection is interfered with to the extent that its acquisition and/or execution is opposed by (a) prior response tendencies caused by certain components of the stimulus in question, and (b) alternative response tendencies in the process of being differentiated. In Broadbent and Gregory's incompatible situation, both b- and c-reaction paradigms involved the former source, but only the b-reaction paradigm also involved the latter source. If their

[8]Note that in this incompatible situation, both b- and c-reaction paradigms equally involve the competing responses that underlie the incompatibility; to the stimulus BID, saying DECK is seen as incompatible with saying BID. ("Incompatibility" may be defined as associative or proactive interference.) Broadbent and Gregory's incompatible situation may be represented as follows:

$$\text{BID} \longrightarrow \text{DECK}, \overline{\text{BID}}$$

c-reaction:

$$\text{DID} \longrightarrow \overline{\text{DECK}}, \overline{\text{DID}}$$
$$\text{BID} \longrightarrow \text{DECK}, \overline{\text{DIM}}, \overline{\text{BID}}$$

b-reaction:

$$\text{DID} \longrightarrow \text{DIM}, \overline{\text{DECK}}, \overline{\text{DID}}$$

The negative tendencies $\overline{\text{BID}}$ and $\overline{\text{DID}}$ at the extreme right are the sources of incompatibility.

compatible situation is now considered, the inhibitive role of to-be-differentiated alternative-response tendencies in choice responding can be examined without the presence of interfering prior associations. Those subjects giving c-reactions had to say BID (R_1) whenever they heard BID (S_1) and refrain from saying either DID or BID whenever they heard DID (S_2). Those giving b-reactions had to say BID (R_1) to BID (S_1) and DID (R_2) to DID (S_2).[9] The results are shown as the lower curve in Fig. 2.4. If anything, c-reactions (mean RT = 292 msec.) took slightly longer than b-reactions (mean RT = 284 msec.). Thus in the absence of proactive interference, that is , in the absence of incompatibility, S_1 and S_2 apparently do not induce reciprocal interference. Two highly compatible systems, therefore, are two independent systems, where the skillful operation of one does not require inhibition of the other. This means that in the compatible condition of Broadbent and Gregory's experiment, S_1 and S_2 were not treated, from the subject's point of view, as related in any way.

What Broadbent and Gregory have shown is that when two stimuli are related from the responder's point of view, successful differential responding requires negative inducement of the alternative(s). Stimuli are related from the responder's point of view only when their central representations interact, that is, only when they elicit to a detectable extent common elements of representation.

Bertelson (1963) gives results that substantiate the role of compatibility in the b-reaction (simple concept formation) paradigm: As compatibility increases, RTs decrease. The mean RTs over 550 stimulus presentations for nine subjects are shown as the open circles in Fig. 2.4 for each of his three levels of S-R compatibility. The bottom point represents his most compatible condition. That increased compatibility may be

---

[9]Corresponding to the representation of the incompatible situation given in Footnote 8, the compatible situation may be represented as follows:

$$\text{BID} \longrightarrow \text{BID}$$

c-reaction:

$$\text{DID} \longrightarrow \overline{\text{BID}}, \overline{\text{DID}}$$
$$\text{BID} \longrightarrow \text{BID}, \overline{\text{DID}}$$

b-reaction:

$$\text{DID} \longrightarrow \text{DID}, \overline{\text{BID}}$$

interpreted as decreased inhibitory involvement receives even
further support from Bertelson's experiment: As compatibility increases, the difference in RTs to "new" and repeated
stimuli decreases. This decline of the transition effect with
increased compatibility means that the composite response
$(R_1, \overline{R}_2)$ of one trial is not offering as much resistance to the
composite response of the next trial $(R_2, \overline{R}_1)$ when the stimulus
of the next trial is "new." That this is the proper interpretation follows from the fact that most of the effect of increasing compatibility is in shortening the RT to "new" stimuli.
These effects are shown in Table 2.2.

TABLE 2.2   Mean RTs (in Msec.) to New and Old Stimuli for
Three Degrees of S-R Compatibility from Bertelson's (1963)
Experiment*

| Stimulus | Compatibility | | |
	Least	Medium	Most
New	443	410	377
	(33)	(33)	
Old	333	320	307
	(13)	(13)	

*Decreases in RT between compatibility conditions are shown
in parentheses.

In light of the discussion thus far, the first major point
to be made is the following: *If the associations $S_1 \rightarrow R_1$ and
$S_2 \rightarrow R_2$ exist, and if S_1 and S_2 go together in some sense,
then the occurrence of S_1 leads to retrieval of both R_1 and R_2.*
This joint retrieval is mediated by the elements common
to S_1 and S_2, that is, by the dimensions that do not change
value from S_1 to S_2 and thereby cause S_1 and S_2 to "go
together." This conclusion is basic; for it is because of this
joint retrieval that inhibition enters the picture of skilled
performance. A recent experiment by Underwood (1965)
emphasizes the joint-retrieval point. Using the Shepard-
Teghtsoonian (1961) recognition-memory paradigm, Under-

wood presented 200 words in sequence, to each of which the subject had to respond "old" or "new" according to whether he thought he had or had not seen the word earlier in the sequence. The interesting finding for our purposes is that when at a later point in the sequence an associate (e.g., ROUGH) of an earlier word (e.g., SMOOTH) was presented, the subject tended to recognize the associate as old. It is as if in responding to the earlier word, its associates were also activated, thereby according the associates what amounts to a functional occurrence in the sequence.

The second major point to be made may be stated as follows: *If the occurrence of S_1 leads to retrieval of both R_1 and R_2, then skill in performing R_1 involves inhibition of R_2.* This conclusion derives from the literature reviewed above, including the studies by Gynther, Gibson, and Pavlov. The strength of inhibition of R_2 when S_1 is presented was seen to depend directly upon the similarity of, or amount of generalization between, S_1 and S_2, and upon the strength of the $S_2 \rightarrow R_2$ association. This induced inhibition of alternative responses when R_1 is elicited has two notable properties. First, the reciprocal inhibitory effect on R_1 itself summates logarithmically over the number of alternative responses inhibited (e.g., Hyman, 1953). Second, the inhibition so induced perseverates for a finite length of time, thereby transferring its effects to whatever the next response might be. This transfer effect is discriminative in that the size of the consequent response decrement depends on how the successive eliciting stimuli relate to each other.

PART III

It may be fairly clear by now what form the definition of "concept" is to take. However, a certain amount of circumlocution may be helpful before offering the intended definition. It might be said that an organism "has a concept" when in making one response he must simultaneously inhibit a particular set of other responses. When an organism says "It is green" and means that it is not red, it seems reasonable to assert that the organism has a concept of color. When an organism says 'It is green" and means that it is not ripe, it seems reasonable to insist that the organism is not at the moment exercising his concept of color, rather he is exercising, or has, a concept of maturity or readiness. Almost certainly the underlying nervous activity associated with the former utterance of "It is green" is different from that associated with the latter utterance, where the difference lies in whatever it takes to inhibit the response "red" as compared with whatever it takes to inhibit the response "ripe." In short, then, the following definition seems appropriate: *A concept is a set of mutually induced response tendencies.*[10]

In conjunction with this definition, there are four points of clarification or elaboration to be made. The first three have already been treated in detail above, hence they can be disposed of briefly. First, it may be asked what causes or mediates this mutual induction. In terms of the present analysis, it is s_c, the set of contextual or common cues, that does the mediating; that is, s_c causes the reciprocal excitation and inhibition that interrelate the response tendencies making up the concept. Suppose, for some limited purpose an organism were required to divide his world into S_1 things and S_2 things, giving the response R_1 to instances of S_1 and R_2 to instances of S_2. Upon the occurrence of an S_1 object or event, the following representation seems descriptive:

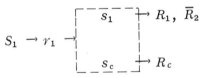

whereas should an exemplar of S_2 occur, the following may be written:

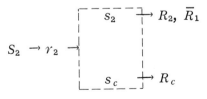

<hr />

[10] The mutual induction (positive and negative) here referred to is seen by the present writer as precisely the mutual induction referred to by Pavlov (1927, Lecture XI).

In this case, s_c (those aspects of the world that jointly do not systematically change between S_1 and S_2 and are attended to by the organism) causes the activation of whatever response tendencies have occurred in its presence in the past, namely R_1, R_2, $\overline{R}_1$, and $\overline{R}_2$. Thus R_c is a composite response made up of R_1 and R_2, together with their negative tendencies, and thereby is the concept involved in relating S_1 with S_2.

Second, it may be asked what causes a particular one of the set of mutually induced response tendencies to occur. The answer is that dimensional variation that jointly distinguishes S_1 from S_2 and is attended to by the organism. Thus although s_c causes the composite response tendency R_1, R_2, $\overline{R}_1$, $\overline{R}_2$, the specific cue s_1 causes the composite response tendency R_1, $\overline{R}_2$, hence the net result is the overt response R_1. Note that it is the negative tendency $\overline{R}_1$, which has become conditional upon s_c, that is responsible for the R_1 response decrement observed in the studies cited earlier.

Third, it may be asked where all these response tendencies come from. It has been one of the aims of this paper to argue that they arise from simple discrimination learning, which is the conditioning of inhibitory tendencies to related but different stimuli. Thus in learning to say "green" to objects that reflect electromagnetic energy with wavelength λ = 540 mμ, the child simultaneously learns to inhibit the response "green" to objects that reflect energy of λ = 610 mμ (red). To so proceed, in conjunction with the converse condition (learning to say "red" when λ = 610 mμ, but to refrain from saying "red" when λ = 540 mμ), is to acquire, or to form, the concept of color.

The fourth point that requires comment has to do with what is best called concept labeling. If R_c is a concept elicited in situation S_1 (which has s_c as a component), then what has occurred is the activation of a set of reciprocally exciting and inhibiting response tendencies. Note that no requirement of consciousness is involved. Thus an organism can have a concept, or make use of a concept, without being aware of it, and certainly without having a special name or labeling response for it. But a labeling response can be learned, and hence awareness of a concept can be learned. Clearly, since s_c is a response-eliciting stimulus, s_c can serve as the unconditional stimulus in a conditioning paradigm where the conditional stimulus is what is called a label (e.g., the aurally-detected utterance "color," or the visual cue COLOR). In this way, certain stimulus events can be said to come to elicit such-and-such a concept (R_c). Conversely, since all responses, including $R_c s$, give rise to stimuli, such response-produced stimuli can, like any other type stimulus, serve as conditional stimuli in a conditioning paradigm where the unconditional stimulus is whatever stimulus is necessary to evoke an arbitrary labeling response. Concept labeling, then, is a learning process superimposed upon the necessarily prior concept-formation process; it is a conditioning process wherein the stimuli (s_c) causing the concept (R_c), or the stimuli caused by the concept, are paired with arbitrary stimuli, which consequently become labels. Cognizance of a concept is thus a learned response, a conditional labeling response.

PART IV

An unpublished study recently conducted in our laboratory by Claude Steiner (1965) bears directly on the analysis given above. It revolved around the idea that orientation toward context becomes habituated in a concept-attainment problem. In other words, the subject, in learning to respond correctly, is seen as coming to inhibit perception of irrelevant stimuli thereby eliminating irrelevant responses. The experiment was divided into three stages.

Stage I. The stimuli were triads of colored (red, yellow, green) shapes (circle, square, triangle). On each trial, two such triads, an S_1 and an S_2, were presented simultaneously, side by side, on a screen. Triads where all three shapes were different but the outside two shapes were of the same color were instances of S_1; triads where all three shapes and colors were different were instances of S_2. The subjects' task was to learn, to a 10/10 criterion, which triads were instances of S_1 and to press one of two buttons according to whether the S_1 instance was on the right or on the left. On the average, a subject took between 5.1 (median) and 8.2 (mean) trials before beginning his criterion run.

Stage II. After the 10/10 criterion was met, 15 additional trials were given, over which all subjects continued to respond according to their Stage-I solution. During the last 10 of these 15 post-solution trials, a new dimension was added: One, but not the other, of the two presented triads was heavily cross-hatched. For the subjects in Group ICE (irrelevant cue exposure), the new dimension correlated zero with instances of S_1 and S_2; for the subjects in Group RCE (relevant cue exposure), the presence and absence of cross-hatching on a given triad was perfectly correlated with whether or not the triad was an instance of S_1; for the subjects in Group NCE (no cue exposure), the cross-hatching dimension was not introduced at all.

Stage III. All subjects solved, to a 10/10 criterion, a new problem based on the cross-hatching dimension. For Groups ICE and RCE, Stage III was therefore a shift task; for Group NCE, Stage III began with the introduction of the new dimension. The solution dimension of Stages I and II was not represented in Stage III. Except for the cross-hatching, all triads were made up of three different shapes, each differently colored. Thus the three groups were treated identically in Stages I and III, differently only in Stage II.

Prior to the Stage-I, -II, -III sequence, all subjects were pretrained on an auditory tracking task. Depending upon which earphone carried a soft tone, the subject depressed either a left or a right footpedal. During the Stage-I, -II, -III sequence, the subjects engaged in the tracking task only during Stage II, the stage in which they continued to respond to the visual stimuli according to their Stage-I solution and, depending upon the cue-exposure condition, in which they experienced the new dimension. Neither tracking nor tones occurred in Stages I and III.

The reason for the tracking task in Stage II was to provide information on the extent to which attention was in fact invested in the new dimension: the more a subject switched attention away from the tracking task toward the new dimension, the longer would be his RT to the incoming tones.

Consider first the resulting relation between performance decrement on the tracking task due to a shift in attention to the new dimension and performance on the shift task (Stage

III). Steiner argued that to the extent that the subject
(a) attended to the new dimension, as evidenced by a decrement in tracking-task performance, and (b) considered the
new dimension to be irrelevant, from his point of view, to
Stage-II criterion performance, then to that extent would the
subject acquire receptive inhibition relative to the new
dimension, thereby impeding solution of the shift task (Stage
III). which was based on that dimension. In keeping with this
expectation the correlation, for Group RCE, between performance decrement on the tracking task (increase in RT upon
initiation of the new dimension) and per cent saving[11] on
the shift task was -.80 ($p < .01$). This means that the more
a given subject attended to the new relevant but redundant
dimension when it was introduced in Stage II, the more trials
it took him to solve on that dimension in Stage III. The corresponding control calculation for Group NCE, for whom the
new dimension was not introduced in Stage II but who nevertheless had to solve on that new dimension in Stage III, appropriately gave a correlation of .07.

Consider next a comparison of the three groups in Stage
III. For each of the groups, the median trials to criterion was
figured for both Stage-I and Stage-III solutions. From these,
the percent saving was calculated. These are shown in
Fig. 2.5. It is clear that cue exposure during Stage II resulted
in considerable impedance in Stage III. This, together with the
negative correlation between disruption in Stage-II tracking
and percent saving in Stage III, indicates that those subjects
who payed the most attention to the new dimension in Stage
II were least able to utilize that dimension in Stage III.
Thus the interpretation proffered at the outset of this section
seems completely reasonable: Perception of a dimension
previously attended to but not utilized becomes inhibited.
Indeed, the inferred inhibition toward the new dimension was
so strong in some subjects that four of the ten subjects in
Group ICE and three of the ten in Group RCE could not solve the
shift task in 100 trials. Several non-solvers, upon being
questioned after the experiment, insisted they could not see
any distinguishing dimension among the Stage-III stimuli, and

---

[11]Percent saving was calculated by the formula $(ttc_{III} - ttc_I)/$
$(ttc_{III} + ttc_I)$, where ttc_I, for example, reads "Trials to criterion on the
Stage-I task."

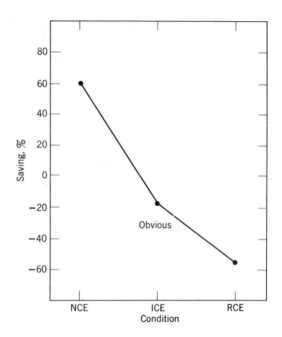

Fig. 2.5   Percent saving on shifting to the second problem as a
function of cue exposure condition. (From Steiner, 1965)

expressed discovery upon being shown that some stimuli
were heavily and obviously cross-hatched and others were
not. (That in normal circumstances the cross-hatch dimension is an easy one to solve on is attested to by the fact that
the median number trials to criterion for Group NCE in Stage
III was 2.)

    In Steiner's experiment, not all of the conditions of which
are reported here, the solution concept of Stage I was expand-
ed in Stage II by the addition of a new dimension. However,
the circumstances were such that the subjects continued to
respond as they had been responding in Stage I. Thus the new
dimension came to be represented as "do not respond to
cross-hatching," which means that an induced inhibition of
perception of the cross-hatching dimension was incorporated
into the orienting response of each trial. That there was
more negative transfer to Stage III for Group-RCE than
Group-ICE subjects indicates that orientation toward the new
dimension was more strongly inhibited when it was introduced

on a relevant schedule than when it was introduced on an irrelevant schedule.

Note that what is relevant from the observer's point of view may in actuality be irrelevant from the learner's point of view. Failure to recognize this possibility can give rise to defective formulations of concept attainment. For example, the considerable negative transfer from Stage II to Stage III for Group-RCE subjects is in direct opposition to Bourne and Restle's (1959) cue-conditioning and cue-adaptation model. This predicament is traceable to the non-relativistic nature of their model: From the model's point of view, the new dimension of Stage II is seen as relevant, whereas from the subject's point of view, the new dimension is seen as irrelevant. Bourne and Restle's model is in complete agreement, however, with the finding of negative transfer for Group-ICE subjects, since the points of view of the subject and the model happen to coincide. In a similar vein, Bower and Trabasso (1964) must predict no differences among Groups NCE, ICE, and RCE in transfer from Stage II to Stage III. This is because, in their model, once the correct responses have been conditioned to the appropriate values (categories) of the solution dimension, no other dimension can be sampled. In other words, a process has been assumed that does not allow the subject even to see the new dimension of Stage II, to say nothing of acquiring differential, transferable responses to it. Similar comments apply to Restle's (1962) strategy-selection model.

PART V

An organism may be said to be utilizing a concept when (a) he responds differentially to S_1 and S_2, *and* (b) his response to S_1 requires inhibition of his response to S_2. If R_1 does not mean $\overline{R}_2$ (not-R_2), then in responding differentially to S_1 and S_2, no conceptual process is involved. Thus, to define "attainment" in the phrase "concept attainment," an organism attains a concept when, presumably for adjustive reasons, he finds mutual induction of alternative response tendencies necessary for skilled behavior.

It is important to the analysis outlined in this paper that the statements of the foregoing paragraph not be seen as restricted to overt responses, but as equally applicable to receptive (orienting, perceiving) responses as well. Indeed, the present writer suspects that in time it may prove sufficient to limit the application of this analysis to receptive responses alone, for they are the determiners of cue distinctions and of how, in general, the organism samples impinging energy.[12]

To come back, more or less, to the intent of the critical comments that were made at the outset, two evaluative statements seem appropriate. First, there appears to be no reason why the present formulation should be deemed non-relativistic. The notion of a concept here elaborated is in no way contingent upon an external observer's point of view; no constraint on the organism to match an arbitrary criterion set by an observer is involved. Yet at the same time, the

---

[12]The view that selective behavior may be accounted for primarily in terms of orienting responses has been elaborated by Spence (1960). Orienting-response-produced cues are seen as the distinctive stimuli with which appropriate responses are associated. This means that what is transferred from situation to situation, and hence what underlies adaptability and adjustment, depends primarily on the orienting tendencies that relate the organism to those aspects of his environment that have proved critical for success in the past. The relation between this position of Spence and the analysis given by Lawrence (1963) is worth noting. For Spence, the orienting response is elicited by the total configuration and serves to focus the organism's receptive facilities on only selected aspects of the configuration. Lawrence, on the other hand, postulates a more subtle coding response (p. 189f) that is not elicited directly by proximal stimulation but that occurs after reception in order to modify the input. Lawrence eschews the receptor-adjustment hypothesis of Spence and others on the grounds that such orienting responses are necessarily controlled by the very stimuli that control the overt responses to be explained. But such a charge overlooks the idea that configurational characteristics serve to direct attention to subproperties of the configuration, which may or may not change when the configuration changes. In other words, Spence's receptor-adjustment responses are no less coding responses than those postulated by Lawrence. In removing the clearly necessary selector mechanism to a more internal location, Lawrence does not offer a substantially new idea, rather he tries to make the difficult point that receptor adjustment, if taken as strictly a peripheral process, is inadequate to handle all the complexities of stimulated behavior. For such reasons as this, no attempt has been made in the present paper to draw a line between what is meant by terms like "orienting response" (Spence, 1960), "orientation reflex" (Sokolov, 1963), and "coding response" (Lawrence, 1963). Just because they can be operationally distinguished according to external criteria does not imply they do not serve the organism in essentially the same way.

processes here seen to underlie concept attainment are such that their characteristics can be inferred fairly safely from such diverse measures as RTs and per cent choices. Certainly none of the inferences are task-bound.

Second, the present formulation hopefully in no way contradicts what applicable neurophysiological facts we have on hand. It involves resolution of excitatory and inhibitory tendencies acquired through conditioning. The composition rule employed herein is that excitatory and inhibitory tendencies oppose each other, which seems perfectly compatible with the opposition of excitatory and inhibitory processes at the neural level. Presumably, concern for such matters is implicit in our inclusion of physiological pursuits as relevant to psychological thought.

CHAPTER 3   *James G. Holland*
                                   University of Pittsburgh

DISCUSSION OF PAPERS BY
LYLE E. BOURNE AND EDWIN J. MARTIN

There is no rigid definition of "concept," as the vast differences in these two papers have made clear. The authors not only mean different things by concept formation; their approach and methods are unalike. For Martin, concept formation is not a uniquely verbal process but, like simple discrimination, an instance of stimulus control. A child learns to call an object which is more or less spherical and not too large or too small a "ball," and to inhibit calling it red or green when his behavior reflects the concept "ball." This view of concept formation enables Martin to draw on a wide range of discrimination experiments, including one in eyelid conditioning, for his theoretical constructs to form a rigorous theory.

Bourne, on the other hand, considers concept formation to be the learning of relevant "attributes" and "rules" by which instances can be categorized as examples or non-examples of the concept. Rules and attributes seem to be a highly verbal matter. In Bourne's experiments, a subject comes to "know" a rule either through verbal instruction or induction from examples. This view sets concept formation apart from the rest of learning. The author can draw little on previous theoretical formulations, and proceeds to design some arbitrary tasks as a vehicle for investigating concept formation as he has defined it.

But which of these two best characterize natural concept formation? Or if both do, what types of cases are characterized by one and what type by the other? The difference between them seems to be the difference between learning words directly and learning dictionary definitions of words. It's hard to imagine one of Bourne's experiments as an analogue of early concept learning in the child. A child fairly quickly will learn to identify "cars" before he can name attributes or rules applying to the classification of objects as "cars" or "non-cars." Nor would concept formation in lower animals be readily handled by Bourne. A variety of lower organisms have learned the oddity problem, matching to sample tasks, and have acquired learning sets. The defining rules for these tasks always appear in the experimenter's write-ups. Apparently the experimenter identifies rules, but it's hardly parsimonious and certainly not empirical to assume a similar verbal process in the animal.

Concept learning by animals is rare because conditions are seldom conducive for such; however, it is no less real for its rarity. In a recent study, Herrnstein and Loveland (1964) arranged to have pigeons respond when there was a person shown in a view of a landscape and not to respond when there was no person. In establishing this discrimination, over twelve hundred unselected scenes, principally from Southeast Asia, were used. Those scenes that contained people were the positive stimuli; those without, the negative stimuli. The views of the people varied greatly as to dress, number, position in the field, and presence or absence of intervening objects. The scenes were presented one at a time on a translucent screen in an experimental chamber. A pigeon was reinforced on an average of once a minute for pecking the key when a scene was being projected that contained a person. Responses were not reinforced in those scenes in which the experimenter judged that there was no person shown in the scene. Within 7 to 10 sessions, clear signs of discrimination between scenes containing people and those without people were found, though the performance continued to improve over a period of months. The pigeons clearly had a concept of "person." But the concept was established through procedures rather like ordinary discrimination learning, except that many different postive stimuli were presented relatively few times each, and similarly, many different stimuli constituted the negative cases and appeared only one or a few times. Therefore, concept formation cannot be viewed as distinctly human or verbal.

Even though one can easily question whether Bourne's formulation characterizes all instances one would call concept formation or not, it still may be appropriate for some types of concept formation. One may ask whether the tasks designed for his subjects are mere arbitrary games created by an ingenious experimenter, or whether they are in fact analogues of important human tasks. Although the child learning a new label cannot articulate the attributes and rules, the author of a dictionary does exactly that. The entomologist, attempting to classify a newly discovered species seems, at least superficially, to be acting like one of Bourne's subjects. A six-year old child speaks in a manner which reflects all of the "rules" of structural linguistics, but only after he becomes an adult and studies to become a linguist does he learn to examine the language to extract its rules. These special scholarly activities may be analogous to Bourne's experimental tasks, but they are very rare occurrences indeed, for new insects are seldom discovered, and a large number of linguists working for a long period of time have succeeded in discovering only a few rules of language. Even then, they seem to be often following carefully formulated procedures of their discipline rather than any direct rule learning.

The development of arbitrary experimental situations is often a useful approach in science, provided the task is chosen to provide ready experimental analysis of the important controlling variables. It is possible that this is the case in Bourne's experimental settings. However, as Bourne himself comments, few systematic generalizations have emerged from the series of experiments that he has thus far performed. But the future may provide such a system, and the energy and ingenuity with which Bourne approaches his task would encourage us to think that such a happy conclusion might be reached.

By now it must be apparent that this author agrees with Martin that concept formation is not a unique process but a case of discrimination learning. As Martin says, there is a line from generalization to discrimination, and finally to concept formation as the number of different stimuli involved in training is increased. He formulates a theory of concept formation in which inhibition becomes the central concept. He even goes so far as to define a concept in terms of this theoretical construct. The claim is made that "a concept is a set of mutually induced response tendencies." This orientation to concept formation is new, ingenious, and has the rigor associated with the hypothetico-deductive approach to theory construction. One of the advantages frequently quoted for such an approach is that theory can be proven wrong, and indeed this one can as I shall illustrate below.

Martin observes that discrimination between stimuli "evolves only at a cost." This cost is provided by the inhibition and the generalization of inhibition resulting from the introduction of negative stimuli. He demonstrates this with several experiments which indicated that, after the initial conditioning of a stimulus to a response, the addition of a second stimulus during which responses were not reinforced (i.e. extinction) lowers the response strength to the original positive stimulus. Since he primarily bases his case on a change of response strength for a single stimulus on a same stimulus continuum with the second negative stimulus, it might be instructive to take a more empirical approach and examine data in which the whole range of stimuli on that continuum is examined. This is clearly a question of the shape of the stimulus generalization gradient which has successfully been measured directly (Guttman, 1956). Data provided by Terrace (1964) are shown as Group 1 in Fig. 3.1. The technique for this measurement of generalization is to first reinforce responses on a variable interval schedule in the presence of the positive stimulus. In the case of Group 1, there is no discrimination training as such, so during training there has been only one stimulus, a 580 mu light illuminating a translucent key in the standard experimental chamber for operant conditioning in pigeons. The variable interval schedule results in stable responding with reasonable resistance to extinction. To test for generalization, a test session is initiated in which reinforcement is not available, but during which lights of differing wave lengths are presented in random order for brief 30-sec periods. In Fig. 3.1, Group 1, which had only the S^+ training, shows the familiar peak in the gradient at the S^+ value of 850 mμ with responses in general falling off as the stimuli move either direction from the S^+ value. However, if instead of presenting only S^+ during initial training, standard discrimination training is used, the shape of the gradient is changed. This can be seen in the data from Terrace's Group 3 shown in the third column of Fig. 3.1. There is virtually no responding below the wavelength

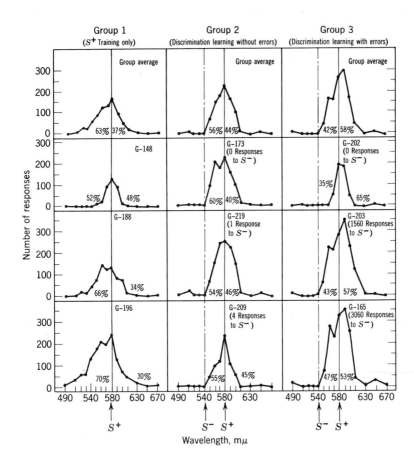

Fig. 3.1 Generalization gradients for each bird and average gradients for each group. Each point represents the number of responses emitted to one of the test stimuli presented in the generalization test. The number to the right and the left of the solid vertical lines represents the percentage of the total area under the gradient that lies above and below S^+, respectively. (From Terrace, 1964)

for the negative stimulus or at the negative stimulus (in this instance a 540 mμ light). The interesting point is that the peak of the gradient has moved from the S^+ value to a value in the opposite direction of S^+ from the S^-. This peak shift in the generalization gradient has been interpreted as the effect of generalization of inhibition to the S^-. This interpretation agrees with Martin's theory; however, when discrimination can be established without errors (i.e. without S^- responses) the situation is considerably different. Terrace has successfully developed techniques to establish such error-free discriminations. Group 2 had learned discrimination by such a procedure before the generalization test. This was done by always presenting the S^+ for one-minute intervals during training. The S^- was initially both less bright and of much shorter duration (2 sec). The duration and the brightness were gradually increased in a series of steps until the brightness and duration of the S^- and S^+ were equal. In many instances, with this procedure, the animal learned the discrimination without errors. In the case of the data shown in Fig. 3.1, the three birds made zero, one, and four responses to the S^- during the entire training procedure. When the stimulus generalization gradient is measured after this type of discrimination training, there is no peak shift, and there is no sign of inhibition.

In a second study Terrace (1963) found an additional dramatic difference between discrimination with and without errors. He compared the effects of chlorpromazine and imipramine on the impairment of discrimination performance after both error and errorless discrimination training. These two substances are of the variety commonly known as "tranquilizers" and have long been known to disrupt the performance of a learned discrimination. Terrace confirms this effect by obtaining considerable responding in the presence of S^- after either of these drugs, but absolutely no S^- responding when these drugs are used with birds who have learned the discrimination without errors. Both peak shift and the disruption with these tranquilizers suggest to Terrace that a negative stimulus after discrimination training with errors acts as an aversive stimulus which is inhibitory to responding. The important point, however, is that with his ingeniously developed errorless discrimination, the S^- remains a neutral stimulus rather than an inhibitory one. The fact that discrimination can be readily formed without developing an inhibitory stimulus disproves Martin's claim that discrimination occurs only "with a cost," and it would seem to have similar disastrous effects on the central role he gives inhibition in his theory of concept formation.

In teaching machine work, establishing concepts which are either error-free or have relatively few errors is the rule rather than the exception (Holland, 1960, 1962; Skinner, 1958). The attempt to strike a balance between moving ahead rapidly and avoiding errors usually leads to programs which result in a few errors, but they are often few indeed compared with what would be necessary if the programmer had to establish inhibitory tendencies for each of the various irrelevant stimulus dimensions for a concept.

In conclusion, both of these papers leave us without an adequate systematic development in the area of concept formation; Bourne's, because little systemization developed from his experiments and the generality of his experimental task seems questionable; Martin's, because his theoretical constructs prove insufficient for handling errorless learning.

CHAPTER 4

Earl B. Hunt
University of Washington

UTILIZATION OF MEMORY
IN CONCEPT-LEARNING SYSTEMS*

In pattern recognition a problem solver must develop a rule for identifying objects as members of classes. In the related concept-learning problem every object, or item, can be described by stating its values on each of a finite, known number of attributes. The attributes are usually nominal variables. An example is the well-known psychological experiment in which the subject is asked to learn an arbitrary classification rule for meaningless geometric patterns--for example, "All triangles are called *GEK*." In most psychological experiments, and in the artificial intelligence studies to be reported here, items are presented to the learner one at a time, he (it) guesses the correct classification, and is then told what the correct classification is. From the learner's point of view, the object of the game is to develop an answer adequate enough to classify all objects while minimizing the number of errors of classification and the number of objects required (the organizing set) during the learning process.

I shall mainly be concerned with the learning of fairly complex rules, in which the correct classification of an item can only be determined by examination of a number of its attributes. The particular concept-learning problems to be studied are shown in Fig. 4.1, which depicts five classification rules as trees of sequential decisions. With the exception of Problem 1, none of these decision procedures can be

The computations required for this research were performed at the Western Data Processing Center, U.C.L.A. The support received is grate- fully acknowledged. Mr. Lawrence Press aided in the work by programming the experiments involving CLS-11.

78   Utilization of Memory

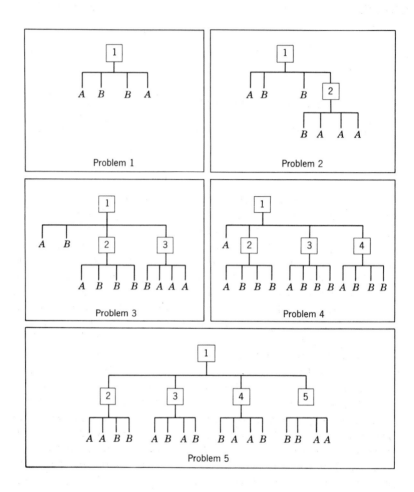

Fig. 4.1   Classification trees used in concept learning study. An
item is classified by first testing for the value of Attribute 1.
Depending on the value, the item is routed to the first, second,
third, or fourth node from the left below the first node. If the node
is numbered the numbered attribute is tested. Otherwise, the item
is classed as an " A" or "B".

expressed as a linear classification rule.[1]

If the correct concept is expressed as a sequential deci- sion process and, hence, depicted as a tree, learning can be thought of as the problem of inferring the correct decision procedure from the information contained in the organizing set. The difficulty of a particular concept-learning problem will then depend upon the complexity of the rule to be learned and the methods of inference used by the learner. This paper discusses the effect of using certain methods of inference upon the performance of a concept learner, without implying that people do, or do not, use any of the methods presented.

Two further specializations of the general problem should be noted. Given two classification processes of equal accu- racy, the procedure which minimizes the number of attri- butes to be examined is considered the preferable one. This is an intuitively reasonable restriction, since in any practical case (e.g. medical diagnosis) the user of a classi- fication rule must pay for the information he requires. Also, a distinction must be made between the organizing set

---

[1]A linear classification rule is one which assigns a number, x_{ij}, to the j th value of attribute i, for all i and j, and then locates a number, X^*, such that if j_k is the value of attribute i of object k, then object k is a member of Class 1 if and only if

$$\sum_i x_{ij_k} > X^*$$

The procedure is easily generalized to more than two classes by con- sidering X^* to be an interval, rather than a point, and requiring that the summation lie within the interval.

An example of a concept which can be formulated as a linear classifi- cation rule is "All *GEK* items are triangles." The appropriate classifica- tion rule is (a) assign the number 1 to the value *triangle* of the attribute *shape*, and assign zeroes to all other values of attributes and, (b) assign an object to class *GEK* if and only if the value of $\sum_i x_{ijk}$ is greater than or equal to one.

An example of a concept which cannot be formulated as a linear class- ification rule is "All *GEK* items have red borders or green centers, but not both." In this example the weight designed to the value of each attribute depends upon the value of another attribute.

This description of linear classification rules differs from that nor- mally given because it has been concerned with nominal attributes with more than two values.   A more conventional description is given by Nilsson (1965).

as it has been presented to the learner and as it is effectively available to him. Showing the learner a new item may not increase his store of information, since presentation of the new item may, in some simple or complex fashion, cause him to lose previously presented information. In most interesting cases we are concerned with learners who have a finite amount of "space" available for storage of information during the learning process, and this space is far too small to store all the information that may be presented. How should the learner organize this limited memory and what is a practical rule for making inferences from the contents of an imperfect memory? The question is particularly challenging because the learner cannot know exactly what to remember until after he has solved the problem. The experiments to be reported will be directly concerned with these questions.

PREVIOUS WORK

In a series of experimental studies, Hunt, Marin, and Stone (1966) considered the question of how a rational problem solver ought to learn concepts, given some intuitively reasonable constraints on the cost factors in problem solving. To set the framework for the current experiments, a brief review of their reasoning is in order.

The activity engaged in during concept learning can be divided into two phases, the action when the learner accepts and classifies items into the organizing set, and the action when the learner examines the current contents of memory in order to develop a new concept. We proposed that a rational learner would only enter the second phase, which presumably entails much more work, following an error of classification, since only then would he receive a signal that the hypothesis he was entertaining was, in fact, incorrect.

We also suggested that concept learning be thought of as a game against an indifferent opponent, Nature. In this game Nature has one move, the choice of a particular decision tree as the correct answer. The learner has two moves, since he chooses both a procedure for storing information in memory and a method for examining the contents of memory. Once these choices are made the game begins.

Items are generated at random, and presented to the learner as described above. The cost of the game to the learner is assumed to be a monotonically increasing function of the number of errors and the number of items observed before solving the problem. This does not imply a zero sum game; cost to the learner need not be interpreted as a payoff to Nature.

The trial hypothesis will itself be a classification tree. Figure 2 depicts a series of steps in the development of such a tree from a known organizing set. Initially all items in memory are marked as "Active at the first node." The CLS (concept learning system) first checks to see if all items active at the node being considered (initially the highest node in the tree) are members of the same class. This is done in Steps 1 and 2. If all items do belong to the same class, the problem is solved. This is shown in Steps 4 and 6. If there are items from two or more classes active at the node an attribute is selected and used to route items from this node (subproblem) to new subproblems. This is done at Step 5. The sorting is based on what subproblems might exist, rather than on what subproblems are represented in memory at the time. For instance, if Attribute 1 were to be selected at a given node, and if this attribute had four possible values, then four subproblems would be established as nodes immediately under the current one, even if no items under consideration had, say, Value 3 on Attribute 1. In using the resultant tree, items would be routed to nodes immediately below the original node if they (a) had been marked as active at the original node and (b) had a specific value on the selected attribute. Thus each of the subproblems is itself a classification rule, and as such may give rise to more subproblems. When a subproblem is reached for which either there are no items in memory or for which all items are members of the same class, the process terminates. The node in question will be an endpoint. If there are items for this endpoint, then the endpoint is marked with the appropriate class name. If there are no items, then the *CLS* procedures described differ in the manner of treatment which will be described below. The problem-solving process as a whole terminates when there are no more subproblems.

In its general spirit, this is an inductive problem-solving version of Newell, Shaw, and Simon's (1959) General Problem Solver (GPS) program for deductive problem solving.

An initially complex classification problem is successively reduced to more and more trivial subproblems in the same way that *GPS* reduces a complex deductive chain to a series of simple steps. There is no arbitrary limit on the complexity of the classification system, although there are some problems concerning allocation of space in a computer program which represents a realization of a *CLS* procedure. On the other hand, for any finite set of items in memory the process always terminates, since the worst one could do would be to generate a tree in which each endpoint identified a single item in memory.

The formulation of Fig. 4.2 pushes the problem solver's move in the game against Nature back to Step 5 of the figure. Hunt et al. experimented with several different attribute selection rules, each of which turned out to have both advantages and disadvantages. Here three rules (moves of the learner) will be considered. To remain consistent with the earlier work, they will be referred to as *CLS*-9, -10, and -11. In addition, some experiments were conducted with a variant of *CLS*-9 which used its memory space in a slightly different way than did the other systems.

ATTRIBUTE SELECTION METHODS

The following notation will be used to describe the algorithms used for attribute selection:

n = number of items active in the subproblem

n_{ijk} = number of active items which are in class k and have value j of attribute i.

$$n_{ij} = \Sigma_k n_{ijk}$$
$$n_k = \Sigma_i \Sigma_j n_{ijk}$$

CLS-9 Strategy: For every attribute i calculate

(1) $$C_1 = \Sigma_j \max_k \{n_{ijk}\}$$

and select as the attribute to be tested at that subproblem the attribute, i^*, which maximizes C_1, providing that

(2) $C_1* > \max_k \{n_{.k}\}$

and

(3) $n > 0$

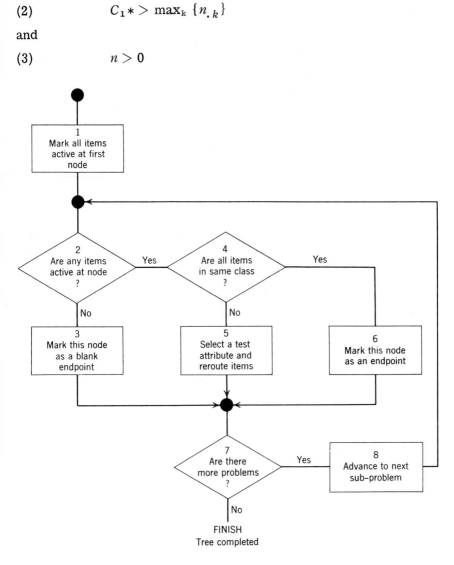

Fig. 4.2   Procedure for developing a new hypothesis by examining the organizing set.

If restriction (2) is not met, there is no attribute such that knowledge of its value permits a more accurate guess of the class membership of a randomly chosen item than could be obtained by making the simple guess that the item was a member of the class most frequently found among items active at this subproblem. If n is zero, then we are dealing with one of the logically possible, but currently non-existent, subproblems discussed previously. In CLS-9 the node corresponding to such a subproblem is made an endpoint but no class name is recorded. This is analagous to a person's refusing to guess the class membership of an object which he has never seen, although he acknowledges the logical possibility. To take a not entirely unrealistic example, CLS-9 would refuse to predict whether a lady senator from Texas will be a Democrat or Republican.

CLS-9 is one of the concept learners investigated by Hunt et al., and we have published an Algol computer program which defines it.[2] The average performance of CLS-9 on a set of problems similar to Problems 1 through 4 of Fig. 1 was substantially equivalent to that of other CLS programs requiring fewer calculations, therefore, from the standpoint of economics of information, CLS-9 might not seem a particularly desirable system. On the other hand, CLS-9 exhibited less variability in performance as a function of the logical form of the problem to be solved than did most of the systems to which it was compared, either directly or indirectly. This is equivalent to saying that CLS-9 provides the learner with a strategy such that his payoff is relatively independent of the move of his opponent. This was one of the reasons for choosing CLS-9 for further study; in many realistic situations reduction of the variability of payoff is considered desirable.

There is another argument for investigating CLS-9, which is independent of the previous experimental results. In the act of classifying an object, it may be necessary to make the classification before all the information desired can be gathered. This situation is familiar to anyone who has had to choose between job, house, or, perhaps, spouse

---

[2]Pages 232 and 233 of the Hunt et al. report were interchanged in printing. The program is correct only if this change is made.

possibilities. In the terminology of *CLS*, a classification must be made before an endpoint is reached. It has been shown that if one is given a fixed organizing set, then the *CLS*-9 procedure develops a decision tree such that each attribute selected in the tree is the one which will maximize the probability of correct classification if sequential testing is terminated immediately after the selected attribute is tested (Hunt, 1965). The proof depends strongly upon the assumption that the organizing set is fixed, and that the tree is developed only once. On the other hand, there is no proof that the same procedure would be either good or bad in a situation in which the organizing set were continuously changing, as it is in the serial-presentation concept-learning situation with which we are dealing here.

CLS-10 Strategy: From one half to one third of the errors made during learning by *CLS*-9 occur because an item is presented which is routed to one of the endpoints in the trial decision tree which represents a subproblem not represented in memory at the time that the tree was built, hence, that endpoint is not associated with a class name (Hunt, et al., p. 111). *CLS*-10 incorporates a heuristic procedure for associating these endpoints with a class name.

CLS-10 is identical to *CLS*-9 except when restriction (3) the nonexistent subproblem condition, is violated. In this case, as before, the node is made an endpoint, but has assigned to it the class name of the most heavily represented class at the node immediately above the endpoint node. Formally, the endpoint is associated with class name k^*, where

(4) $$n_{k}^* = \max_k \{n_k\}$$

and (4) is defined for the set of items active at the subproblem which generated the nonexistent subproblem.

Informally, following the *CLS*-10 procedure, one would say that a lady senator from Texas was a Democrat on the grounds that most senators from Texas are Democrats. This captures the spirit, if not the details, of the difference between *CLS*-9 and *CLS*-10.

CLS-11 Strategy: In *CLS*-11 an attempt was made to use a procedure justified by classical statistical analysis to select attributes. The selection procedure expressed in Equation (1) was replaced by a chi-square maximization procedure. Suppose that there are a attributes eligible for selection at a particular subproblem. In CLS-11 the chi-square for contingency between attribute value and class membership of an item was computed for each of these a attributes, and the attribute selected which maximized the obtained chi-square. Note that so long as each attribute has the same number of values, a condition satisfied in all experiments to be reported, maximizing chi-square is equivalent to minimizing the probability of obtaining such a value if the null hypothesis is true, since the degrees of freedom will be identical for every comparison. CLS-11 was identical to CLS-10 in all other respects.

UTILIZATION OF MEMORY

All programs used what we have referred to previously as a fixed storage system (Hunt et al., p. 31). In such a system the learner's memory can be thought of as containing m slots, each capable of holding a complete description of exactly one item. When an item is presented its description is written into a randomly chosen slot, erasing any previous contents which the slot may have had.

Normally only one description of an item is stored in memory. The possibility has been raised, however, that certain items are "key" representatives of a class or subclass, and therefore pains should be taken to insure that copies of these items are always retained. One way to do this is to store multiple copies of any item thought to contain crucial information. This has the drawback that the multiple copies will write over some unique information, and also that the key items are difficult to identify before the problem is solved. An *a priori* plausible heuristic approach for identifying key items, however, is to regard any item which is classified erroneously as a key item. At least, it will be known that this item contains some information not available at the time that the now disconfirmed trial hypothesis was generated. To test the usefulness of this heuristic approach the CLS-9 program was written so that s additional copies of an item would be stored if the system erred in its trial classification of the item. To identify different conditions using this option, the notation CLS-9-s will be used, where s indicates the number of additional copies stored. Note that storing the additional copies will distort the frequency counts made during the attribute-selection stage.

EXPERIMENTAL PROCEDURE

All the experiments were conducted by Monte Carlo simulation of the appropriate CLS and concept-learning situation using a digital computer. The necessary programs were written in FORTRAN IV. Because of the limitations of the FORTRAN language the programs representing the different $CLSs$ had to be specialized to the particular experimental situation. This is strictly a technical limitation, and does not affect the logic of the simulation in any way. So that this claim may be examined, a listing of the program for CLS-10 is included in this report as Appendix A.

The objects to be categorized were defined by five attributes with four values each, a total of 1024 distinct items. The appropriate classification rules for the different problems are shown in Fig. 4.1. Items were presented at random, without repetition, until a block of 1024 items had been shown. The experiment was terminated when a rule capable of classifying all 1024 items was developed, or after 8192 items had been presented. There were 10 independent replications of every experimental condition.

Ten repetitions of a given CLS with fixed memory size on Problems 1--4 required about five minutes computing time using the IBM 7044/7094 Direct Coupled system.

Experiment I

In this experiment the three $CLSs$ were used to solve problems 1—4, with memory space available for storing 20, 30, or 1024 items. Two versions of CLS-9 were used, 9-0 and 9-4. Two measures of performance were taken, the number of errors of classification during learning, and the number of items presented before the system developed the correct answer.

The mean number of errors made in each condition of the

Utilization of Memory

TABLE 4.1   Mean Errors as a Function of CLS, Memory
Size and Problem in Experiment I

Memory Size	Problems			
	1	2	3	4
CLS 11-				
20	2.6	4.7	13.6	52.6
30	2.4	4.4	9.2	11.9
1024	2.4	4.1	7.0	6.8
CLS 10-				
20	2.5	3.8	6.8	16.1
30	2.4	4.0	6.4	10.1
1024	2.3	3.3	5.9	7.1
CLS 9-0-				
20	2.7	7.6	17.5	185.0
30	2.9	6.0	11.9	18.1
1024	3.2	5.1	7.3	10.9
CLS 9-4-				
20	3.3	10.0	199.8	800.6
30	2.8	6.2	12.4	84.9
1024	3.0	5.4	9.4	9.5

experiment is shown in Table 4.1, and the mean number of items required shown in Table 4.2. The corresponding analyses of variance are given in Tables 4.3 and 4.4. The analysis of variance computations were based on the fully crossed factorial design with fixed effects for each variable (Scheffe, 1959).

Tables 4.3 and 4.4 indicate a plethora of significant results; all main variables and all interactions show reliable effects. Fortunately, the pattern of the data can be explained by a few clear trends. These are revealed both in the data for errors and items presented. Since these two variables are highly correlated, only the error scores will be discussed in detail.

The main effects of problem complexity and memory size are expected. The more complex the tree describing the problem, the harder the problem is to solve. While this is not surprising, it is worth noting that the "Problems" effect

TABLE 4.2 Average Last Error as a Function of CLS, Problems and Memory Size in Experiment I.

Memory Size	Problem			
	1	2	3	4
CLS-11				
20	10.5	24.8	67.1	370.7
30	8.8	29.6	59.7	81.6
1024	8.8	29.3	36.1	45.5
CLS-10				
20	8.5	16.2	45.4	72.8
30	9.9	19.6	33.4	62.5
1024	8.1	26.8	35.0	54.2
CLS-9-0				
20	9.9	51.4	115.5	1346.0
30	7.2	42.7	97.8	114.8
1024	8.5	30.7	46.5	58.3
CLS-9-4				
20	68.2	61.7	901.5	7934.6
30	8.3	31.0	68.1	649.0
1024	8.7	44.4	49.6	51.4

TABLE 4.3 Analysis of Variance of Errors

Source of Variation	Degrees of Freedom	Sums of Squares	Mean Squares	F
1-Programs	3	632584.77344	210861.58984	106.51
2-Memory size	2	588280.23438	294140.11719	148.57
3-Problems	3	765021.69531	255007.23047	128.81
12	6	972420.78125	162070.12891	81.86
13	9	1077394.71875	119710.52344	60.47
23	6	1074108.70313	179018.11719	90.42
123	18	1623609.93750	90200.55176	45.56
Within replicates	432	855252.01563	1979.75003	
Total	479	7588672.87500		

here is much smaller, relative to other effects, than it was in most of our other studies. It is always good to have a larger memory, in the sense that increasing memory size always improves problem performance. However the effect is by no means linear. The difference between having a storage space of 30 or 1024 items is, on the average, less than the difference between 20- or 30-item memories.

TABLE 4.4 Analysis of Variance of Last Error: Experiment I

Source of Variation	Degrees of Freedom	Sums of Squares	Mean Squares	F
1-Programs	3	49304213.00000	16434737.62500	232.28
2-Memory size	2	42795109.00000	21397554.50000	302.43
3-Problems	3	65385284.50000	21795094.75000	308.05
12	6	79782570.00000	13297095.00000	187.94
13	9	111745643.00000	12416182.50000	175.49
23	6	99235377.00000	16539229.50000	233.77
123	18	89731052.00000	9970116.87500	140.92
Within replicates	432	30564806.75000	70751.86719	
Total	479	82284388.00000		

There is a consistent ordering between CLSs.[3] CLS-10 provides the best performance, followed closely by CLS-11, then CLS-9-0, and, at a considerable distance, by CLS-9-4 The size of the average difference between systems 9-0 and 9-4, although undoubtedly the largest, is somewhat exaggerated because of the very poor performance of CLS-9-4 on Problem 4 with a 20-item memory. In this condition solutions were seldom obtained, so the numbers entered in Tables 1 and 2 reflect those which would have been obtained if solution were achieved on the 8193rd item presented.

The interaction effects obtained can be traced to two causes. If an item is sufficiently easy (e.g. Problem 1, which is similar to the sort of problems often used in psychological studies) any CLS with only a modest memory space can solve the problem quickly. However, a given problem will always require for its solution a characteristic minimum amount of information which must be effectively available to the learner. The amount of information which is so available will depend upon the amount of information in memory at the time and the efficiency of the attribute selection

[3]The paired differences between any two programs are reliable. CLS-10 performs better than CLS-11 in eleven of the twelve possible comparisons in Table 4.1. Correspondingly, CLS-11 exceeds CLS-9-0 in all twelve possible comparisons, and CLS-9-0 exceeds the performance of CLS-9-4 in ten of twelve comparisions.

technique being used to process it. Thus on a given problem two CLSs will have different minimum memory requirements in order to reach a solution, or alternately, to produce equivalent performance figures on a problem which they both solve.

For any CLS program there is evidently a point in problem complexity beyond which, given limits on patience and available computer time, the system simply cannot go. Up to this point, which differs for different CLSs, there should be a regular relation between difficulty, problem complexity, and memory size. This can be shown by close examination of Table 4.1. A pure effect of problem complexity can be shown by contrasting the columns within a given row (memory size) and block (CLS) of the table. We ask at which column the regular relation between problem difficulty and problem complexity breaks down. It is approximately true that with every increase in problem complexity the number of errors doubles, for a constant system and memory size, so long as the relationship is orderly. Therefore, the arbitrary measure of "breakdown" has been set as the first point in a given row and block at which the number of errors exceeds three times the number of errors in the column immediately to the left. These points are marked in Table 4.1. Note that where they occur they define the upper right-hand corner of the block (the region of low memory and high problem complexity) as a region in which that system, in effect, cannot function.

Similarly, it is possible to obtain pure measures of the effect of increased memory by comparing adjacent rows within a given block and column, since this holds CLS and problem complexity constant. Here we ask at what point increasing memory size no longer leads to an increase in performance. Again selecting an arbitrary criterion, let us say that effective memory increases will be indicated by decreases in the average number of errors by at least .5 errors. In the lower left-hand corners of the blocks of Table 4.1 boundaries are marked beyond which such a reduction is no longer obtained. Below and to the left of these boundaries performance is determined solely by the complexity of the problem and the power of the CLS used.

Experiment II

Extrapolating from the results of Experiment I, it should be possible to locate areas in which previously functioning systems will break down, either due to an increase in problem complexity or decrease in memory size. It should also be possible to find "isodifficulty" points, points at which different systems give identical performances because of variations in memory size. A final particularly interesting equivalence, for a given CLS, is the point at which system performance over the range of problems being considered is no longer improved by increases in memory size. If we regard memory as a purchasable commodity, this point represents the point beyond which the marginal gain is zero, and therefore it is the point beyond which memory should not be increased.

Upon examination of the data from each replication of the 1024-item memory conditions of Experiment I, it was found that the last error always occurred within 75 items for CLS-10 and 150 items for CLS-9-0 and 9-4. Accordingly these two conditions were run directly. A new condition, CLS-9-2, was also run with a 150-item memory as a partial check to see if there was any evidence for a non-monotonic relationship between performance and the number of copies of errors stored in memory.

In order to produce system breakdown under stated conditions, CLS 9-0 and 9-4 were run with 15-item memory sizes, to see if this moved the point of problem unsolvability to a lower level of complexity (Table 4.6). CLS-10 was used with a 1024-item memory in an attempt to solve Problem 5, which represents a greater level of complexity than any problem ever solved by a CLS in an error-correction concept-learning situation.

As in Experiment I, the data for total errors and last error were highly correlated, so only the former will be discussed. Table 4.5 shows the results of using 75- and 150-item memories. For ease of comparison the results from the relevant 1024-item memory conditions of Experiment I are included in Table 4.5. It can be seen immediately that the smaller memory sizes result in substantially the same performance as the appropriate 1024-item control condition. Also equivalent, if not superior, performance can be obtained from CLS-10 with a 75-item memory as from CLS-9-0 or

TABLE 4.5 Mean Errors Using Different CLS Systems and Memory Size, with Comparison Data from Experiment I.

CLS and Memory Used	Problems			
	1	2	3	4
CLS 10, 75 items	2.3	3.6	6.5	7.8
CLS 9-0, 150 items	2.7	5.4	9.5	8.7
CLS 9-2, 150 items	2.7	5.7	8.1	9.8
CLS 9-4, 150 items	2.3	5.4	8.4	9.8
From Experiment I:				
CLS 10, 1024 items	2.3	3.3	5.9	7.1
CLS 9-0, 1024 items	3.2	5.1	7.3	10.9
CLS 9-4, 1024 items	3.0	5.4	9.4	9.5

TABLE 4.6 Mean Errors using Small Memory Asteriks Indicate Unsolvable Problems.

Program and Memory size	Problem			
	1	2	3	4
CLS 9-0, 15 items	2.3	7.6	122.2	*
CLS 9-4, 15 items	3.1	23.6	*	*

9-4 with a memory twice as large. This comparison provides one meaningful way of evaluating the additional power derived from the heuristic procedure incorporated in CLS-10.

Problem 5 proved too difficult for CLS-10, even with a 1024-item memory. Several attempts have been made to solve this problem using different systems, but without any success. Occasional solutions have been recorded, but by far the more usual case is that the problem is still not solved before the limit of 8192 items is presented. (Having memory space available for 1024 items does not assure that 1024 unique items will ever be placed in memory at any one time. If this does happen, any of the CLSs described here will solve any classification problem for this universe of items.) In addition, with a very large memory the time required to develop a decision tree becomes prohibitive. Of course, the problem could always be solved by adding more memory and getting a faster computer. This is not the point; there is no intrinsic value to solving the problem. What is important is that this problem

represents a point beyond the capability of our current generation of concept-learning systems, and hence can serve as a tar-
get for future programs.

DISCUSSION OF SPECIFIC RESULTS

In spite of the attraction of the CLS-9 attribute-selection
procedure for constructing concepts from a fixed organizing
set, it is clearly not an optimal procedure in a concept-
learning situation in which the organizing set is enlarged one
item at a time. There is a substantial improvement in
performance if the attribute-selection strategy of CLS-9 is
amplified to include the heuristic procedure for guessing the
answer to logically possible, but presently unencountered,
problems. This guessing technique is evidently a powerful
tool and should be used in future CLSs.

Negative evidence was obtained for two other CLS modifications. Attribute selection by chi-square maximization,
although justifiable by classical statistical reasoning, did not
result in any improvement in performance over CLS-10.
If anything, there was a decrease in performance. Similarly,
the strategy of storing multiple copies of erroneously classified
items is evidently a bad way to utilize a limited memory space.
Negative conclusions are always disappointing, but since both
suggestions seemed, $a priori$, to be reasonable ones the
conclusions are not without value. Going beyond the conclusions strictly permitted by the data, it seems unlikely that any
other classical statistical technique for attribute selection will
do much better than CLS-11. Any such technique is bound to be
highly correlated with the chi-square technique in its selection
of attributes and, therefore, should give equivalent performance. Future systems will probably rely upon the simple
counting technique since the computing required to obtain the
necessary statistics exceeds the computing required by CLS-
10.

On the other hand, failure to find any method for improving
the use of fixed storage memories does not leave me with the
feeling that the single copy, random-storage method is at all
satisfactory. This seems unlikely because of its simplicity
and obvious wastefulness. There are two different approaches

which could be followed. One is to use memory space to store information about past answers instead of information about individual items. Such a change would entail a complete reworking of the *CLS* technique, as the development of a new hypothesis would then require modification of an old one instead of reexamination of the contents of memory. The resulting concept learner might look much more like Feigenbaum's (1961) *EPAM* model of verbal learning, which uses the answer storage type of memory, than it would the present *CLS*. A less drastic change is to make a *CLS* selective in the attributes which it stores during learning. A simple modification, which is currently being investigated, stores information only about those attributes which are examined when an item is classified. Thus each item requires less space in a fixed-size memory. We have done enough preliminary work to know that this, alone, does not produce a more efficient memory utilization scheme than the random-storage method, but some variant of selective storage may do so.

The observation that there are trade-offs between problem complexity, memory size, and system performance, and that the exact trade-off varies from system to system is hardly surprising. It does suggest that a *CLS* be viewed as moving in a "system space" somewhat analagous to the performance envelope of an aircraft. A possible system space is illustrated in Fig 4.3. The plane of this figure is defined by the dimensions memory size and problem complexity. System performance can be thought of as a surface above the plane. The surface slopes uniformly downward to the right for all points in region *A*, the surface above the line defining the maximum effective memory size. Here memory size is so large that further increases do not help, so system performance is determined solely by problem difficulty. In regions *B* and *C* the surface is infinitely low, since in these areas the problems are too hard for the system. In region *B*, however, there is some hope that one could move the system to a point at which it could perform by adding more memory. In region *D* the performance surface slopes upward toward its "northern" boundary with region A and downward toward its "eastern" boundary with region *C*, illustrating the interactive effects of problem complexity and memory upon system performance.

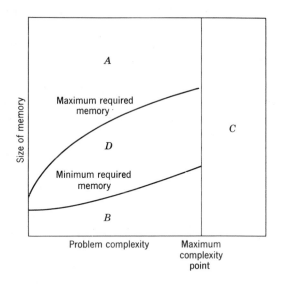

Fig. 4.3 Hypothetical system space in which a *CLS* problem combination can be located. The performance can be thought of as a surface located above this plane. The function relating the height of the surface to the coordinates of the plane depends on the region of the plane. See text for further explanation.

The interesting problem is to describe in more detail the contours and boundaries of this surface. We have some clues about them. There is evidently a precipitous decline as we approach the boundaries between region *D* and *B* or *C*. Throughout our studies of *CLS* performance we have seen little warning before increases in problem complexity or decreases in memory size suddenly plunge a *CLS* into a region of unsolvability. (This remark must be tempered by an expression of concern for the fineness of the measure of problem complexity, although I strongly suspect that the conjecture is correct.) On the other hand, the flattening which takes place at the boundary between regions A and D seems to occur much more gradually.

The space in which a CLS may move must be determined in a much more precise manner. This will require both the development of better measures of system resources and problem complexity and the conduct of experimental studies designed to explore the space for specific systems.

GENERAL DISCUSSION

The previous sections have been concerned with a particular series of experiments conducted in a fairly narrow framework. The results are offered as a small step toward our understanding of the many problems involved in the empirical study of rational thought. More generally, the work does have speculative interest for the general field of artificial intelligence and, by analogy, may provide ideas of use in psychology. The reader should make a clear distinction, however, between the actual experimental results and the less tightly reasoned discussion of their implications.

Marschak (1965) has pointed out that problem solving is an economic problem, that, in his words,

"...The highest profit may not be worth a good night's sleep. Nor does it usually pay to compute numbers to the tenth digit. The existence of costs of decision, or of thinking for that matter, must modify our choice of decisions, and even the course of our reasoning."

This argument is directly applicable to artificial intelligence research. From the viewpoint of the user of a problem-solving automaton there are two costs, the cost of installing the system and the operating cost which may be adjusted as problems are encountered. (In CLS there is the cost of programming a new system, and the cost of using the system with different sizes of memory.) The learner wants an artificial intelligence such that he can achieve reasonable solutions for the problems he expects to encounter by adjusting system variables which are under his control. To do this, he must know the system's performance envelope.

The problem with an analysis of this sort is that it is almost too general. Ashby (1956, 1960) has introduced almost the same terms in his discussions of systems with regions of stability, and of ultrastable systems. He then applies the systems space approach to discussions of heating units, ghosts, and the behavior of the brain. Similarly, Rosecrance (1963) uses Ashby's terms to analyze international politics from Louis XV to De Gaulle. To show that a system-space analysis of artificial intelligence devices is useful, one must show both that it can be applied to more than one system, and that some general laws can be found which relate the discovered functions in the space to the characteristics of the device being studied.

There are reports which suggest that the sharp boundary between solvable and unsolvable problems is a characteristic of intelligent devices or, if you prefer, problem-solving procedures in general. Newell, Shaw, and Simon's Logic Theorist program either solved symbolic logic problems in a few steps or not at all (Newell, Shaw, and Simon, 1957). Recently a version of their General Problem Solver program (Newell et al., 1959) has been installed as an operating system[4] and used to solve problems in symbolic logic, simple algebra, and inequalities. After examining the solutions achieved (or not reached) by the program, I have the feeling that the systems-space approach is reasonable. If the *GPS* solves a problem, the difficulty of the solution seems intuitively to be related to the complexity of the problem and to the system variables (in this case depth of recursion permitted and number of axioms provided). Unsolvable problems seem to be completely outside this relation. The program often terminates without making any discernible progress toward its goal. Nothing more definite can be said until we have better characterizations of the system and of problem complexity. It is interesting to note that many problems can be described by a tree graph in much the same manner as we have desscribed concept-learning problems. Several measures based upon the structure of the graph have been proposed to evaluate the difficulty of a problem. Slagle's (1962) measures for allocating resources in symbolic integration problems are a good example. We lack a systematic survey of these methods and a critical evaluation of the extent to which the graphic

---

[4] The modifications and programming required to develop this version of *GPS* have been carried out by J. R. Quinlan of the Western Data Processing Center, U.C.L.A.

notation is superficial or reveals basic commonalities across different problem areas.[5]

Finally, what do the *CLS* experiments have to say about human concept learning? Nothing, except by analogy, since no direct comparison was made between *CLS* and human performance. On the other hand, such comparisons have been made, and the analogy is not entirely irrelevant to psychology. There are two points in particular which I should like to call to the attention of the student of human learning.

One is the discontinuity between hard and unsolvable problems. This is particularly interesting because measures of complexity of a problem based upon its tree representation have been shown to be reasonable predictors of the difficulty of concept-learning problems for humans (Bourne, this volume; Hunt *et al.* 1966, section III; Neisser and Weene, 1962). In practically every concept-learning experiment there are non-solvers. Is it possible that these subjects differ in kind, rather than degree, in their techniques for learning concepts?

A somewhat related point is that equivalent performance can be obtained from non-identical systems if memory sizes are also varied. It would be very difficult to tell, from the "protocol" of one of the experiments reported here, whether the program being used was *CLS*-10 with a small memory or *CLS*-9-4 with a large one. It should be possible to devise independent tests of a person's ability to remember information and to make inferences from a known organizing set. How, then, would these measures interact in predicting his performance in the conventional serial presentation concept-learning task?

---

[5] Professor Newell has pointed out that unless problems are generated by some systematic procedure, to ensure that all points in the problem space are covered, the results of empirical studies of problem solving by artificial intelligence may be misleading. Specifically, in the Logic Theorist studies the problems were taken from those studied by Whitehead and Russell in the *Principia Mathematica.* It may be that these problems fall into two sets, fairly simple problems and very difficult ones, with nothing in between. In the *CLS* studies this criticism is less forceful, since the procedure of choosing problems by increasing tree complexity in a straightforward way offers some insurance that different points in the problem space will be covered. The criticism, however, is applicable to the *GPS* studies which we have performed.

SUMMARY

As part of a series in artificial intelligence experiments, four different computer programs for concept learning were tested on five problems of varying complexity. The amount of information which a program could store while solving the problem was varied independently. Program performance could be described as a function of the location of a given study in an abstract space defined by problem complexity and the amount of memory available.

The results were discussed in terms of previous work on concept learning and for their implications in the general fields of artificial intelligence and the psychology of human learning.

Appendix A

PROGRAM FOR CLS-10 EXPERIMENT

```
$JOB            0,5,2000      2562B EARL HUNT WDPC CLS 10 P4 TEST
$ID             2562A CLS 10 SOURCE DECK
$EXECUTE        IBJOB
$IBJOB 2562C    MAP,FIOCS
$IBFTC LEARN    M94,XR7,NODECK
        DIMENSION MEMRY (7,1024),ITREE(120,2),IRTE(40,2),ITEM(6)
        DIMENSION ITEMS (1024,5)
        LOGICAL CHECK
        INTEGER CURNT,RCTRL
        COMMON RCTRL,MEMRY,MSIZE,ITEM,ISIZE,ITREE,CURNT,IRTE,ITRACE
 100    FORMAT(19,I3,I2)
 101    FORMAT(I4,I2,I4)
 102    FORMAT(2I1)
        READ(5,100) RCTRL,ICONS,LX
        DO 86 LSX = 1,LX
        READ (5,110) IRPTS,ITRACE,LIMIT,ISTRES
 103    FORMAT(I2)
 104    FORMAT(20H ITEMS AFTER SHUFFLE)
 113    FORMAT(16(1X,5I1))
 112    FORMAT(24H ADDED ERROR STORAGE IS ,I2)
 110    FORMAT (2I2,I5,I2)
        READ(5,101) IN,ISIZE,MSIZE
C THE OUTER BLOCK PERMITS REPETITION WITH NEW PROBLEMS
        DO 86 JJI = 1,ICONS
        READ(5,103) L
        DO 1 I = 1,L,1
   1    READ(5,110) (IRTE(I,J),J = 1,2)
C IF ITRACE = 1 FULL REPORT IS GIVEN. IF ITRACE
C = -1 DETAILS OF HYPOTHESIS DEVELOPMENT ARE
C GIVEN. IF ITRACE = 0 ONLY ERROR COUNT IS
C GIVEN
   1500FORMAT(28H PATTERN RECOGNITION PROBLEM/20H NUMBER OF PROBLEMS ,I2/
       413H MEMORY SIZE ,I4,20H ITEMS PER PROBLEM ,I4/15H CORRECT ANSWER)
        PRINT 150,IRPTS,MSIZE,IN
 151    FORMAT(1H ,2I2)
        DO 33 I = 1,L,1
  33    PRINT 151,(IRTE(I,J),J = 1,2)
 152    FORMAT(26H RANDOM NUMBER CONTROL IS ,I9)
        PRINT 152,RCTRL
        PRINT 112, ISTRES
C ESTABLISH BASE DATA FOR RUN
        JLAST = 0
        JTOT = 0
        CALL STIMLI (ITEMS)
        IF(ITRACE)34,35,36
 153    FORMAT(21H DETAILED TRACE IS ON)
 154    FORMAT(13H TRACE IS OFF)
 155    FORMAT(22H EXTERNAL TRACE IS ON  )
  34    PRINT 153
        GO TO 37
  35    PRINT 154
        GO TO 37
  36    PRINT 155
  37    DO 50 KPROB = 1,IRPTS,1
C ESTABLISH BASE DATA FOR PROBLEM
        LAST = 0
        NBASE = 0
        CURNT = 0
```

```
      JSET=0
      DO 30 K=1,MSIZE,1
      DO 30 L=1,6,1
30    MEMRY (L,K)=0
      DO 31 I=1,120
      DO 31 J=1,2,1
31    ITREE(I,J)=0
      JERROR=0
C ESTABLISH DATA FOR ITERATION
90    CHECK = .TRUE.
      CALL SHUFLE (ITEMS,1024,5)
      IF(ITRACE) 38,39,38
38    PRINT 104
      DO 43 K1= 1,1024,16
      K2= K1+15
43    PRINT 113,((ITEMS(I1,I2),I2 = 1,5), I1 =K1,K2)
39    CONTINUE
      DO 6 N=1,IN,1
      DO 4 J=1,5
      ITEM(J) = ITEMS(N,J)
4     CONTINUE
      CALL CLASS(1,IMARK)
      IANS=IMARK
      ITEM(6)=IMARK
      IF(JSET) 3,3,2
3     JSET=1
      ITREE(1,1)=IMARK
      ITREE(1,2)=0
      GO TO 10
2     CALL CLASS(0,IANS)
10    CALL MEMSTR(CURNT)
      IF(IMARK-IANS)5,6,5
5     JERROR = JERROR+1
      LAST = N+NBASE
C SECTION CHANGED FOR DIFFERENTIAL STORAGE OF ERRORS
      IF (ISTRES .EQ.0) GO TO 76
      DO 75 KTH=1,ISTRES
75    CALL MEMSTR (CURNT)
76    CONTINUE
      IF (CHECK) CHECK = .FALSE.
105   FORMAT(7H ERROR 12)
      IF(ITRACE)40,16,40
40    PRINT 105,JERROR
108   FORMAT(10H MEMORY IS)
109   FORMAT(1X,6I1)
      PRINT 108
      DO 15 I= 1,MSIZE,1
      IF(MEMRY(1,I))16,16,15
15    PRINT 109,(MEMRY(J,I),J=1,6)
16    CONTINUE
      IATX=ISIZE-1
      CALL DECTRE (120,IATX,4,2)
      IF(IN-N)41,41,51
51    CONTINUE
106   FORMAT(12H NEW TREE IS)
41    CONTINUE
      IF(ITRACE.EQ .0) GOTO 12
      PRINT 106
107   FORMAT(1H ,2I1)
      IFWRD=2
      DO 11 I=1, 120
      IF(I-IFWRD)21,12,12
21    PRINT 107,(ITREE(I,J),J=1,2)
      IF(ITREE(I,2))11,11,22
```

```
   22 IFWRD=ITREE(I,2)+4
   11 CONTINUE
   12 CONTINUE
    6 CONTINUE
  156 FORMAT(25H TOTAL ERRORS ON PROBLEM ,I2,2X,I3)
C CHECK TO SEE IF NEW REPETITION IS NEEDED
      IF (CHECK) GO TO 91
      NBASE = NBASE + IN
      IF(LIMIT-NBASE) 92,92,90
C REPORT RESULT OF RUN
  157 FORMAT (9H PROBLEM ,I3,18H TERMINATED AFTER ,I6,6H ITEMS)
  158 FORMAT (20H LAST ERROR ON ITEM ,I4)
  159 FORMAT (15H END OF RUN OF ,I4,9H PROBLEMS/
     126H AVERAGE NUMBER OF ERRORS ,F7.3,20H AVERAGE LAST ERROR ,F8.3)
   92 PRINT 157,KPROB,LIMIT
   91 PRINT 156,KPROB,JERROR
      PRINT 158,LAST
      JTOT =JTOT + JERROR
   50 JLAST = JLAST + LAST
      X = JTOT
      Y = JLAST
      XRPTS = IRPTS
      X = X/XRPTS
      Y = Y/XRPTS
      PRINT 159,IRPTS,X,Y
   86 CONTINUE
      STOP
      END
$IBFTC CLASS   M94,XR7,NODECK
      SUBROUTINE CLASS(M,IMARK)
      DIMENSION MEMRY(7,1024),ITREE(120,2),IRTE(40,2),ITEM(6)
      INTEGER ICURNT,RCTRL
      COMMON RCTRL,MEMRY,MSIZE,ITEM,ISIZE,ITREE,CURNT,IRTE
      I =1
      IF(M)1,1,10
C     CLASSIFY ACCORDING TO CURRENT HYPOTHESIS
    1 IF(ITREE(I,2))2,2,3
    2 IMARK = ITREE(I,1)
      RETURN
    3 J=ITREE(I,1)
      I=ITREE(I,2)+ITEM(J)-1
      GO TO 1
   10 IF(IRTE(I,2))11,11,12
   11 IMARK=IRTE(I,1)
      RETURN
   12 J=IRTE(I,1)
      I=IRTE(I,2)+ITEM(J)-1
      GO TO 10
      END
$IBFTC MEMSTR  M94,XR7,NODECK
      SUBROUTINE MEMSTR(CURNT)
      DIMENSION MEMRY(7,1024),ITREE(120,2),IRTE(40,2),ITEM(6)
      INTEGER CURNT,RCTRL
      COMMON IRCTRL,MEMRY,MSIZE,ITEM,ISIZE,ITREE,JUNK,IRTE
      J=RANDIT(1,MSIZE)
      IF(J-CURNT)2,2,1
    1 J=CURNT+1
      CURNT=J
    2 DO 3 I=1,ISIZE,1
    3 MEMRY(I,J)=ITEM(I)
      MEMRY(ISIZE+1,J)=1
      RETURN
      END
```

```
$IBFTC SELECT M94,XR7,NODECK
       SUBROUTINE SELECT (INDEX,ICURNT,IATRIB,IVALUE,ICLASS,IANS,IRSN,IT)
C      SUBROUTINE SELECTS TEST AT NODE INDEX.ON RETURN IF IANS=IRSN=0
C      THERE ARE NO ITEMS ON THIS NODE. IF IANS +0 AND IRSN=0 THERE
C      ARE ITEMS BUT ALL OF THE SAME CLASS, ABS(IANS). IF IANS=0 AND
C      IRSN=0 THERE IS NO ATTRIBUTE WITH MORE HITS THAN THE BEST
C      GUESS CLASS, WHICH IS NAMED BY IANS. IF IANS AND IRSN=0
C      IANS IS THE NAME OF THE ATTRIBUTE WHICH GIVES BEST CLASSIFYING .
C      FIRST STEP IS TO INITIALIZE AND ALLOCATE
       DIMENSION MEMRY (7,1024),ITEM(6),FREQ(4,5,2),ICNT(2)
       INTEGER FREQ
       COMMON IRCTRL,MEMRY, MSIZE,ITEM,ISIZE
       KKK =ISIZE + 1
       IPROB=-1
       DO 1 I=1,ICLASS,1
       ICNT(I)=0
       DO 1 J=1,IATRIB,1
       DO 1 K=1,IVALUE,1
     1 FREQ(K,J,I)=0
C      THIS SECTION ESTABLISHES FREQUENCY AND PROBLEM EXISTENCE
       DO 6 I=1,ICURNT,1
C      CHECK ALLOWABILITY OF THIS ITEM
       IF(MEMRY(KKK,I)-INDEX) 6,61,6
C      ITEM IS ACTIVE
    61 IT =MEMRY(ISIZE ,I)
       ICNT(IT)=ICNT(IT)+1
       IF(IPROB)2,5,3
C      PASSAGE IF NO ITEMS LOCATED BEFORE THIS ONE
     2 IPROB=IT
       GO TO 5
C      PASSAGE IF ONLY ONE CLASS SEEN SO FAR
     3 IF(IPROB-IT)4,5,4
     4 IPROB=0
C      FREQUENCY TALLY CONTINUES
     5 DO 51 J=1,IATRIB,1
       K=MEMRY(J,I)
       IF(K)51,50,50
    50 FREQ(K,J,IT)=FREQ(K,J,IT)+1
    51 CONTINUE
     6 CONTINUE
C      FREQUENCIES HAVE BEEN TABULATED,MAKE PROBLEM TEST
       IRSN=0
       IF(IPROB)7,9,8
     7 IANS=0
C      NO PROBLEMS
       RETURN
C      ALL ITEMS OF SAME CLASS
     8 IANS=-IPROB
       RETURN
C       ITEMS OF VARIED CLASSES, BEST GUESS REQUIRED
C      SECTION FOR FINDING BEST BLIND GUESS
     9 IT=1
       DO 11 I=2,ICLASS,1
       IF(ICNT(I)-ICNT(IT))11,11,10
    10 IT=I
    11 CONTINUE
C      NOW FIND BEST GUESS FROM ATTRIBUTES
       IANS=IT
       MAX=ICNT(IT)
       DO 18 I=1,IATRIB,1
       IWIN=0
       DO 14 J=1,IVALUE,1
       JWIN=1
```

```
      DO 13 K=2,ICLASS,1
      IF(FREQ(J,I,K)-FREQ(J,I,JWIN))13,13,12
   12 JWIN=K
   13 CONTINUE
   14 IWIN=IWIN+FREQ(J,I,JWIN)
C     CHECK AGAINST ACCURACY OF BEST GUESS
      IF(IWIN-MAX)18,18,15
C     BETTER THAN BEST PREVIOUS GUESS, CHECK AGAINST BLIND GUESS
C     FOLLOWING STATEMENT COULD BE REDONE BY ASSIGNMENT
   15 IF(IRSN)16,16,17
   16 IRSN=1
   17 IANS=I
      MAX=IWIN
   18 CONTINUE
C ANSWER FLAGS IN PLACE, REPORT
      RETURN
      END
$IBFTC SHUFLE M94,XR7,NODECK
      SUBROUTINE SHUFLE(ITEM,K,IATRIB)
C SHUFFLES K ITEMS OF LESS THAN 10 ATTRIBUTES
      DIMENSION IBUF(10),ITEM(K,IATRIB)
      DO 1 I=1,K
      JX=RANDIT (1,K)
      DO 1 J=1,IATRIB
      IBUF(J)=ITEM(JX,J)
      ITEM(JX,J)=ITEM(I,J)
    1 ITEM(I,J)=IBUF(J)
      RETURN
      END
$IBFTC STIMLI  M94,XR7,NODECK
      SUBROUTINE STIMLI(ITEMS)
C SETS UP SUBROUTINES FOR 5 X 4 CASE
      DIMENSION ITEMS (1024,5)
      IT=1
      DO 1 I=1,4
      DO 1 J=1,4
      DO 1 K=1,4
      DO 1 L=1,4
      DO 1 M=1,4
      ITEMS(IT,1)=I
      ITEMS(IT,2)=J
      ITEMS(IT,3)=K
      ITEMS(IT,4)=L
      ITEMS(IT,5) =M
    1 IT=IT+1
      RETURN
      END
$IBFTC DECTRE  M94,XR7,NODECK
      SUBROUTINE DECTRE(MAXHT,IATRIB,IVALU,ICLASS)
      DIMENSION MEMRY(7,1024),ITEM(6),ITREE(120,2),IRITE(40,2)
      INTEGER CURNT,RCTRL
C     THIS IS THE SUBROUTINE FOR DEVELOPING A TREE FROM A FIXED CONTENTS
C     OF MEMORY
      COMMON IRCTRL,MEMRY,MSIZE,ITEM,ISIZE,ITREE,CURNT,IRITE,ITRACE
C     CLEAN OUT OLD TREE FIRST THING
      KKK = ISIZE + 1
      DO 7 I=1,MAXHT
      DO 7 J=1,2,1
    7 ITREE(I,J)=0
      INDEX=1
      NEXT=2
    1 CALL SELECT (INDEX,CURNT,IATRIB,IVALU,ICLASS,IANS,IRSN,IT)
      IF(IRSN)2,2,5
```

```
C THIS SECTION IS MODIFIED FOR CLS-10 BEST GUESS PROCEDURE
2      IF(IANS) 3,9,4
  100  FORMAT(20H ALL ITEMS OF CLASS 12)
    3  IANS=-IANS
       IF(ITRACE)91,8,8
   91  PRINT 100,IANS
       GO TO 8
  101  FORMAT(15H BEST GUESS IS 12)
    4  IF(ITRACE)92,8,8
   92  PRINT 101,IANS
       GO TO 8
C      PASSAGE THROUGH THIS SECTION INDICATES TEST SELECTION
    5  IBASE=NEXT-1
       DO 6 I=1,CURNT,1
       IF(MEMRY(KXK,I)-INDEX) 6,12,6
   12  MEMRY(KXK,I)=IBASE+MEMRY(IANS,I)
    6  CONTINUE
  103  FORMAT(6H TEST ,12,4H IS ,12)
       IF(ITRACE)94,93,93
   94  PRINT 103,INDEX,IANS
   93  CONTINUE
       ITREE(INDEX,1)=IANS
       ITREE(INDEX,2)=NEXT
       ITX=NEXT+ IVALU-1
       DO 15 JTX = NEXT,ITX
   15  ITREE(JTX,1)=IT
       NEXT=NEXT+IVALU
       GO TO 9
    8  ITREE(INDEX,1)=IANS
    9  INDEX=INDEX+1
       IF(NEXT-INDEX)10,10,1
   10  DO 11 I=1,MSIZE,1
       IF(MEMRY(1,I))13,13,11
   11  MEMRY(KXK,I) = 1
   13  RETURN
       END
$IBFTC RANDOM  M94,XR7,NODECK
       SUBROUTINE RANDOM(R,MIN,MAX,IRCRL)
       X = IRCRL
       SM1=3435973837
       SM2=6871947674
       X=3.0*X
       IF(X-SM2)1,1,3
    1  IF(X-SM1)2,2,4
    2  XMAX=MAX
       XMIN=MIN
       R=X/SM1*(XMAX-XMIN)+XMIN
       IRCRL=X
       RETURN
    3  X=X-SM2
       GO TO 2
    4  X=X-SM1
       GO TO 2
       END
$IBFTC RANDIT  M94,XR7,NODECK
       FUNCTION RANDIT(MIN,MAX)
       COMMON IRCTRL
       CALL RANDOM(R,MIN,MAX+1,IRCTRL)
       RANDIT=R
       RETURN
       END
```

CHAPTER 5   *Lee W. Gregg*
                        Carnegie Institute of Technology

INTERNAL REPRESENTATIONS
OF SEQUENTIAL CONCEPTS*

Much psychological literature has described concepts as nouns that name shared characteristics of objects or events. Where the properties of the stimuli are easily described, the name of the concept becomes the name of the attribute values common to a partitioning of the stimuli into a subset of positive instances. For the learner, the functional utility of the concept comes about because these names, these nouns, define equivalence classes. Manipulations can be performed on the class names which become powerful tools for human problem-solving behavior.

My intent is to extend the usefulness of these nouns by providing verbs and adjectives to assist them. The verbs are information processes; the adjectives are associated information usually defined by a particular context. It is not enough to know that a person "has" the concept "round." More critical for predicting his behavior in a problem-solving task is a knowledge of the form in which that concept name is represented in memory, how the concept becomes available as an idea for generating hypotheses, or when such a concept will be invoked to bring order to a chaotic problem environment. It is important to recognize that concepts and their internal representations are constantly shifting as new experiences demand greater or lesser degrees of abstraction and as new tasks strain the boundaries imposed by a particular

The studies reported here were supported by the Public Health Service, Department of Health, Education, and Welfare, under Research Grant M-07722.

107

form of representation. This fluidity should caution us against naming unchangeable concepts.

In this paper, I will attempt to show that a number of alternative representations of a concept grow out of the same learning experience. The nature of the representation depends strongly on the ways initial encoding schemes are applied to the elementary features of the task. The evidence will be drawn from a learning experiment in which subjects are to learn a sequence of switch settings. Since analyses of the data are within the framework of an information-processing model, let me try to develop, briefly, a rationale for adopting this approach, and attempt a re-statement of the problem faced by those who wish to understand the growing literature on human cognitive processes.

CONTENT OF CONCEPTS

In 1951, Vinacke was reluctant to give a single precise definition of a concept; rather he contented himself with a summary of their essential features. He pointed out that concepts were not direct sensory data but that they are derived from previous experience. He stated that concepts are responses, symbolic in nature, that "tie together, or link, or combine discrete sensory experiences." The only clue to the nature of the concept, apart from what it does, is contained in the phrase "symbolic in nature."

The idea of a concept as a symbol or a name of something is clear. What is not clear is the background of learning that makes formation and use of the name possible.

Vinacke (1951, p. 5) illustrates that there is much more to be understood with:

> ...it appears that concepts should be placed in a broader, more dynamic context than has been the case up to now. They must be regarded as selective mechanisms in the mental organization of the individual, tying together sensory impressions thus aiding in the identification and classification of objects. But concepts involve more than the integration of sense impression ... for they are linked with symbolic responses which can be activated without the physical presence of external objects. Concepts can be given names.... and used to manipulate experience over and beyond the more simple

> recognition function. . . . Thus, a symbolic response does not
> have a fixed, permanent meaning but represents a momentary
> focusing of experience upon a particular stimulus situation. . . .

Before we attempt to state precisely what we think the
dynamic context is and how the selective mechanisms work to
integrate sense impressions, or, alternatively, to integrate
both sense impressions and other symbolic data generated by
the cognitive system, we must examine the substance of the
sensory experiences that provide the content of concepts.

Hovland (1952) proposed a concept model in which specific instances are created by combinations of the values of
attributes. Given a number of attributes or dimensions, each
having two or more values or levels, it is possible to define
a particular concept by specifying the appropriate value or
values of one or more relevant attribute. Various classes of
concepts can be described by means of this model.

The emphasis for each of these types of concepts is on the
characteristics of the stimuli. The focus of research was on
the selection of relevant from irrelevant dimensions so that
concept attainment or identification became the study of how
subjects discovered the particular set of absolute or relative
properties of the stimuli.

While the imaginative work of Bruner et al. (1956)
shifted attention to the processes by which subjects do this,
their framework for describing the content of concepts was
essentially the same as Hovland's. Hunt's (1962) survey of
the field further elaborated the ideas relating short-term
memory load to the discovery mechanisms within that common
framework, introduced a new emphasis.

Hunt's analysis of concept learning led him to seek a
more general notation for describing concepts in terms of the
operators of symbolic logic. The logical connectives specify
the rules for combining attribute values. This elaboration of
the information theoretic ideas raised the following question.
If the learner must describe both the properties of objects and
the connective relationships among them, how is the learning
effort distributed between these two subtasks? In his discussion of a simulation model for conditional focusing, Hunt
examined several heuristics for determining when such
shifts might occur. Clearly more empirical work was needed.

Haygood and Bourne (1965) took on the job, distinguishing more clearly between attribute-learning and rule-learning aspects of conceptual behavior.

Attribute learning, rule learning, and the strategies subjects employ in concept-identification tasks are interesting problems in their own right, and, of course, provide information relevant to the learning of concepts. But we want to know much more about the specific information content that the learner brings with him into the new problem-solving tasks.

CONCEPT LEARNING:
A RESTATEMENT OF THE PROBLEM

It is an easy thing to define concept attainment or identification in terms of the discovery of appropriate naming responses for well-defined attribute-value arrays. "Well-defined" simply means that there is agreement by most users of a particular language on the meaning of a verbal label. Concept-attainment or concept-identification tasks then become instances of very simple S-R learning. "Red circles are positive." Concept acquisition, on the other hand, requires the formation of "basic associations" in a "situation in which a simple set of instructions would not suffice." The quotes are from Kendler (1964) who fails to see that words like "basic" and "simple" beg the definitional question. It is impossible to describe a set of basic associations common to even a highly selected group of young children. A simple set of instructions would have to be those understood by the learner; and this implies that we know in advance what concepts the learner has already acquired. In the extreme, every subject in an experiment might have to receive a different, simple set of instructions.

The dilemma, then, seems to be that of choosing an appropriate starting point. Where should one begin the analysis of conceptual behavior if he does not wish to fall prey to an infinite regress to more and more "basic" levels of association?

At the moment, there seems to be only one starting point that is feasible and completely unambiguous, that is, where the subject enters the experimental laboratory.

The implication of this choice is that any study of concept

learning must pay as much attention to what the subject is like before the learning as after. More specifically, it poses the problem of characterizing the internal representations of those concepts the subject brings with him to the task and asks us to discover in what important respects those characterizations are changed as a result of the learning. The approach focuses on the individual subject, and imposes on the investigator the task of developing techniques that will make explicit many aspects of behavior that are ignored as covert in most investigations.

Sequential Concept Learning

Central to the search for ways of discovering internal representations of human concepts is a series of experiments in which subjects learn a sequence of switch settings. The subject is seated at a table. Before him is a panel on which there are four toggle switches. The switches can be moved to the left or to the right. Above the row of switches is a spring action lever switch and a pilot light (later a buzzer was used instead of the light). The subject is told that he must search for a particular arrangement of the four toggle switches so that the light will come on when the lever switch is depressed. He is told that when he finds that setting, he is to remember it and continue searching for new switch settings; the apparatus steps automatically from one setting to the next. He is told, that there is a certain number of settings to be learned. The settings are to be learned in a particular order; repeated trials will be given, with the same settings in the same order, until he can produce the sequence without error.

This serial learning task is complicated by the fact that the subjects must first discover the correct settings; hence, it is not surprising that for most subjects their early efforts soon are directed toward the subgoal of finding a procedure for testing different switch settings such that all possibilities are exhausted, no settings are skipped.

In constructing the specific sequences which the subjects are to discover, it is possible to create redundancy in various ways. The task as viewed by the subject then becomes a search for pattern. That subjects expect to find order, even when the sequences actually are random and of indefinite length, was one of the unique findings of Feldman (1963) in his study of binary choice behavior. In adopting this set, subjects in the switch-throwing task develop hypotheses based on familiar concepts.

One of the first experiments used a sequence in one-to-one correspondence with the first 16 binary numbers (0000, 0001, 0010, 0011, 0100, ..., 1111). Let us explore, briefly, the first few responses of a group of 15 subjects. What are the hypotheses that subjects generate in performing this task?

Response Patterns of Individual Subjects

	First Attempted Setting				
Binary Pattern	300	301	302	303	304
RRRR	RRRR	RRRR	RRRR	RRRR	RRRR
RRRL	LRRR	LLLL	RRRL	RRRL	LLLL
RRLR	RRRR	RRLL	RRLR	RRLL	RRLL
RRLL	RRRR	RRRR	RLRR	RLRR	RLRR
Binary Pattern	305	306	307	308	309
RRRR	RRRR	RRRR	RRRR	RRRR	RRRR
RRRL	LLLL	LRLR	RRRL	RRRL	LRRR
RRLR	RRLR	RRLL	RRLL	RRLL	RRLL
RRLL	RLRR	RLRR	RRLL	RLRR	RLRR
Binary Pattern	310	311	312	313	314
RRRR	RRRR	RRRR	RRRR	RRRR	RRRR
RRRL	LRRR	LLLL	RRRL	LRRR	RRRR
RRLR	RRLR	LRRR	LRRL	RRLR	RRLL
RRLL	RRLL	RLRR	RRRR	RLRR	RLRR

Fig. 5.1

On the left-hand side of Fig. 5.1 are the first 4 correct switch settings; the L's and R's stand for left and right. The actual responses for each of the subjects are just those first attempted. Remember that they continued trying settings until the correct one was discovered.

All of the subjects began with the setting RRRR, given

them through the instructions. Four of the 15 tried the setting, LLLL, as the second; one tried the setting RRRR again
(314). Nine of the 15 tried either RRRL or LRRR; 5 with the
L on the right, 4 with the L on the left. One tried LRLR.

For the third setting, after having experienced the sequence RRRR followed by RRRL, we found 8 subjects testing
RRLL as their initial setting. Four of the subjects tried
RRLR; and there were 3 subjects who tried other settings.
The setting RRRR was tried by subject 300 on this occasion
and on every other for the rest of the first trial. He was following a systematic search procedure. There were 2 other
atypical responses.

On the fourth correct setting, 10 of the 15 subjects first
tried RLRR. Two subjects tried RRLL and were correct
since both of these subjects had by this time thought of the
binary number sequence and held it as a hypothesis. Subject
300 continued his systematic search and 2 subjects tried the
setting RRRR.

The probability that as many as 10 or more of the 15
subjects would choose a particular setting, that is, the setting
RLRR, by random selection on a particular trial is exceed-
ingly small. We can calculate just how small by letting $n =$
the number of subjects acting independently, and $k = 10, 11,$
..., n. If it is equally likely that any one of the settings will
be chosen, p, the probability of selecting a particular setting,
is 1/16. Hence,

$$P(NH: 1 \geq 10) = \sum_{k}^{n} \frac{n!}{k!(n-k)!} \ p^k \ (1-p)^{n-k}$$

$$= \sum_{k=10}^{15} \frac{15!}{k!(15-k)!} \ \left(\frac{1}{16}\right)^k \left(\frac{15}{16}\right)^{15-k}$$

$$= 2.039 \times 10^{-9}$$

Since the setting RLRR is an incorrect setting, we cannot
attribute the departure from random selection to learning
effects. After all none of these subjects had as yet discovered the correct setting at this first try.

Of course what the subjects said was, in fact, that the
settings might be following a pattern. For most of these

subjects, the protocol made explicit that some variant of a concept "moving across" determined their choice at that time. Neither their hypothesis nor the actual settings they produced were generated randomly. At least it was this conviction that led us to transcribe tape recordings of the subject's comments, and to analyze in detail the relationships between what was said and the circumstances (including the switch-throwing responses) under which these reports were made. We have reported elsewhere the general techniques for developing an information processing model from such an analysis (Laughery and Gregg, 1962). For the present, it is enough to restate the assumptions made in constructing the model and to outline its general features.

Theoretical Assumptions

In general, an information processing theory assumes that a set of symbolic processes can be stated in sufficiently explicit ways that, when organized in the form of a computer program, the computer will run. The symbolic processes are rules governing the manipulation of symbols. The symbols represent environmental objects and behavioral events for both subject and experimenter. Let me simply state that it is impossible for most of us to be explicit enough to produce a running program on the first attempt. The role of the computer in part becomes that of a disciplinarian whose effective punishment is the silent treatment.

More specifically, the construction of the problem-solving model rests on the following assumptions.

1. At the level of description in which verbal and motor acts are the objective responses, each response is produced by a completely deterministic mechanism. No random variables were introduced into the program to "improve" the simulation.

2. The processor is a discrete, serial device. In this self-paced task, complications arising from the simultaneous action of experimenter and subject did not arise.

3. The program, or theory, is an explanation of the behavior of an individual human learner. To describe group data or average effects would require running the program more

than once and reducing the individual response data. Individual differences, to the extent that they may exist, require changes in the program structure or initial state.

The program was written in IPL-V (Newell et al, 1961), a list processing language designed for nonnumerical applications.

Features of the Model

The model distinguishes two modes or phases of behavior — search and hypothesis testing. In the search mode, settings are generated either from an organized set of search concepts or from a list containing arbitrary arrangements of a variety of such concepts. In the hypothesis-testing mode, settings are also generated in two ways. A subject with no prior knowledge of the exact sequence may analyze one or more of the recent settings and select a hypothesis on the basis of a match against a concept already available to him. The concept "moving across," appearing as it did early in the first trial, would be an example of this. In later trials, however, the subject may have partial information about the sequence. The model provides a memory list-structure for such information. If the information available is insufficient to produce a unique switch setting, a hypothesis based on partial information may be formed.

In general, the model postulates that hypothesis testing behavior is tried first. If a hypothesis is found, that is, a switch setting is generated, the setting is tested. If the test fails, the model branches immediately to the search mode. Of course if it succeeds, the next setting is tested.

Unfortunately, this brief statement of the workings of a program was not exact enough for the computer. The computer wanted to know what a "concept" was and what a "setting" looked like. And here, then, arise the issues of internal representation.

Encoding Individual Switch Settings. "All Chinamen look alike to the occidental." And so do the switch settings, at least for a time, to the subject. This is not surprising when we think of the sequence in terms of the letters "L" and "R" as presented in Fig. 5.1. The binary valued list is the extreme case of intralist similarity. In fact, in a serial verbal learning experiment using these materials, only 17 of 30 subjects reached the criterion of one perfect recitation by the end of an experimental session lasting approximately 40 minutes. However, the settings are learned eventually.

What are the cues that are used to identify uniquely the 16 settings? One of the first to emerge and one that almost every subject mentions explicitly is a partitioning of the settings according to the Form of the setting. Eleven of the 15 subjects in the exploratory experiment did so. The Form of the setting refers to the number of switches having each of the positional values. Hence, there are 3 possible forms for the 4-switch task: 4-1, with all switches to the right or to the left; 3-1, 8 settings of which RLLL and LRRR are examples; and 2-2, the 6 combinations of 2 right's and 2 left's. Obviously, Form alone is insufficient to determine a particular setting but it does provide the kind of partial information mentioned earlier. Subjects would frequently remember or think they remembered that the "next setting was a 3-1." For many subjects, the Form of the settings became the basis for a systematic search procedure.

Next, subjects remember the Major Symbol. "It was a 3-1 setting, three rights, I think." Form and Symbol uniquely determine the settings, RRRR and LLLL. The Symbol value halves the 3-1 settings, but has little relevance for the 2-2's.

By remembering the location in the array of switches that differ from the background defined by the Major Symbol, subjects are able to discriminate all 16 settings. The location values usually are given as numbers 1, 2, 3, 4; and usually originate at the left-hand side of the linear string of switches.

Although other descriptions of the switches are often found, about which more will be said, the simulation model used only those already mentioned. A switch setting is generated then by specifying values of the three attributes, Form, Major Symbol, Location of Differences.

Encoding Sequential Concepts. In the context of the switch-throwing experiment, a sequential concept is an order-defining rule relating two or more settings. For example, the pair of settings (RRRR, LLLL) is related by the rule, "Change all switches to the other binary position." Since the computer, like the subject, can change only one switch at a time, the programmer must make clear which switch is to be changed first, second, third, and fourth. Similarly, the pair (LLLL, RRRR) can be thought of in terms of the same rule; and so can the pairs (RLRR, LRLL) and (LRLR, RLRL). The rule may be the same, but the sequences are different.

Now it happens that you and I, in reading the above brief description, have made the implicit assumption that the first member of the "ordered pair" is the left-hand setting within the parentheses. Unfortunately, today's computers are unable to jump to such conclusions. To be completely explicit, we must tell the computer which switch setting to change via the rule; or, more generally where it might find that setting, that is, the location in the subject's memory. Of course one may assume that the setting to which the concept is to apply is the current setting stored for the human subject in the physical world of real switches on the display panel. If this assumption is made, it should be done with the awareness that a piece of memory is embedded in the task. Whether or not it is used depends on the strategy the subject adopts for learning.

If a concept is stated only in terms of the rule, while the object of the transformation is specified indirectly, the rule will sometimes not apply. Consider this re-statement of the previous rule:

"Change all switches from the right to the left position." The sequences (LLLL, RRRR) , (RLRR, LRLL) and (LRLR, RLRL) cannot, now, be subsumed under the rule. If we add the phrase "unless the switch is already in the right-hand position, then..." we are talking about different concepts depending upon what instructions complete the phrase. This poses an interesting and unsolved problem. To what extent are tests of applicability an integral part of the conceptual repertoire? The issue is whether we ever learn a concept in isolation from other information prescribing, however grossly, the domain of its use. Have you ever tried to take the logarithm of "APPLE"?

In constructing the simulation model, it became clear that there were two types of sequential concepts corresponding roughly to what might be called visual pattern sequences and motor pattern sequences. The distinction is implied in the foregoing discussion of possible rules. The distinction and the psychological relevance may be clearer if we examine a specific response pattern. Assume that the switches started all left,

(LLLL). The responses are:

$$\begin{bmatrix} RLLL \\ LRLL \\ LLRL \\ LLLR \end{bmatrix}$$

The subject produced the setting RLLL by moving the first switch, $s1$, to the right position. What he did to produce the second switch setting was to return the switch on the extreme left from the right to the left.

$$\begin{bmatrix} LLLL \end{bmatrix}$$

Then he moved the second switch from left to right.

$$\begin{bmatrix} LRLL \end{bmatrix}$$

Suppose we replace the response matrix with a change-operator matrix of 0's and 1's where we interpret a component, a_{ij}, as follows:

$$\text{if } a_{ij} = 0, \text{ then } f(s_{ij}) = \begin{cases} L \text{ if } s_{ij} = L \\ R \text{ if } s_{ij} = R \end{cases}$$

$$\text{if } a_{ij} = 1, \text{ then } f(s_{ij}) = \begin{cases} L \text{ if } s_{ij} = R \\ R \text{ if } s_{ij} = L \end{cases}$$

The change-operator matrix then becomes:

$$A = \begin{bmatrix} 1\,0\,0\,0 \\ 1\,1\,0\,0 \\ 0\,1\,1\,0 \\ 0\,0\,1\,1 \end{bmatrix}$$

and it describes the motor responses required to produce the original sequence of settings. Notice that in the first row there is a single 1, while the three remaining rows each have two 1's. Let me make two comments: First, the matrix is not as tidy as it might be; and second, tidy or not, it is perfectly possible for a subject to fixate such a pattern of movements and, without specific attention to which direction the changes were made, manipulate the switches blindfolded. The significance of these remarks is simply that the motor acts need not require memory of the visual-spatial characteristics of a setting. The setting-to-be-changed is stored on the panel.

Suppose, on the other hand, that the subject uses a little of his own memory. He chooses, for whatever reasons, to carry around in his head just one switch setting — a visual model, perhaps, of the most typical switch setting. Since the sample response pattern we are now considering starts with the setting (LLLL) , he may select it. The change-operator matrix applied to that base setting would look like this.

$$B = \begin{bmatrix} 1\,0\,0\,0 \\ 0\,1\,0\,0 \\ 0\,0\,1\,0 \\ 0\,0\,0\,1 \end{bmatrix}$$

This matrix is neater than matrix A. Each row contains a single 1. Of course, to actually produce the sequence of settings, the subject must perform physically the manipulations described by matrix A. Nevertheless, since man is a visually dominant creature, we would have to put our scientific bets on B as the more frequently encountered generator for the given response pattern.

Both types of sequential concepts were included in the model. The internal representations for each prescribed a base setting, either RRRR or LLLL for the visual response concepts, and a change operator. In the case of the motor-response concepts, either the last correct setting (subject stored it) or the last attempted setting (the current one on the switch panel) became the base. The following change operators were used:

1. Same $C1 = \begin{bmatrix} 0000 \end{bmatrix}$
2. Opposite $C2 = \begin{bmatrix} 1111 \end{bmatrix}$

3. Moving across $C3 = \begin{bmatrix} 1\,0\,0\,0 \\ 0\,1\,0\,0 \\ 0\,0\,1\,0 \\ 0\,0\,0\,1 \end{bmatrix}$ $C3' = \begin{bmatrix} 0\,0\,0\,1 \\ 0\,0\,1\,0 \\ 0\,1\,0\,0 \\ 1\,0\,0\,0 \end{bmatrix}$

4. Fill in $C4 = \begin{bmatrix} 1\,0\,0\,0 \\ 1\,1\,0\,0 \\ 1\,1\,1\,0 \\ 1\,1\,1\,1 \end{bmatrix}$ $C4' = \begin{bmatrix} 0\,0\,0\,1 \\ 0\,0\,1\,1 \\ 0\,1\,1\,1 \\ 1\,1\,1\,1 \end{bmatrix}$

5. Change two

$$C5 = \begin{bmatrix} 1\,1\,0\,0 \\ 1\,0\,1\,0 \\ 1\,0\,0\,1 \\ 0\,1\,1\,0 \\ 0\,1\,0\,1 \\ 0\,0\,1\,1 \end{bmatrix} \qquad C5' = \begin{bmatrix} 0\,0\,1\,1 \\ 0\,1\,0\,1 \\ 1\,0\,0\,1 \\ 0\,1\,1\,0 \\ 1\,0\,1\,0 \\ 1\,1\,0\,0 \end{bmatrix}$$

Selecting a subset of these concepts for a particular computer run is equivalent to stating a hypothesis about the cognitive state of the learner at the start of the experiment.

Learning Strategies. An executive routine organizes the search and learning behavior of the model. Figure 5.2 is a simplified version of one such strategy. The initial concepts are contained on the list *CO*. An effective search process

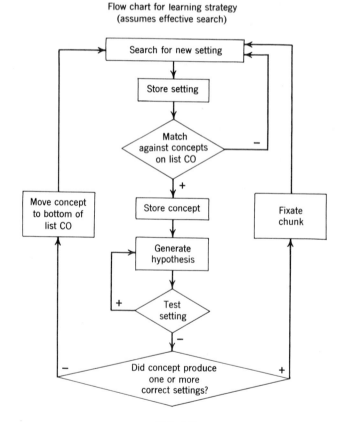

Flow chart for learning strategy
(assumes effective search)

Fig. 5.2

guarantees that the correct settings will be discovered by the program. As new settings are found, a match is attempted against the concepts on list CO. If a concept on CO is capable of generating that setting, a hypothesis, namely the next setting called for by that concept, is generated. An unsuccessful test leads to an evaluation of the concept. If the concept produces one or more correct settings, really two or more since the initial match on the concept was obtained, the "chunk," however great, is fixated. If the concept fails to produce a correct hypothesis, it is moved unceremoniously to the end of the list.

This incomplete account of the simulation model should be enough to suggest the general nature of a theory based on process description. The program did learn the binary sequence, building a compound concept from parts of the simpler ones. It also learned some random sequences but did so in about as many trials as on the more highly structured one. Obviously, more information was needed about the transition from initial to terminal state. In particular, a more exact description of the final concept seemed desirable.

SOME EXPERIMENTAL RESULTS

Three groups of 12 subjects each learned sequences of length 16 on the 4-switch task. Group 1 (Random) learned sequences selected by means of a table of random numbers; 3 subjects were assigned to each of 4 different lists. Group 2 (Patterned) learned the lists $P1$ through $P4$ shown in Fig. 5.3. Again there were 3 subjects assigned to each of the lists. All 12 subjects of Group 3 (Binary) learned the sequence shown in the first column of Fig. 5.3; the binary numbers from 0 to 15 where R = 0 and L = 1. Four subjects were replaced because of apparatus failures. Two subjects assigned to the binary list were rejected because they knew the binary numbers, however, three subjects in the other groups who had this knowledge were retained. The subjects learned the sequences to a criterion of one perfect recitation. An experimental session lasted one to one and a half hours, and the subjects returned for a second or a third session after an interval of about one week.

Each setting tested by the subject during the course of

Binary Count and Patterned Sequences

Binary	P1	P2	P3	P4
8421	2814	1428	4281	8142
RRRR	RRRR	RRRR	RRRR	RRRR
RRRL	RRLR	LRRR	RRRL	RLRR
RRLR	LRRR	RRLR	RLRR	RRRL
RRLL	LRLR	LRLR	RLRL	RLRL
RLRR	RRRL	RLRR	LRRR	RRLR
RLRL	RRLL	LLRR	LRRL	RLLR
RLLR	LRRL	RLLR	LLRR	RRLL
RLLL	LRLL	LLLR	LLRL	RLLL
LRRR	RLRR	RRRL	RRLR	LRRR
LRRL	RLLR	LRRL	RRLL	LLRR
LRLR	LLRR	RRLL	RLLR	LRRL
LRLL	LLLR	LRLL	RLLL	LLRL
LLRR	RLRL	RLRL	LRLR	LRLR
LLRL	RLLL	LLRL	LRLL	LLLR
LLLR	LLRL	RLLL	LLLR	LRLL
LLLL	LLLL	LLLL	LLLL	LLLL

Fig. 5.3

learning and the time of the response to the nearest second was recorded automatically. Since the instructions encouraged the subject to "think aloud," a microphone and tape recorder were used to record the verbal protocol.

Table 5.1 is a summary of the mean performance measures. The subjects of Group 1 (Random) took almost three times as many trials to reach criterion as did those of Group 3. The mean for the subjects of Group 2 (Patterned) is about half that of the Group 1 subjects. On the average, subjects who received the binary list took just over an hour to learn; Group 3 (Random) subjects required almost 2 hours, Group 2 (Patterned) subjects fall somewhere between.

Total first trial errors reflect the effort and time devoted to search. The means of 189.4 and 180.8 for Groups 1 and 2 are higher than the mean of 125.2 for Group 3. However, 2 subjects in Group 3 learned in a single trial in which very few errors were made. The expected value of first trial errors on the assumption of random selection without replacement is

TABLE 5.1 Summary of Mean Performance Measures Based
on Twelve Subjects in Each of The Experimental Groups

	Trials to Criterion	Total Time	Total 1st Trial Errors
Group 1 — Random	12.0	109.0	189.4
Group 2 — Patterned	5.5	81.6	180.8
Group 3 — Binary	4.1	66.7	125.2

128 errors, a value close to that of the Group 3 mean and well below the means of the other groups. Random selection without replacement implies that the subjects exhibit perfect memory for the settings already tested — an effective search strategy. It appears that most subjects are not effective searchers on the first trial.

Figure 5.4 plots the group mean number of correct responses for the first 15 trials. Two of the 12 subjects in Group 3 had not reached criterion by the fifteenth trial, taking 19 and 20 trials to learn. Groups 2 and 3 are similar in rate of acquisition but differ markedly from Group 1.

In Figs. 5.5, 5.6, and 5.7 individual learning curves for half of the subjects in each of the groups are presented. The subjects selected for this are not necessarily typical of the group mean performance, although the overall differences of Fig. 5.4 can be detected. The reason for exhibiting these particular curves is to show the range of behaviors that occur in all three groups. For example, Subjects 127 and 131 of Fig. 5.5 (Random) are not much worse than Subject 220, Fig. 5.6, a subject who learned one of the patterned sequences. And Subject 322, Fig. 5.6, shows little or no increase in correct responses up to and including trial 6. That subject's (322) performance to that point is inferior to all other experimental subjects, regardless of group. Similarly, Subject 110, Fig. 5.5, learned a random sequence in just 3 trials. His performance was exceeded only by 2 subjects, 306 and 314 in Group 3, Fig. 5.7.

The point is not that individual differences are great, but rather that a great deal of information must be contained in these discrepant behaviors. Given that such performance differences exist, we would like to know if these differences are related to different terminal states. Can we find evidence

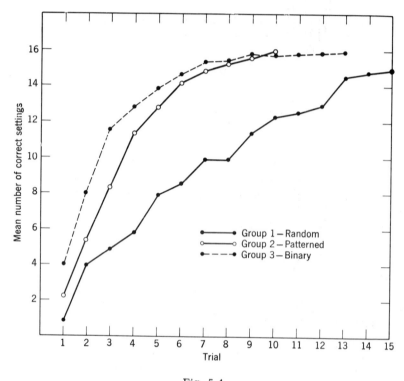

Fig. 5.4

to confirm or disconfirm the notion that the concept of the binary sequence is a linear re-combination of parts of previously learned, conceptually more primitive, sequences? Is there sufficient evidence to describe in some detail the memory structure of a concept?

Much of the analysis that follows rests on the post-experimental interview in which the following three questions were asked.

1. How did you go about learning the sequence?
2. How did you finally get them in the right order?
3. Is there anything else you can tell me about the way you learned or moved the switches, for example...? If not specifically mentioned by the subject, this last question became the vehicle for determining the subject's estimate of the number of switch settings in the sequence, the way he named (or numbered) the individual switches, and, finally, whether he could describe the sequence as a pattern.

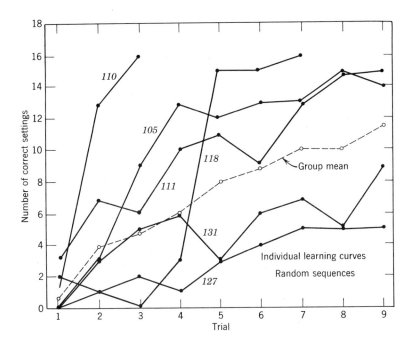

Fig. 5.5

The tape recordings of the verbal protocol during learning were transcribed and collated with the switch-throwing responses.

Protocol analysis is a problem-solving task. Its goal is to construct an internally consistent set of statements about the behavior in question. Usually this involves formulating a descriptive metalanguage suitable for later translation into a computer language. In a sense, the analysis searches for the intersection of two sets -- the set of programmable statements, S, of the logical possibilities and the set of observations, O. Obviously the size of the set, $S \cap O$, is bounded by the size of either set. Therefore, the number of observations should be as large as possible. Where there are many observations, multiple points of contact can be found between statement and observation. The more of these there are, the greater the plausibility of that statement.

Ultimately, the set of statements is constrained by the requirements that (a) no statement shall conflict with any

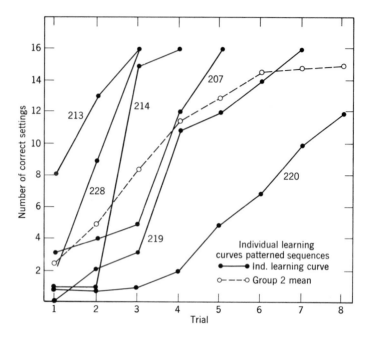

Fig. 5.6

observation and (b) the set is sufficient to produce the behavior via a running program. Statements of the set, even though they may be programmable individually, may still not produce a program capable of generating the behavior.

In the next section is a description of the binary concepts derived from the protocol analyses of the subjects of Group 3 who learned that sequence. The analyses end prior to the running-program stage. The descriptive metalanguage is adapted from the one used by Simon and Kotovsky (1963) in their analysis of series completion problems.

Representations of the Binary Sequence

Table 5.2 presents a summary of the terminal encodings for the 12 subjects of Group 3. For each subject, trials to criterion and total time measures are given together with the information relevant to a specification of the subject's concept

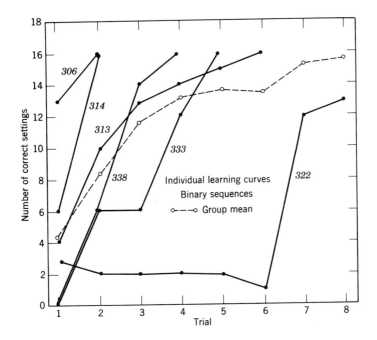

Fig. 5.7

of the binary sequence. The column headed "Base" refers to the switch setting used by the subject in his final encoding. For 8 of the subjects this setting was RRRR, which was also the initial setting in the sequence. One subject used the setting LLLL; two used the last correct setting as a base; and one subject, Subject 322, learned the sequence without a base, as such. The column headed "Switch Labels" gives the numerals subjects used to name the switches. The numbers 1,2,3,4 mean that a subject called the first switch on the left "switch one" and the switch on his extreme right "switch four." Remember that this is the terminal designation. Some subjects arrived at this specific naming only after other labels for the switches had been tried. Only one subject, Subject 322, failed to come up with a fixed designation for the 4 switches. The parentheses used in Table 5.2 mean that the group of switches were thought of as a single unit. Subject 303, for example, treated

TABLE 5.2 Summary Table of the Representations of the
Binary Concept

Subject	Trials to Criterion	Total Time	Base	Switch Labels	Concept
3416302	2	86	RRRR	1, 2, 3, 4	Serial, Mixed Dictionary
3416303	2	6	RRRR	(1, 2), (1, 2)	Double Cycle, No Dictionary
3416304	8	72	RRRR	4, 3, 2, 1	Serial, Change Operator
3416305	2	15	RRRR	1, 1, (1, 2)	Compound, No Dictionary
3416306	1	5	RRRR	1, (4, 2, 1)	Double Cycle, Octal Dictionary
3416313	5	23	RRRR	8, 4, 2, 1	Double Cycle, Binary Dictionary
3416314	1	7	RRRR	1, 2, 3, 4	Compound, Change Operator
3416316	5	97	Last	1, 2, 3, 4	Compound, Two Segments
3416317	3	151	RRRR	1, 2, 3, 4	Serial, Change Operator
3416322	13	207	None	None	Serial, Decimal Dictionary
3416333	4	107	LLLL	1, 2, 3, 4	Serial, Change Operator
3416338	3	24	Last	1, 2, 3, 4	Serial, Change Operator

the 2 switches on the right as one pair and the 2 switches on the left as a second pair.

Let me dispose of Subject 322 at this time. The way he learned the binary sequence obscured whatever base and switch labels he might have used early in the learning. His learning curve is shown in Fig. 5.5 which exhibits no learning over the first six trials. However, the subject actually learned two sequences of switch settings in this period. His approach to the problem of discriminating among the 16 switch settings was to repeat them in a fixed order during search; that order was as follows: RRRR, RRRL, RRLR, RLRR, LRRR, RRLL, RLRL, LRRL, RLLR, LRLR, LLRR, RLLL, LRLL, LLRL, LLLR, LLLL. Each time Subject 322 searched for a new setting he rehearsed the above response pattern. Ultimately, he gave each of the settings in that pattern a label corresponding to the decimal number of its serial position. Thus RRRR =1, RRRL = 2, ..., LLLL = 16. On about the sixth trial the subject had firmly established this pattern. He could now begin learning. What he learned, of course, was the serial list of 16 decimal numbers corresponding to the serial numbers of the switch settings in his search pattern; namely: 1, 2, 3, 6, 4, 7, 9, 12, 5, 8, 10, 13, 11, 14, 15, 16. His learning was further impeded because he alternated between calling his first setting the zeroth setting and the first setting. Nevertheless, Subject 322's representation of the sequence is an example of one of the three general kinds of concepts uncovered by the analysis. In the column headed "Concept" in Table 5.2, we have called Subject 322's representation, serial, with a decimal dictionary.

Serial Representation. Obviously what we mean by a serial representation is that the subject learned a single list of items such that the production of a setting derives from the information contained in a list item. There is a one-to-one correspondence between items on the learned list and the settings in the sequence. In order to set the 4 switches to successive settings, the subject must keep track of his place on the list. We will use the symbol $M1$ to stand for a place-keeper in memory. The operation "Next of $M1$" replaces the current location with the one that follows in the list. Following Simon and Kotovsky (1963), the expression $(M1, N(M1))$ is equivalent to, "respond with the object named in $M1$," and then perform the operation, "find the next on the list." Enclosing the expression in parentheses means to repeat this operation as long as there is a next item.

For Subject 322, the list that we have referred to is a list of decimal numbers from 1 to 16. Any one of those numbers is transformed into a specific setting by the process that Subject 322 learned during search. To indicate that this is an indirect mechanism, we will change $M1$ to $D(M1)$. We can think of the response process for producing the specific switch setting from an arbitrary label as a dictionary lookup. Since the numbers that Subject 322 used were the decimal numbers this dictionary consists of entries, decimal numerals, and a definition for each associated switch setting. A final statement of Subject 322's concept is as follows:

List: 1,2,3,6,4,7,9,12,5,8,10,13,11,14,15,16

Dictionary: 1 = RRRR, 2 = RRRL, 3 = RRLR, 4 = RLRR, . . . ,
           16 = LLLL
Initialize: $M1 \leftarrow 1$, List
Iteration Sequence: $(D(M1), N(M1))$

Six of the 12 subjects in Group 3 learned serial representation of the binary concept. Subject 302 also used a dictionary, but the other 4 subjects used a process for obtaining
the switch settings from the serial list that we have called a
"change operator." Change operators were discussed in an
earlier section. The idea quite simply is that a switch label
designates a column location in the change operator matrix,
and successive settings descend through the rows of the matrix. The serial lists that the subjects learn is a list of the
switch labels.

An example of a subject who learned a serial representation but did so by using a change operator is Subject 304.
The subject learned a serial list where the items of the list
were the names of the switches to be changed.

List: 0,1,2,(1-2),3,(3-1),(3-2),(3-2-1),4,(4-1),(4-2),
      (4-1-2),(4-3),(4-3-1),(4-3-2),(4-3-2-1)
Initialize: $M1 \leftarrow 0$, List
Change Operator: $A = |\text{List}|$, RRRR
Iteration Sequence: $(A(M1), N(M1))$

The switch settings are generated by applying the change list
to the base; in this case, the setting RRRR.

What is the difference between a dictionary look-up and a
change operator? The change operator can be thought of as a
rule for generating settings, whereas the dictionary definition
of a setting is a paired-associate item. The name of the dictionary entry, the stimulus member, can be completely arbitrary; the integrated response member is a string of symbols
describing the setting. In the case of the change operator,
however, processing requirements and the labels must be cohesive.

Cyclical Concepts. Row 2 of Table 5.2 describes Subject
303's representation. Notice that the switch labels are paired.
This subject reported that he thought of the switches as "the
pair on the left" and "the pair on the right." Subject 303 noticed that the pair on the right exhibited a cycle that was re-

peated. He also noticed that the same values were repeated in the left-hand pair for every cycle of the right-hand pair. The serial list that Subject 303 learned was a short one of length 4. He said he learned the pair values visually so that his representation of one cycle was (RR), (RL), (LR), and (LL). This report, if true, would indicate that Subject 303 needed neither a dictionary nor a generator to go from the contents of his memory to the position of the switches on the panel. Moreover, the same list served him in a double role. But since there were 2 cycles he had to keep track of 2 locations on the fixated list. Let $M1$ and $M2$ be Subject 303's place-keepers for the pair on the left and the pair on the right, respectively. We can now represent the concept that this subject used to generate the binary sequence:

List: (RR), (RL), (LR), (LL)
Initialize: $M1 \leftarrow$ RR, List; $M2 \leftarrow$ RR, List
Iteration Sequence: $((M1, M2, N(M2)), N(M1))$

Three of the 12 subjects used variants of the double cycle concept. Subject 306 grouped the 3 switches on the right into a triad, thought of a panel of a computer he had once seen where the lights were a group of 3, and remembered that they had called it an octal code. His description of the octal numbers showed that he had memorized pairs of light positions and numbers. His basic list, $L1$, was the octal numbers 0 through 7. But he had one switch left over. What he did was to put its 2 values on a separate list, $L2$, which contained the symbols R and L. His iteration sequence was:

List 1: 0,1,2,3,4,5,6,7
Dictionary: 0 = RRR, 1 = RRL, 2 = RLR, ..., 7 = LLL
List 2: R, L
Initialize: $M1 \leftarrow$ R, List 2, $M2 \leftarrow$ 0, List 1
Iteration Sequence: $((M1, D(M2), N(M2)), N(M1))$

For Subject 313 the switch-throwing problem reminded him of a radiation counter. Notice that it took Subject 313 five trials and 23 minutes to learn the sequence even with this headstart. His final representation, however, is probably closest to what a mathematician would say if asked to describe the binary number sequence. He, in fact, used a binary dictionary where R = 0 and L = 1, and computed each new setting by adding and carrying. For him, the concept was:

List: 0,1
Dictionary: 0 = R, 1 = L
Initialize: $M1 \leftarrow M2 \leftarrow M3 \leftarrow M4 \leftarrow$ 0, List
Iteration Sequence: $((((D(M1),\ D(M2),\ D(M3),\ D(M4),$
$N(M4)),\ N(M3)),\ N(M2)),\ N(M1))$

Compound Concepts. Only 3 of the 12 subjects developed compound concepts in the sense that this idea was used in the original simulation program. A compound concept like both of the others requires the fixation of one or more lists. The difference, however, is in terms of the iteration sequences. In the serial concept the process of "finding next" proceeds without interruption. In the cyclical concepts, the iterations are nested so that the cue for changing to the value of a superordinate comes from the completion of a list cycle. For the compound concepts, the structure of the binary sequence is broken up into separate parts. For example, Subject 316 learned the binary sequence in two distinct segments corresponding to the first half and second half of the problem sequence. He encoded the changes from his base, the last correct setting, in terms of the switch labels 1, 2, 3, and 4 from left to right. Now if we examine the binary sequence and generate Subject 316's list for the change operator, we see that the second half of the list is the same as the first half.

Setting	Switch to be Changed	Setting	Switch to be Changed
RRRR	1 2 3 4	LRRR	1 2 3 4
RRRL	4	LRRL	4
RRLR	3 4	LRLR	3 4
RRLL	4	LRLL	4
RLRR	2 3 4	LLRR	2 3 4
RLRL	4	LLRL	4
RLLR	3 4	LLLR	3 4
RLLL	4	LLLL	4

However, subject 316 did not recognize this. He thought he was learning two different lists. And when asked about the pattern in the post-experimental interview, he said only that he thought there was a place in both where the numbers went, "4, 234, 4." There are reasons for this subject's confusion, but our point here is that the iteration sequence for generating the binary pattern has a quite different form from the nested iteration of the cyclical concepts and from the simple structure of the serial concept.

To represent Subject 316's concept we take into account that the subject thought that there were two different lists by giving separate names to the subject's internal representation of the lists — call them List 1 and List 2.

List 1: (1-2-3-4),(4),(3-4),(4),(2-3-4),(4),(3-4),(4)
List 2: $(1-2-3-4)^1,(4)^1,(3-4)^1,(4)^1,(2-3-4)^1,(4)^1,(3-4)^1,(4)^1$
Change Operator: $A = |M1|$, Last Correct
Initialize: $M1 \leftarrow$ List 1, $M2 \leftarrow (1-2-3-4)$
Iteration Sequence: $((A(M2), N(M2))$, Reset $(M1,M2))$

At the time when this subject reached criterion, the only relationship perceived by the subject between the two distinct parts of his representation was that the first half preceded the second half. The new operation "Reset" is introduced to suggest the way the learning is encapsulated. After completing the response sequence corresponding to the first half, the act of resetting $M1$ and $M2$ establishes the new "initial" conditions, $M1 \leftarrow$ List 2 and $M2 \leftarrow (1-2-3-4)^1$, for generating the second half of the sequence.

Both of the remaining subjects, 305 and 314, noticed the cycle RR, RL, LR, and LL in the right-hand pair of switches. Unlike Subject 303, these subjects did not see that the pair of switches on the left followed that same pattern. Instead they formed internal representations in which the left-hand switches were treated separately. What they learned was a compound of the cyclical pattern and a description of the states of the other switches. The entire sequence was broken down into four distinct segments. For Subject 305, the concept appeared to be:

List 1: (RR), (RL), (LR), (LL)
Initialize: $M1 \leftarrow$ R, $M2 \leftarrow$ R, $M3 \leftarrow$ (RR), List 1
Iteration Sequence: $(((M1), (M2), (M3), N(M3))$, Reset
$\qquad\qquad\qquad\qquad ((M1), (M2))$
Where: Reset $= M2 \leftarrow$ L; then
$\qquad\qquad M1 \leftarrow$ L, $M2 \leftarrow$ R; then
$\qquad\qquad M2 \leftarrow$ L

The reset operation seems much more like paired-associates learning than serial-list learning. For each distinct segment cues arising from the completion of the cycle and the current state of the switches are sufficient to define the subject's place. Associated with these cues are the specific responses involved in resetting the switches not in the cycle.

We could easily argue that only 6 of the subjects learned an integrated pattern description. The serial-concept learners were simply recoding the 16 settings and a serial list by any name is still a list. The subjects that learned cyclical and compound concepts, in general, effected a greater reduction in the encoding process. Fewer items were fixated in "arbitrary" orders. Segmentation of the list depended to a greater or lesser extent on an integrating rule.

On the other hand, we could maintain that all of the subjects exhibited terminal behaviors that were really much the same. All variants of the representations were recodings of the original sequence involving one or more serial-learning components. The very large differences in performance measures reflected the interaction between the perceptual encoding of settings and previously learned concepts applied to the problem-solving task.

Just how great the performance differences were is indicated by a comparison of the 6 subjects who learned either the cyclical or compound concepts with the 6 subjects who learned a pure serial representation. There was a 2-1 ratio in trials to criterion, 5.50 trials for the serial concept learners and 2.67 trials for the others. Total learning time was even more striking, 108 minutes for the serial learners and 26 minutes for the cyclical or compound rule learners.

We suspect that some rather powerful effect is at work to produce such differences among a group of relatively homogeneous college sophomores. In the next section we will attempt to account for much, though not all, of the differences by examining the very early behaviors of the subjects in Groups 1 and 2. We will see that the ways subjects label, or fail to label, the switches and settings on Trial 1 predict total time and total errors during acquisition.

THE ROLE OF VERBAL LABELS

An efficient encoding scheme is one that reduces the number of items that have to be fixated in arbitrary ways. Before the subjects can encode a switch setting, however, the stimulus material must be distinguished. We have already seen that the selection of a base and a set of labels for the switches make it possible for the subject to develop an effective encoding. For the subjects of Group 3 it is difficult to separate the initial encoding from the concept solution. Discovery of the pattern by the subjects in Group 3 came about too rapidly, except in the case of Subject 322. If the subjects were simply identifying the concept of the binary numbers, this would suggest that they already had the coding scheme available to them. The patterned and random lists for Group 1 present greater opportunities for investigating initial behavior, even though the subjects of Group 2 learned about as fast on the average as did those of Group 3. The sequences learned by the subjects of Group 2 exhibited certain regularities but no *a priori* concept serves to name the sequences.

Many of the subjects had a great deal of difficulty learning the patterned and random sequences. The difficulties can be classified into three types.

1. Indefinite descriptors: Demonstrative pronouns such as "these" and "those," "this one" and "that one," were used by subjects in referring to the switches or settings. These words worked all right as long as the switch setting being described was in front of the subject, but obviously created difficulties in subsequent recall.
2. Insufficient descriptors: The information that the subject used to encode the settings, though stable and specific, is still inadequate to completely specify a unique switch setting. Most generally this was seen in subjects using only the form of the switch setting to describe it, that is, "the last one is a three-and-one setting."
3. Inconsistent descriptors: Here the subjects were precise enough and definite enough but their encoding schemes were unstable. From time to time either the base setting or the way the switches were labeled changed.

Can we distinguish differences among the subjects'

behavior in labeling switches and switch settings? If so, what is the effect of establishing efficient encoding schemes early in the learning? Trial 1 protocols for the 24 subjects in Group 1 and 2 were analyzed with respect to: (a) decisions stated by the subject to use a systematic approach, and confirmation of this in his response behaviors, or (b) a statement in the post-experimental interview that on the first trial the subject selected a base and labeled the switches also verified through the response sequences, or (c) specific evidence of the lack of consistency with regard to base and switch labels. Tables 5.3 and 5.4 summarize the results of the "content analysis" of the Trial 1 data. Six of the subjects in Group 1 and five of the subjects in Group 2 selected a base and labeled the switches on the first trial, thus meeting the prerequisite for an efficient code. In Table 5.5, the performance measures for the efficient

TABLE 5.3 Initial Coding Schemes for Individual Subjects
of Group 1: Random Sequences

Subject	Trials to Criterion	Total Time	Base	Switch Labels	Switch Position Names R	L
3416110	2	67	None	L, CL, CR, R	Evening	Morning
3416118	6	176	None	1, 2, 3, 4	X	X
3416131	15	124	None	1, 2, 3, 4	X	X
3416105	10	43	RRRR	1, 2, 3, 4	X	X
3416123	13	100	RRRR	4, 3, 2, 1	X	X
3416129	11	117	RRRR	1, 2, 3, 4	X	X
3416111	9	95	LLLL	8, 4, 2, 1	1	0
3416124	20	74	LLLL	1, 2, 3, 4	X	X
3416126	10	154	None	None	X	X *
3416108	19	99	None	None	mixed	
3416121	14	99	None	None	X	X
3416127	15	160	Last	None	X	X

*Form of setting.

and inefficient subjects of the combined groups is compared with respect to total learning performance. Trials to criterion were not significant. Total learning time, about 112 minutes for the inefficient subject versus about 69 minutes for the efficient subject was significant; total first errors were also significant, about 220 for the inefficient versus 136 for the efficient. The overall effect suggests that the initial strategy, whether a deliberate cognitive decision or a piece of elicited

TABLE 5.4 Initial Coding Schemes for Individual Subjects
of Group 2: Patterned Sequences

Subject	Trials to Criterion	Total Time	Base	Switch Labels	Switch Position Names R	L
3416209	4	21	RRRR	1, 2, 3, 4	X	X
3416228	2	105	RRRR	8, 4, 2, 1	X	X
3416239	5	115	None	None	X	X*
3416213	2	26	RRRR	1, 2, 3, 4	X	X
3416215	5	76	None	None	1	0
3416220	9	85	None	None	X	X
3416207	4	125	None	None	R	L
3416212	9	130	None	None	X	X
3416219	6	66	None	Mixed	X	X*
3416214	3	57	RRRR	1, 2, 3, 4	X	X
3416210	11	127	None	None	Mixed	*
3416237	6	44	RRRR	1, 2, 3, 4	X	X

*Form of setting.

TABLE 5.5 Comparison of the Mean Performance Measures
of "Efficient" and "Inefficient" Subjects of Groups 1 and 2

Efficient	Trials to Criterion	Total Time	Total 1st Trial Errors
N = 11	7.9	69.2	135.9
Inefficient N = 13	9.4	113.8	220.3

behavior characteristic of the subject in problem-solving tasks, is highly effective.

An efficient encoding scheme, apart from reducing the number of arbitrary associations, should increase the discriminability of individual switch settings. This would suggest that the number of settings tried during search would also be reduced. The mean number of settings attempted divided by first errors for each subject over the first four trials of the experimental session were computed. Figure 5.8 is a plot of the means for the efficient and inefficient subjects for Groups 1 and 2. Only for those subjects who received the patterned lists did the initial encoding scheme appear to help during search. The differences between efficient and inefficient subjects receiving the random lists are not significant. Evidently,

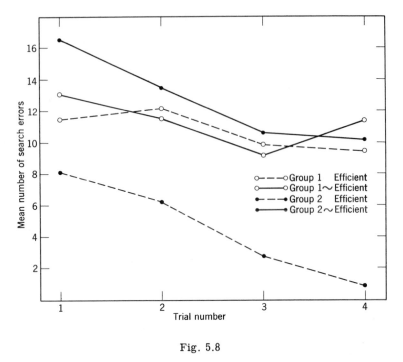

Fig. 5.8

the effects of labeling play a more important role in patterned discovery than in search.

IMPLICATION AND SPECULATION

Although we may speak of concepts as the names of logical abstractions, their representation in human memory must be concrete. Specific serial lists, associative connections (cueing features for the iteration sequences), and rules relating these elements must exist before we can say that the subject has learned a concept. Without them, the subject is incapable of generating any behavior whatever. This is the "dynamic context" Vinacke may have had in mind.

Concepts are the names for coherent sequences of information processing acts carried out by an individual in performing a particular task. The sequence need not be a fixed, serial one; decision rules leading to alternative outcomes are possible components of the "coherent" sequence; information-gathering processes may be incorporated. Coherent is not intended as a criterial property, but is rather used in a descriptive sense. The term "information processing acts" implies that a discrete, serial mechanism is capable of accepting symbols as input and producing symbols as output; the issue of these symbols being covert or overt, conscious or unconscious, explicit or implicit, psycho- or motor is unresolved. A particular individual may have a name for a coherent sequence that is different from the name applied to the identical sequence by another. Conversely, two people may have the same name as a result of a common language but quite different information processes associated with it. Of course, the name itself may be an entirely private symbol, not necessarily a part of any communicable language system.

A great deal of work is implied by the techniques of analysis and by the strategy for organizing our research findings into simulation models of behavior. Anyone who has attempted to write a large-scale computer program realizes that that program never works correctly the first time. A number of de-bugging runs are necessary. The approach, though difficult, seems to be a fruitful one. New techniques and experimental designs are called for to bring the analysis of process to a more rigorous level.

Let me mention briefly some of the directions in which these ideas have taken us.

Analysis of Temporal Relationships in Verbal Strings.

Serially-integrated components of a concept may be likened to Miller's (1956) chunks, and should have the following characteristics: (a) responses based on a well-integrated chunk should exhibit a uniform and small inter-element response interval, and (b) breaking into the middle of the serial chain should produce performance decrement in terms of errors or delays. In an experiment on induced chunking (McLean & Gregg, 1967), 5 groups of 15 subjects each learned a serial list of 24 letters of the English alphabet; e and i were omitted to reduce the occurrence of meaningful words in the random lists. The independent variable was the number of letters displayed on a particular presentation; 1, 3, 4, 6, or 8 letter-group segments of the list.

The results were that any one of the induced chunking conditions was superior to the one-letter-at-a-time condition. In fact, subjects learned the serial lists in about half the time required for serial learning of the individual letters. Upon reaching the criterion of one perfect recitation, all subjects were asked to say the list backward. We measured interletter response intervals for both the last trial and the backward recall. The effects of letter grouping were clearly apparent in the last trial, and were amplified still more in the backward recitation. The structure of memory, even for a simple serial list, can be thought of as a compound concept where sub-units of the list are organized in a more complex structure. We are currently attempting to trace the development of the hierarchical structure from initial to terminal performance.

Short-term Memory Implications.

The number of different place-keepers is a rough measure of the diversity of a concept's structure. The keeping-track experiments (Yntema and Mueser, 1962; Lloyd, Reid, and Feallock, 1960) and work in our own laboratory (Olshavsky, 1965; Simon and Kotovsky, 1963) suggest that when the number of place-keepers exceeds only 2 or 3, substantial decrements in performance occur.

Place-keepers are relatively content free — they are locations which, if verbalized, might be ordinal position names, "first," "second," "third," etc. In fact, the characteristic of all short-term memory experiments is massing of intra-list similarity; successive items differ from those that have preceded only in positional arrangement. We might suspect, then, that conceptual organizations are constrained by the number of place-keepers human short-term memory can tolerate. If the conditions during acquisition of a concept or utilization of a concept make differential demands that strain the limits of human cognitive behavior, we can expect failure on the part of the subject and modification of the conceptual structure to conform to the task requirements.

Consider the consequences of encoding the binary sequences in terms of regularities exhibited by individual

switches. For the patterned and binary count sequences, one
of the switches simply alternates from the left to the right
position; a second is in double alternation; another cycles every
fourth occasion; and the last, every eight times. This description is perceptually clear when the setting matrix is available
for visual inspection as in Fig. 5.3.

This particular representation is easy to learn in the sense
that almost all of us are able to apply the concept of "cycle" or
"alternate" and can fixate a series of four digits, for example,
8,4,2,1 or 1,4,2,8. It is effective for generating the binary
sequence column by column. With paper and pencil, the rows
of the binary sequence are a free concomitant of the procedure
for producing the columns. This representation, however, is
not a good one for producing one row of the sequence at a time.
Four place-keepers are required, and the task, without additional information or memory aids, that is, paper and pencil, is
almost impossible.

Only one subject, 306 in Group 3, learned a concept roughly
in this way. Why so few? Our conclusion is that the conditions
of the experiment — discovering one setting at a time — made
it unlikely that subjects could ever observe "simultaneously"
the column regularities. Only by fixating substantial segments
of the row sequence is it possible for the subject to detect the
column by column variation. For example, in the sequence,

RRRR
RLRR
RRRL
RLRL

Column 2 is the alternating column while Column 4 is in double
alternation. The two columns in which changes have occurred
are necessarily the ones with the shortest periods. Column 2,
at the end of the segment, has completed two cycles; Column 4,
just one. Yet, without recoding, the subject must fixate a serial
list of 16 individual letters, namely RRRR, RLRR, RRRL,
RLRL. The punctuation marks for the groups are probably
free. To examine any column, say Column 4, the subject must
generate the fourth symbol in each group, keeping track as he
does so, of his place within the group. As successive symbols
are obtained, he must remember them and he must keep track
of the groups. Stated in this way, the task is indeed formidable.
Even so, runs as short as length 4 scarcely are enough to

verify the single or double alternations. And, at this point, the subject can know very little of the sequential properties of Columns 1 and 3. His most tenable hypothesis is that these columns will remain the same.

Symbolic behavior of the sort we have just described can never lead to simultaneity in the same sense that impressions of two objects occupying spatially distinct locations are simultaneous. Apparent simultaneity comes about from the close temporal contiguity of the symbols in short-term memory. It seems likely that the symbols themselves are of an auditory nature, but precisely what symbols provide the content of the short-term memory depends on the encoding scheme adopted by a given subject. The role of short term memory processes in simple concept learning is much better understood than in this more complex problem solving and learning task. Let me suggest that a fruitful line of inquiry is one that views short-term memory not as a unitary process, but as a set of processes evolving from relationships between the demands imposed by a task environment and the set of cognitive mechanisms the subject brings to bear in dealing with that environment.

CHAPTER 6   *Bennet B. Murdock, Jr.*

University of Toronto

DISCUSSION OF PAPERS
BY LEE W. GREGG AND EARL B. HUNT

Before discussing the papers of Lee W. Gregg and Earl B. Hunt, I would like to review briefly some of the background literature on concept learning. This literature should serve as a context in which these two papers can be evaluated. After this survey I shall turn to the specifics of the papers themselves.

If one starts with the review of the concept-formation field made by Vinacke in 1951 and then looks at some of the recent developments, one cannot help but be impressed with the progress that has been made. Our theoretical analyses are much more sophisticated and our experimental studies much better designed and executed. Computer simulation is becoming more and more accepted as a test of the adequacy of theoretical formulation. Nevertheless, there is still considerable diversification of theory and terminology. In this connection let me cite a recent metaphor suggested by Julian Jaynes (1966) by which he compares physics and psychology. He likens physics to mountain climbing. The direction (through blizzard, mist, or searing sun) is always upward. Each new generation gets equipment, ropes up, and follows the leader. By contrast, psychology is like a huge entangled forest. The multitudes pass through, each one equipped with ear-plugs and blinders, certain that he alone has found the way, and calls on others to follow. As the papers in this symposium attest, the concept-learning field is no exception.

After the Vinacke paper, an article by Hovland in 1952 may well have marked a turning point in the field. He suggested an information-type analysis of concept learning, separated positive and negative instances, and (perhaps most important) presented a dimensional analysis of the stimulus

143

materials. In particular he clearly separated such variables as total number of dimensions (or attributes), number of relevant and irrelevant dimensions, number of levels of each dimension, and the minimum number of positive and negative instances required to specify a concept as a function of the above variables. The well-known experiment of Hovland and Weiss in 1953 was an experimental test of some of these ideas.

The book by Bruner, Goodnow, and Austin in 1956 called attention to conjunctive, disjunctive, and relational concepts. With two or more relevant dimensions a conjunctive concept is the intersection while a disjunctive concept is the union of the subsets. Furthermore, they distinguished among various types of strategies (in particular, between scanning and focusing) and the effectiveness of these strategies as a function of type of concept and cognitive strain (or memory load) required. Their emphasis on "keeping track" may well have been the precursor of subsequent studies in short-term memory (e.g., those of Yntema at Lincoln Labs and Lloyd and Reid at Virginia). Finally, their emphasis on the payoff matrix and its role in the decision process sounds not unfamiliar today.

In 1959 Bourne and Restle proposed a mathematical theory of concept identification based on a theory of discrimination learning. Essentially it dealt with the learning of conjunctive concepts, with the number of relevant and irrelevant dimensions as two main experimental variables. Two processes were postulated, strengthening the relevant cues and adapting out the irrelevant cues.

In 1961 the Shepard, Hovland, and Jenkins monograph dealt with the learning of classifications. They used 6 different classifications of stimuli which varied in binary fashion along 3 dimensions. If we use the terminology of Garner (1962) to describe these classifications, we can say that Level I of Shepard et al. represents a direct contingency, Level II is a first-order interaction, and Level VI a second-order interaction. That is, using the illustrative example of Shepard in Fig. 1 (p. 3), the positive instances in Level I were all black stimuli. In Level II, black triangles and white squares were positive but white triangles and black squares negative. Thus, Level I had 1 relevant but 2 irrelevant dimensions, Level II had 2 relevant and 1 irrelevant dimension (the latter being size) but the appropriate classification depended on the joint properties of color and shape. Finally, Level VI involved all

3 dimensions: Triangles if large were positive when black, if small were positive when white; squares on the other hand if large were positive when white; if small were positive when black. The remaining classifications (Levels III, IV, and V) were intermediate between Levels II and VI (see Garner, 1962, p. 329).

Essentially, this study of classification learning did two things: It showed that the 70 possible classifications could be reduced to these 6 levels, and it showed that these 6 levels differed consistently in terms of ease of learning. The order of difficulty was, as you would expect, easiest for Level I and most difficult for Level VI except that there was a cross-over between Level VI and Levels III-V with practice (see Fig. 6, p. 8).

In 1962 there were two important books dealing with concept learning. One, of course, was that of Hunt; the other, by Garner, treated concept formation as one of many topics. To discuss them in reverse order, Garner considered a concept-formation problem as one involving multidimensional equivocation. The multidimensionality refers to the ensemble of stimuli used in the task, which must vary in more than one dimension. The equivocation refers to the mapping of stimuli into responses, and the requirement for concept tasks is a many-to-one mapping; that is, more stimuli than responses. Shepard et al. distinguished between identification and classification; equivocation implies classification. By way of contrast, early studies of choice reaction time and absolute judgment were unidimensional and with one-to-one mappings. It can be argued that studies of paired-associate learning and signal-detection represent the other 2 cells of the matrix; but according to Garner the concept of a concept is conjunctive.

Garner likened concept formation to free-recall verbal learning in that in both it is more the form of internal structure of the subset of stimuli than the specific characteristics of the stimuli themselves. Under certain conditions Garner's internal and external constraint will parallel relevant and irrelevant dimensions; and is perhaps analagous to the distinction made by Bruner et al. between concept attainment and concept formation. Roughly speaking, formation is external constraint, attainment is internal constraint which points up a problem of traditional S-R analysis of concepts. Since Dollard and Miller (1950), concept formation has been interpreted in terms of labeling and acquired equivalence of cues, and even today it is claimed that, "Concept learning may be defined as the acquisition of the same response to a number of stimuli having certain characteristics in common" (Dominowski, 1965, p. 271). But as Bruner et al. point out, it is attaching stimuli to responses rather than responses to stimuli, the concept is the classification rule, and the response itself is trivial.

One of the provocative aspects of the Garner model is that the selection of subsets and the form of redundancy can be analyzed in much the same terms as those used by statisticians in discussing fractional replications and confoundings in higher-order experimental designs. Thus, Winer (1963) discusses the use of modular arithmetic to analyze confoundings in randomized-blocks designs, and the Levels I, II, and VI of the Shepard, Hovland, and Jenkins study involving confounding, or blocking, of a main effect, first-order interaction, and second-order interaction, respectively. So in the Whitman and Garner paper (1963) on concept-learning, or the Garner and Whitman paper (1965) on free recall; in his terms simple contingencies are easier to learn than higher-order interactions. The advantages of a combinatorial analysis of this sort is its generality to multidimensional stimuli; and the interesting question will be to see if concept learning does show invariance within n^{th}-order interaction terms.

The book by Hunt proceeds in a different direction from that of Garner. Rather than explore the higher reaches of multidimensionality, it relaxes the restriction of one bit of response uncertainty and uses the methods of symbolic logic to distinguish among conjunction, inclusive and exclusive disjunction, biconditional, etc. Inclusive disjunction is A and/or B while exclusive disjunction is A or B but not both; biconditional is both or neither. Hunt explores the role of memory in concept-formation, and suggests a decision tree as perhaps the most promising type of information-processing model.

The Simon and Kotovsky paper in 1963 dealt with acquisition of concepts for serial patterns. Essentially the task was extrapolation; given a sequence such as *abxcdxefxghx*, what letter comes next? Their main hypothesis about human concept attainment in this sort of situation was that "Subjects attain a serial pattern concept by generating and fixating a pattern description of the concept" (p. 538). The two problems are to propose mechanisms that (a) given a description can generate the pattern, and (b) can induce the pattern from the given letter string. Of the two the latter seems more formidable; the technique used here was to note periodicity, then find alphabetical or identity relationships both within and between periods. The given problems differed in complexity, and those problems failed by various program variants were also failed more often by human subjects. It is interesting that the authors note that, "A closer investigation of the program's failure with the hard problems showed that the difficulties arose specifically in keeping track of the lists associated with distinct positions in immediate memory. The program was incapable of organizing the parts of the pattern into an overall structure when two immediate memory positions were involved" (p. 544). Again we have the "keeping track" problem and the rather severe limitations of immediate memory.

A caveat on computer simulation of cognitive processes has been offered by Kendler (1964). He suggests that much greater attention will have to be paid to the behavior which is being simulated and the generality of computer programs. On the other hand, Kendler seems more favorably disposed to mathematical models of concept formation; unlike computer simulation, he feels, they have emerged from the S-R language and methodological tradition. He emphasizes three properties of concepts: They are associations, they function as cues, and they are responses. To this list Archer (1964) adds a fourth: They are words. And he feels the big step in concept formation is from pre- to post-verbalization.

Three more studies will round off this brief and, no doubt, unduely selective review of the concept-formation literature. First, Bower and Trabasso (1964) take issue with the Bourne and Restle model; they propose an all-or-none in place of incremental model. They deal with the Shepard, Hovland, and Jenkins Type I concept, with either 2 or 4 responses. The model is a 2-state Markov chain, and they suggest 2 processes: A stimulus-selection phase whereby Ss come to perceive the relevant attribute, then a paired-associate phase where the classificatory response is learned. As the number of stimulus-response pairings increases the latter proportion of the learning period will be considerable.

The second paper is that of Haygood and Bourne (1965), wherein an analysis of the 14 partitions of two focal attributes are reduced to 5 basic conditions: Affirmation, conjunction, inclusive disjunction, conditional, and biconditional (each with its complement). Discovery of the relevant attributes is separated from the conceptual rule, and they show that it is possible to study the latter unconfounded with the former. Appreciation of the work of both Bourne and Hunt requires at least a nodding acquaintance with logical relationships and terminology; an excellent introduction can be found in the beginning chapters of Kemeny, Snell, and Thompson (1956).

Finally, a study by Suppes (1966) of mathematical concept formation has just appeared in print. While he too finds evidence for stationarity he reports some interesting developmental trends on perceptual invariance in children. I mention this study of Suppes for two reasons: (a) It suggests quite clearly the work of Piaget, though his work is far beyond the scope of our limited coverage; and (b) Suppes points out that, in using oddity problems, a specific stimulus display was never repeated. As he says, many concept-formation studies repeatedly use the same stimulus display on successive trials, which raises the problem of distinguishing between a concept and a specific stimulus-response connection.

Now, let me turn to a specific consideration of the papers by Gregg and Hunt. The problem that Dr. Gregg deals with is sequential concepts and their internal representation. The importance of the serial order problem was stressed by Lashley in his well-known paper (1951), and I think that he and Gregg would certainly be in agreement about the central determinants of this behavior. Also, as Dr. Gregg points out, this work is not unrelated to the Simon and Kotovsky paper discussed briefly above.

However, the Simon paper dealt with the extrapolation of sequences while the Gregg paper dealt with the learning of sequences. In effect, one can consider the Gregg task as a 16-item serial list in which the items were 4-digit binary numbers. The actualization of these numbers was by means of switches, and it is a moot point whether the same results would have been found had the task been conducted on a purely verbal level.

In Garner's terms this task would only half-qualify as a concept-formation task. The stimuli were multivariate in nature; they were 4 binary dimensions that differed only from the Shepard, Hovland, and Jenkins stimuli in that they were successive rather than simultaneous. That is, a switch setting of LLRL is as much multidimensional as a large black triangle; and indeed the latter may be ambiguous until we decide whether the nervous system uses parallel or serial processing. However, there does not seem to be the equivocation characteristic of many concept-formation studies; the switch settings are not classified into negative and positive instances but must be executed in a prescribed fashion.

Instead, I would argue that the task is an investigation along the Bruner lines of strategies used by subjects in serial learning. The role of strategies in learning tasks is of considerable interest to psychologists in the verbal learning area (see Cofer and Musgrave, *Verbal Behavior and Learning*, (1963). By using a task such as this, Dr. Gregg may have gotten strategies out where we can examine them carefully.

To be perfectly honest I have mixed feelings about the benefits to be gained from computer simulation of a task such as this. On one hand, the virtues of simulation and its role as theory or model are too well known to be repeated here. On the other hand, much attention must be focused on possibly irrelevant or uninteresting details of the problem; for example, in the present case, on how the switches are set rather than on what setting is selected. If I understand correctly, Dr. Gregg, in talking about "change operators" is describing the execution of the responses; but this is usually equivocation in most concept-formation studies. Also, the strategy of modeling the program on the way the subjects *say* they learn the task is certainly debatable. While such an approach seems common in computer simulation of cognitive processes, I am by no means convinced one can learn all that much just by asking subjects how they learned. For years I have asked subjects how they tried to remember, and I don't think that I have learned anything useful yet. I would prefer to base a model on experimental data and comparisons than on subjects' verbal reports.

One of the points I found most interesting was the hierarchical organization implied by categorizing the 16 possible switch positions by first the Form of the setting (i.e., 4-0, 1-3, 2-2, 3-1, and 0-4), then the Major Symbol (i.e., either left or right) and finally the Pattern. Dr. Gregg mentioned that in some cases subjects seemed to know, for instance, what the form of a particular sequence was yet were not able to produce the correct pattern. But I think we need more empirical data here.

Finally, I think it is striking how clear the patterning is when you see the whole display but how difficult it must be to infer it given one step at a time. Dr. Gregg has spelled out clearly the importance of memory limitations and the applicability of notions of chunking and recoding. Although these notions are provacative and stimulating, I am not convinced we have exploited them as effectively as we might; and feel it may be that the chief significance of the work Dr. Gregg has discussed will be to work out in detail the interrelationships between demands of the task, memory load, encoding, and acquisition of sequential concepts.

Dr. Hunt's paper is quite impressive, and is a further indication of how the concept-formation area has progressed in recent years. However, I feel that a full appreciation of this paper requires a careful reading of their recent book, *Experiments in Induction* (Hunt, Marin, & Stone, 1966). In the book not only is it possible to develop the theoretical notions and rationale more fully, but also the details of the prior models, *CLS* 1-8, are developed chronologically.

Perhaps one reason why this work is impressive is that, at least at a low level, it will pass a "Turing Test." That is, not only is the model explicit enough so that a computer will output the solution to a concept-learning problem but also the computer displays essentially the same ordinal relationship among problem types as do human subjects. That is, the order of difficulty for both is essentially conjunction, inclusive disjunction, implication, exclusive disjunction, and biconditional (see Chapter 6 in Hunt, Marin, and Stone). Which is not to say that humans really use an information-processing approach of this sort; but on the other hand, how many other models of concept learning are this explicit?

In the present paper Dr. Hunt disavows extrapolation from artificial intelligence to natural intelligence. However, it is interesting to note that some of the assumptions of his model are receiving support at the experimental level. Thus, Estes and Taylor (1964) have recently found support for a serial processing model in a situation involving brief visual displays and a search-and-detection task. In another vein, Mowbray (1964) has provided some very clear evidence for a single-channel hypothesis in a task involving auditory shadowing. And, of course, the limitations in short-term memory built into the model are abundantly exemplified by many recent experimental studies.

There is one problem however that bothers me a bit about this matter of computer simulation, and though the point is not new it seems appropriate here. If one takes the program as a model for man, in effect, he is espousing a psychological theory or model. I have always been led to believe that there should be a constant interplay between theory and experiment. That is, data suggest or modify theory which in turn lead to new experiments. And it is the latter which seems to be lacking here; the extensive work on computer simulation does not seem to have fed back and led to new and insightful experiments in psychological literature. The interplay between theory and data seems tenuous at best, and at times each seems to occur in splendid isolation.

By way of conclusion, let me come back to my original point—there is wide diversity among theoretical viewpoints. Not only is the gulf there; it seems to be getting wider as models and theories become better developed and more sophisticated, which perhaps suggests what may be the chief virtue of a symposium such as this: Communication channels (S-R connections?) are laid down between the two sides. Let us hope they are used.

CHAPTER 7

Lloyd R. Peterson
                                                    Indiana University

SEARCH AND JUDGMENT IN MEMORY*

Consider a traditional analysis of the verbal learning process. A list of items is presented for a number of trials. The progress of learning is measured by calculating the proportion of correct anticipations on successive trials. It seems clear that this measure of learning might just as appropriately be called a test of memory. An anticipation on Trial N is a test of memory for the presentation on Trial $N - 1$. A similar kind of process would seem to be involved as is studied in a short-term memory experiment. In either case, it is customary to treat the period from cue to response as a whole, and to gather data based on the outcome terminating the test.

Many relatively sophisticated theoretical treatments of learning have dealt only with the final outcome of a trial. In the tradition of behaviorism, they have avoided any temptation to postulate hypothetical processes and have taken as the unit of analysis the period from cue to response, even though this may involve a considerable number of seconds. Substantial achievements have resulted from the use of this approach. However, it would seem both desirable and possible to explore the composition of this test interval, sometimes called the anticipation interval or the recall interval.

It is interesting that in experiments dealing with problem solving and concept learning there has been considerable

The help of several assistants in conducting research described in this paper is acknowledged: Richard Cooley, Joan Dionis, Marcia Johnson, and Jean Schneck. Experimentation was facilitated by NSF Grants GB-704 and GB-3977 to Indiana University.

attention directed to hypothetical events occurring within the individual test interval. Problem solving has been said to involve two factors, the generation of possible solutions, and the recognition of the correct solution (Miller, 1951). Concept identification has been analyzed into two components, discovering the relevant dimension, and learning the responses assigned to specific values of that dimension (Bower & Trabasso, 1963). In the simplest concept identification experiments this load on memory is not great, and the learning involved may be acquired with a single experience. If there are only two values of the relevant dimension to be assigned to two response alternatives, the subject need remember only one pairing. This is an easy task. It is only when there are many values of the relevant dimension that the role of the learning component becomes significant. Interest in the discovery stage of concept identification suggests to the experimenter the strategy of minimizing the requirements of memory.

There is evidence, however, that considerations of memory even enter into the discovery stage of concept learning (Levine, 1963). The subject processes whatever information he can remember. The very hypotheses which he tests to account for remembered information are influenced by memory. The subject does not immediately retest a hypothesis which has been disconfirmed. Sampling of strategies or hypotheses, if it is to be called sampling, is not with immediate replacement. It seems plausible that hierarchies of strategies, whose likelihood of occurrence is ordered on the basis of past experience, exist within the subject. Further, it seems reasonable that relative positions of individual hypotheses change as a result of experimental tests. These hypotheses do not automatically eventuate in responses on the basis of their relative momentary excitatory potential. Rather, the subject is assumed to examine hypotheses and test them implicitly against the information available. Overt response may be based on a hypothesis which originally ranked low in the subject's hierarchy.

This view of concept learning as a search through hypotheses that become available to the subject will be applied in this paper to retrieval processes in general. Recall, whether it be in a short-term memory test, in anticipation of a list of items over trials, or whatever, will be considered to consist of a scanning or search of available memory traces which is terminated by a judgment concerning a response to be made explicit. This is not a novel approach, and some selected instances from the history of verbal learning experiments will be mentioned. The point of view will then be used to interpret some recent experiments. Finally, we will describe efforts to simulate the retrieval process on a computer.

To begin with, let's consider what happens when a subject free associates. There is a relatively automatic aspect of recall which the experimenter attempts to measure by asking the subject to respond freely to some stimulus without stopping to think about his response. There is also a reflective aspect to recall in which the subject doesn't usually say the first thing that he thinks of, but edits his verbal behavior. Similarly an attempt to remember something in the everyday world has a dual aspect. There may be a sequence of free associations, one leading to another, as the individual ignores many recollections that are irrelevant to his search. Something may finally be recalled which ends the search with the individual recognizing that a particular recollection was that which he sought. He may be confident that his recall is accurate even though the occurrence of the recollection has been delayed. This suggests that there is an important difference between those two characteristics of recall.

The concept of recall as a search process goes back at least as far as William James (1890, p. 251). However, the evidence for it is not confined to introspection, and the most pertinent evidence may well be that from verbal learning experiments. Relevant research can profitably be traced back at least as far as McKinney and McGeoch (1935). They investigated the possibility that the findings of retroactive inhibition experiments could be accounted for by competition. This is the notion that at the time of recall responses from interpolated learning compete with responses from initial learning. Objective evidence for this competition was found in the intrusion of responses from a second serial list into recall of an original serial list. It appeared that some intrusion errors had been recognized and rejected as such by the subjects. Written recall was required and intrusions had been scratched out by some subjects. Subjects also reported after the experiment that they had thought of intrusions in recall but had rejected them. The interpolated lists consisted of synonyms for the original list, and several subjects reported recalling a word from the second list, recognizing it as being from that list, and then finding the correct word by thinking of synonyms for the recalled word. This editing of responses by the subject was considered to account for the fact that the number of such errors was not great enough to explain all of the retroactive inhibition.

Melton and Irwin (1940) later studied the retroactive inhibition paradigm by varying the degree of second-list learning. Presumably, the greater the degree of second-list learning, the more it should compete with first-list responses. This should be observed in poorer recall of the first list and the appearance of intrusions from the second list. They found that the number of overt intrusion errors was not proportional to the degree of second-list learning. It seemed clear that some retroactive inhibition was produced by implicit intrusions. This was indicated by expressions of disgust and other more direct statements. Subjects sometimes started to say a syllable and the rejected it as incorrect. The concept of unlearning seems in part to have been added to interference theory as a supplement to competition to account for the consideration that rejection of intrusion errors, through the subject's recognition that they were erroneous, did not guarantee that the subject would think of the right response.

Decision characteristics of the subject at the time of recall were considered by Underwood (1945). On the basis of paired-associate studies he introduced the concept of list differentiation. In addition to associative strength of the interpolated responses, the amount of interference was also considered to be a function of the degree of differentiation of competing response systems. The better the two lists were learned, the better the subject would be able to differentiate between them. Further, the shorter the time interval between the end of interpolated learning and the attempt to recall, the better should be the differentiation. This would explain why intrusions were fewer and omissions more numerous in the condition having the greatest number of trials on the interpolated learning. Recall of the original list typically followed the interpolated list after only a short interval, in the condition with the largest number of trials on the interpolated list. In the conditions with fewer number of trials on the interpolated learning there were substantial rest intervals filled with irrelevant activity separating the end of the interpolated learning from the beginning of recall. This was necessary in order to equate the time from the end of original learning to recall for all conditions. Underwood obtained some evidence that the more recent the interpolated learning the fewer the intrusions. Recency of exposure permitted the subjects to recognize intruding responses as incorrect.

In this connection we have run an experiment varying time from the end of the interpolated learning to recall independent of the degree of learning on the interpolated list. For one experimental group, 15.5 minutes of joke reading filled the interval before recall. For the other group one minute separated interpolated learning from recall. Significantly more intrusions were found with the long-interval group (1.67 per subject) than with the short interval group (.30). In spite of this there was no significant difference in number correct.

The finding of increased numbers of intrusions as time passes since the intruding responses were seen is a kind of inverse recency effect. The more recently a response has occurred the more available it should be to a subject. Yet, paradoxically, the more recently it was seen the less likely it was to be given. A similar kind of finding was reported recently in a guessing task (Peterson, Brewer, and Bertucco, 1963). An analysis of errors showed that the more recently the subject had seen a word in the memory drum, the less likely he was to give it. The task resembled a serial-rote-learning task in that the subject anticipated the next word as he looked at a word in the drum. However, it was modified into a guessing task by changing the order of words on every trial. Numbers correct were analyzed as a function of position, as in traditional serial learning. It was found that correct guesses increased with proximity to the end of a trial. Omissions also increased as the end of a trial neared. It was concluded that the subject could remember what words had already appeared on a given trial and use this memory to maximize his guessing by rejecting responses that he recognized had already occurred on that trial. Increase in omissions presumably resulted from the failure of acceptable responses appearing after the rejection of other responses. A similar guessing strategy was found with subjects in a paired-associate learning task. This is further support of the view that subjects in learning a list engage in decision behavior which does not necessarily result in the automatic production of the first response that occurs to them.

It is not entirely clear, in all cases, what differences between items and lists are used by the subject to discriminate. Sometimes a discrimination of time, or unknown events correlated with time, seem to be involved. When the discriminative cues at time of recall are made obvious, an efficient editing of intrusions becomes possible. An example is when each of two successive paired-associate lists has responses of a different class. We have used numbers as responses in one list and single letters in the other. The stimuli were the same in both lists, eight nonsense syllables of high association value. For the 18 subjects going from either numbers to letters or letters to numbers in successive lists, there were no intrusions on the first trial of relearning the first list. The 18 subjects learning either numbers or letters in both lists did produce a significant number of intrusions (1.28 per subject). In spite of the difference in number of intrusions, there was no significant difference in number correct for these two groups. The relatively rapid rate of presentation, two seconds per exposure, may not have offered enough opportunity to replace rejected intrusions with correct responses.

A measure of the likelihood of occurrence of a response in recall, as distinct from the subject's judgment of the correctness of response, has been investigated by means of a technique called *modified free recall* (Underwood, 1948). Here, the subject is freed of the constraint of having to give a right response, instead he is instructed to respond with the first of a class of responses that occurs to him. Evidence for the operation of a decision process is seen in the fact that this response; is not always the one which the subject vocalizes when he is instructed to give the response appropriate to a particular list.

An experiment by Briggs (1954) compared modified-free-recall measures with traditional recall in a retroactive interference paradigm. In the second list new responses were paired with stimuli from the first list. Subjects were given modified-free-recall tests at various times after learning the second list. The subject was instructed to give the first response, of the two that had been paired with that particular stimulus, that occurred to him. Traditional recall measures of the appropriate first-list responses were also taken. The modified-free-recall tests showed that first-list responses were quite low in frequency of occurrence immediately after second-list learning. In time there was recovery of these first-list responses. In contrast, the traditional recall measures, in which subjects were instructed to give first-list responses, showed little change with the passage of time. It would seem plausible to conclude that immediately after second-list learning the subject recognized a response from the second list as wrong with reference to traditional recall instructions, and waited to speak until a first-list response occurred to him.

The above interpretation of retroactive interference is supported by a latency study of Postman and Kaplan (1947). Latencies of anticipations in relearning after an interpolated list were longer than in a condition in which there was no interpolated list. This effect of the interpolated list persisted after differences in number of errors between the two conditions had disappeared. This could be interpreted as implying that likelihood of occurrence of first-list responses recovered more slowly than recognition of error. The subjects simply waited out errors until the correct response occurred to them.

Further support for this interpretation is found in paired-associate studies by Underwood, (1950a, 1950b), in which long recall times were permitted. The result was that with increased time for recall, retroactive inhibition decreased markedly, and under similar conditions proactive inhibition disappeared completely.

An interpretation of interference as competition among available responses suggests the kind of decision process which is found in psychophysical tests. Postman and Page (1947, p. 376) commented a number of years ago: "When 0 is asked to recall or recognize something he has learned, he needs to abstract from a complex of traces, to reconstruct an event whose traces have become intertwined to varying degrees with the traces of other events." The authors had shown that the accuracy of judgment of the height or width of rectangles was affected by retroactive events in a way similar to that of memory experiments.

SHORT-TERM RETENTION

Short-term retention experiments have also provided data

on events within memory tests. In the recall of individual items, long recall intervals may be permitted and the characteristics of recall over these extended periods observed. The experiment consists of presenting a single item, say a trigram, having the subject engage in some irrelevant verbal activity for a few seconds, and then asking for recall of the item. There is good evidence that the aftereffects of previous tests compete at the time of recall with the most recently presented item (Keppel and Underwood, 1962), since recall of the first item is significantly better than recall of succeeding items. Furthermore, letters from the immediately preceding test item frequently intrude in recall of the current item. The experiment can be conceptualized in terms of memories from previous tests occurring during the recall interval while the subject is attempting to discriminate the most recently presented item. Now, if there were no decrease in the availability of traces as the experiment progresses, then the subject would be presented with an increasingly difficult task as the memory traces from previous presentations accumulated over the experiment. However, the evidence indicates that interference from previous tests levels off after the first few tests in the session. This, added to the finding that intrusions show a strong recency effect, suggests that either the traces from preceding presentations become less available with time and/or the action of intervening events, or the subject is better able to discriminate intrusions as the time since their presentation increases. The evidence that lengthening of the intertrial interval results in better retention (Peterson and Gentile, 1965) might fit either interpretation.

Yntema and Trask (1963) have measured recency discrimination of words presented in a recognition task. In their experiment, a long succession of words was presented to the subject on cards, and at various points in the sequence he was tested by being shown two words at once. His task was to indicate which of the two words he had seen most recently. The longer the interval separating the original presentations of the two items, the more accurate was the discrimination behavior. Further, the shorter the interval from the most recently presented item to the test, the better the discrimination behavior. This seems reasonable on the assumption that the subject is discriminating time by some means. The greater the difference in times the easier should be the discrimination.

Then, if whatever is being discriminated in relation to time changes in a negatively accelerated manner, the shorter the time since the last item, the easier should be the discrimination.

One experiment shows the effect of discriminatory behavior in a striking fashion. Wickens, Born, and Allen (1963) presented a subject with a sequence of tests on items made up of digits or letters. The activity minimizing rehearsal during the retention interval was color naming. They found the customary decrease in retention after the first few tests. Then a test was given in which letters constituted the message for subjects who had previously been tested on digits. Recall of this item from a new class, letters as compared to digits, was found to be as good as recall on the first test of the session. Switching to a new class eliminated the interfering effect of the previous tests. It does not seem likely that the availability of the previous items decreased as a result of the new class being used. Rather, it seems that subjects can remember class membership, that letters were used in the most recent test, and they can edit their responses on the basis of that information.

There remains the question of how the subject can discriminate recency in the case where the current item is of the same form class as previous messages. In what sense do items bear "time tags," as Yntema and Trask (1963) have written? One possibility is that the memory trace varies in strength, and the subject discriminates the amplitude of this trace (Konorski, 1961, p. 122). Another possibility is that an item becomes embedded in a context of other successive events, and can be discriminated relative to this stream of events. We have run a recognition experiment in our laboratory which attempts to differentiate between these two explanations. A succession of words, one at a time, is presented to the subject. Occasionally a word has a question mark after it, and the subject has been instructed that when he sees this test item he is to estimate how many other items have been shown since he last saw the test word. Some of the words had been presented twice before being tested, others had been presented only once. A strength interpretation would seem to predict that items which had been presented twice should be judged more recent than items which had been presented only once. A single trace represents the stored item and the trace should be stronger with repetition. On the other hand, if the subject judges recency by the context in which the word appeared, two traces should be involved based on two presentations. Hence his judgment of how many items have intervened since the last of the two presentations should be at least as great as in the case of one presentation. To the extent that both traces may be present at the time of the test and he can keep the most recent presentation distinct from the earlier presentation of the same item, his judgment should be the same as in the case of a single presentation.

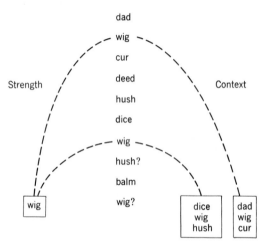

Fig. 7.1 Single and multiple trace conceptions of recognition
memory.

Figure 7.1 schematizes the two conceptions. The sequence of words is part of a block of words that was presented to the subjects. It can be seen that tests and presentations are interspersed in such a way that various conditions overlap. In the example shown, presentation and test of "HUSH," a single presentation condition with two intervening items, is completely contained within the sequence of events testing "WIG."[1]

Figure 7.2 depicts the mean judgment of recency in two

[1]Dr. Frank Restle has reported data on ratings of recency after one presentation of an item (Psychonomic Society, 1965).

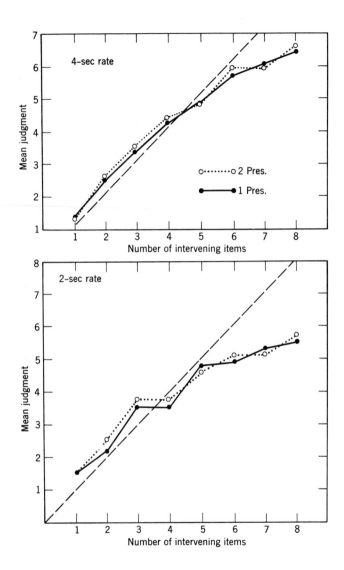

Fig. 7.2   Ratings of recency at 2 rates of presentation.

independent experiments. One was run with the memory drum set at a 2-second rate and the other at a 4-second rate. Within a given presentation rate each subject was tested 4 times in each of the 16 conditions of testing. Twenty-eight subjects were run at each rate. Tests were of the same duration as presentations. The diagonal in the figure indicates perfect judgment. It can be seen from the figure that subjects were on the average fairly accurate in their judgments of recency for items tested after up to 5 intervening items at the 2-second rate. At the 4-second rate subjects did a little better, being close to the ideal through 6 intervening items. In both cases subjects tended to overestimate small numbers of intervening items. The underestimates of the larger numbers of items probably reflect a guessing tendency for which there is a ceiling effect.

The point to be made about Fig. 7.2 is that there is no consistent difference between recency judgments after one as compared to two presentations. There is no support for a strength interpretation of the discrimination of recency, in spite of the fact that two presentations can be assumed to have produced a greater likelihood of being recognized as having occurred in the experimental session. It seems highly unlikely that the two presentations were too far apart for the earlier to affect the later. Four intervening items separated the two presentations in every case. By some means the subjects were able to distinguish the most recent occurrence of a word from earlier occurrences and judge the recency of that event. Of course, not only did the two occurrences have different words preceding and following them, but the subjects could undoubtedly recognize on the second occurrence that they had seen this word before. This recognition may have helped to make the second occurrence distinctive from the first.

Returning once more to the testing of individual items, we have run an experiment in which subjects were given extended time, up to 20 seconds, in which to recall the current item. If an incorrect response was given, the experimenter said, "Wrong," and the subject continued to try to produce the correct response. The subject could make as many responses as he liked in the 20 seconds. We were interested in whether competition from the previous tests would be reduced by telling the subjects that a response was wrong. To what extent did the subject make the correct response? (Ninety-six subjects were

run for six tests on trigrams having no letters in common.)
The trigram was presented in a memory drum for 2 seconds,
and then a number from which to count backward was presented. A rest interval of 10 seconds was given after the 20-
second recall interval was concluded. Figure 7.3 depicts the

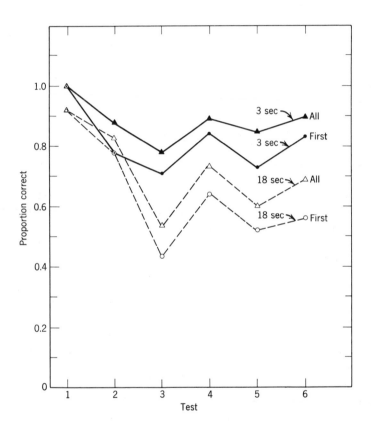

Fig. 7.3   Recall of trigrams after 3 or 18 sec of counting.

results for 3- and 18-second retention intervals. (Only 24
subjects were tested at each of these intervals in the first test
of the session. The remaining subjects were tested at 0 and
9 seconds on the first test. Succeeding data points are based

on 48 subjects each.) The particular retention interval that followed another was counterbalanced over the group of subjects. It can be seen from Fig. 7.3 that subjects were able to some extent to recall correctly after an initial wrong response. To what extent this was guessing we can't say. The point to be noted is that they were by no means able to correct themselves in 100% of the cases. Many responses were simply not available. They may have become unavailable by action of the recall process, or they may have been altered or lost during the retention interval activity. Note that there was some slight forgetting on the initial test of the session. It should also be considered that the trigrams, low association value CCCs, were not well-integrated units. A part of the recall task was the ordering of the elements. To the extent that this ordering was inefficient there can be said to have been intra-item interference, although it should be noted that this type of interference seems to be effective only in interaction with previous test items.

The experiment points up a limitation on the decision-making ability of subjects. Even when they are able to discard some information with the help of the experimenter, they cannot necessarily produce the correct response. If the response is not unitary in composition, it may be unavailable.

LATENCIES FOLLOWING THE LAST ERROR

From the point of view of this paper the measurement of latencies is of considerable significance. If the subject is permitted unlimited recall time, and a set of highly available responses is used, once the capacity to recognize a right response has been achieved, errors should cease. However, if recall time is short, as during anticipation periods at a rapid rate of presentation, the subject may not think of the correct response and hence be charged with an error even though he could recognize the correct response if it had occurred. A finding which fits in with these considerations is that latencies decrease after the subject has stopped making errors. The capacity to recognize the correct response when the subject has thought of it may be achieved before response speed reaches its maximum.

We have reported (Peterson, 1965) a paired-associate experiment investigating latencies after the last error. Subjects were given 20 trials on a list of 10 pairs presented in a memory drum. The subject was permitted as much time as he desired to make a response during the anticipation period. Correction or confirmation was made by a 2-second pairing of items after the subject had made his response. In analyzing the data, sequences of trials for individual pairs were adjusted so that latencies could be averaged for a subject after the last error on a pair. As Fig. 7.4 shows, decreasing latencies were

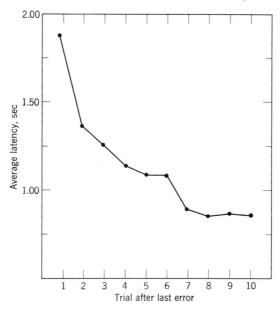

Fig. 7.4 Latencies after errors on individual pairs of associates cease.

found over a group of 15 subjects for 8 trials after the last error.

Latencies on trials before the last error did not show any reliable trend. The frequency correct did show an increasing trend for several trials before the last error. Even so, the proportion correct on the trial before the last error was only .43. Considering that on the trial following the last error, recall reached 100% and continued there, it is clear that this does not remotely resemble a negative growth function. Of course, the selective factor involved in the criterion must be recognized, and it is plausible that some of the responses on the first trial after the last error reflected guessing rather than learning. However, 8 responses were used, and guessing strategies during a trial of the type discussed earlier were minimized by having fewer responses (8) than stimuli (10). In view of these considerations the increment in the vicinity of the first criterion trial was notably large. Further, the largest decrease in latency came on the second trial after the last error. The neighborhood of the last error should therefore be a period of considerable interest to students of paired-associate learning. The evidence does not support a learning model in which pairs are learned on a single trial with performance at a guessing level prior to that. There is an improvement before the last error as shown by the number of correct responses. There is also improvement after the last error, as indexed by the decreasing latencies. In spite of these evidences of gradual change, there also seems to be a discontinuity in the region of the last error that is only partly the result of the criterion artifact.

The findings may be integrated to some degree by the distinction between implicit occurrence of a response and the subject's judgment regarding vocalization of the response. The frequency data may largely reflect the subject's ability to recognize the correct response when it occurs, although it would surely also depend on the availability of the response for recognition. The latency data after the last error would be assumed to index changes in the implicit occurrence of the response. The changes in occurrence would be considered to be slower than those of the recognition function and continue after recognition had reached its maximum.

FREE RECALL AND CONFIDENCE

The discontinuity observed in the neighborhood of the last error made it seem desirable to obtain response measures, other than proportions correct, and latencies in this region. Latencies before the criterion trials involve selection problems, since the response of interest does not occur on every trial. An attempt was made to find a response measure which could reflect graded strength on all trials. The first measure that was tried in an attempt to unpack the anticipation interval was a kind of successive free recall. The subject was instructed to respond freely with all of the words in the list during each anticipation interval, and the measure of the strength of the correct response was taken to be its rank in the sequence of free responses. Following the free recall during a given anticipation interval, the subject was instructed to make a considered judgment as to the correct response. He then ended the extended test by rating his confidence in his considered response. He pressed one of three keys to distinguish a response which he felt was a casual *guess*, *probable*, or *certain*. All three of these measures—free recall, estimate of correct response, and confidence rating—were taken during the anticipation interval for each pair on each trial of a paired-associate task.

Twenty-four introductory students at Indiana University served as subjects. The learning materials were presented in a memory drum which was wired to turn once, give a 2-second exposure, turn again, and stop. The subject initiated a repetition of the cycle by pressing one of three keys.

The stimuli were ten *CVC* trigrams of 5 to 20% Archer association value (1960). The responses were 10 familiar single-syllable words. Each word was randomly paired with one of the trigrams. Two orders of the list were used with each subject.

The subject was told initially that he was participating in an experiment in thinking. He was instructed to give multiple free associations to words that the experimenter spoke. The words table, chair, book, boy, and car were used as practice stimuli. The subject was then introduced to a practice task which combined free recall with paired-associate learning. He was given two words, and instructed to respond with these two words in whatever order they occurred to him as he looked at a nonsense syllable. He was warned not to adopt a stereotyped order. When the two words had been said without pausing, the subject was to decide which of the two words was correct for the nonsense syllable that he was looking at. The subject was to speak this word aloud, and then press one of three telegraph keys placed in front of the drum. If he was just guessing, he was to press the key labeled "Guess." If he was certain that he had given the correct word, he was to press the key marked "Certain." If he thought his decision was correct but wasn't sure, he was to press the key marked "Probable." Pressing any key would turn the drum to an exposure of the nonsense syllable together with the correct word. The subject was taken through the practice list to the criterion of 4 consecutive correct trials. He was then informed that the responses in the experiment proper would be new responses, and was told that they would be paired with new nonsense syllables.

In the experiment proper subjects were run to a criterion of 5 consecutive errorless trials on the list, or for 90 minutes. After every other trial for the first 16 trials, subjects were reminded to free associate without pausing. Thereafter, such a reminder was given only after every fourth trial.

In analysis the scores of individual pairs were adjusted so that measures could be averaged forward 5 trials from the last error on a pair, and backward 5 trials before the last error. Eight of the subjects were eliminated from the analysis because there were not at least 2 pairs for which the last error occurred at a place suitable for such an analysis. The subjects retained in the analysis were thus from the middle of the range of individual ability, and the pairs entering the analysis were medium in difficulty.

The mean proportions recalled correctly before the last error were plotted as a backward learning curve and it was found that the proportion correct rose gradually to .48 on the trial preceding the last error. This is well above the chance level of .10 and significantly higher than the proportion correct on the fifth trial preceding the last error ($t = 5.5$, $df = 15$, $p < .001$). As in the previous experiment there was an abrupt rise to the trials after the last error. Even allowing for the probability that the first trial after the last error is inflated by guessing, it must be concluded that the greatest rise in frequency correct occurred from the trial before to the trial after the last error. The trial of the last error must, of course, be acknowledged to have been an error by reason of selection.

The free recall data are summarized in Fig. 7.5 forward and backward from the last error, which is labeled Trial 0. In scoring these data, if the appropriate response was not given during the free recall period, and it was given as the decision response, it was given a value one unit greater than the number of free responses. If it did not occur at all, it was given a value two units greater than the number of free responses. (Such cases were not frequent, constituting .03 of the scored pairs at Trial -5; .02 of the cases at Trials -4, -3, and -2; and .05 of the cases at Trial 0.) It may be estimated that

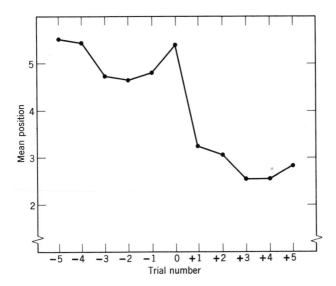

Fig. 7.5   Position of the correct response in a sequence of free recalls. Data are analyzed backward and forward from the trial of the last error on an individual pair, Trial 0.

the appropriate response would occur by chance midway between the fifth and sixth positions. The mean position on the fifth trial before the last error approximates such a value. There was a significant tendency for the appropriate response to appear earlier in the free recall sequence as trials progressed. A comparison of the fifth trial before the last error with the fifth trial after the last error gives a t of 5.93 (df = 15; $p < .001$). On the last error trial there was a marked regression to approximately chance level. Of course, this last error trial was selected in such a way that only errors were made on the decision response, and the subject's free recall scores are thus seen to be related to the traditional measure. Note that whether the first trial after the last error is compared with the last error trial, or the trial preceding the last error, the most rapid decrease in the curve occurred for the trial after the last error.

The confidence ratings for erroneous and correct responses have been plotted separately in Fig. 7.6. "Guess" was scored as 0, "Probable" was scored as 1, and "Certain" was

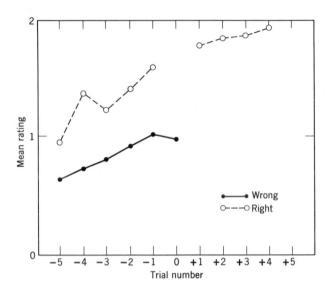

Fig. 7.6   Confidence ratings in the neighborhood of the last error.

scored as 2. Thus the higher the score the greater the subject's confidence. (Scores for four subjects at Trial -5 and one subject each at Trials -4 and -2 were unavailable because no correct responses had been made on these trials among the pairs selected for analysis.) In Fig. 7.6, confidence in right responses is seen to rise markedly before the last error, with little further increase after the last error. There is a ceiling effect to be taken into account, of course. The confidence ratings for wrong responses also tended to rise as trials progressed, but overall were not as high as those for the right responses. Pooling each subject's confidence ratings for right responses and comparing them with wrong responses, the mean confidence in right responses before the last error was found to be higher than that for wrong responses over the same range ($t = 2.71$, $df = 15$, p $< .05$).

The measures taken during the anticipation period of the present study raise a question as to the extent to which these measuring activities may have changed the course of learning. A comparison of frequency correct before the last error in this study with that in the previous study (Peterson, 1965), in which an unpaced anticipation interval without extra measures was used, shows similar increases prior to the last error. Aside from slowing down the learning rate, there is no strong reason to consider that the free recall and confidence ratings had any unusual effect on what was being measured.

Another question arises in regard to what the free recall measures. Somewhat conflicting instructions were given in regard to this behavior. Subjects were told to say words in the order that they thought of them, and yet they were to avoid a stereotyped order. Other kinds of association measures have used one type of restraint or another, and the fact that trends emerged from the data which were not completely unrelated to those of other measures is indicative of some usefulness for the measure. It cannot be claimed that the free recall measure of the present experiment gives an uncontaminated picture of unedited response strength, but it could be argued that some reflection of basic associative strength appears in the measure. The independence of this measure from the traditional anticipation measure is, however, challenged by a finding that the changes over trials were largely confined to those on which a correct final response occurred.

The confidence ratings hint at a factor which is generally omitted from theoretical treatments of the verbal learning process. The confidence ratings showed steady gain prior to the last error, with the majority of subjects responding at the maximum rating on the trial after the last error. Of course, there was also a tendency for the subject to increase his confidence rating for erroneous responses, so that the rating was not wholly a function of individual pairs. It was related to the subject's estimation of how well he was doing on the list generally. However, confidence in right responses exceeded that for wrong responses, and the course of the improvement suggests that a process is being reflected that is largely completed when errors cease. The factor involved in the confidence rating seems to be the subject's ability to recognize the correct response when it occurs to him.

MODIFIED FREE RECALL

The above study was not completely satisfying, so an experiment using a different measure of basic associative strength was designed. Instead of a string of free recall responses during the anticipation interval, the subject was instructed to give the first of the responses in the experiment that occurred to him. This was to be followed by a considered judgment, but there were no confidence ratings. The learning materials were those of the experiment previously described as measuring latencies. In this case latencies were not attempted, and interest was centered on two measures, frequency of modified free recalls and frequency of considered responses. The subjects were instructed that the first response of the unpaced anticipation interval was to be a *guess*, while the second was to follow a period of *thinking*. Subjects were run to a criterion of 6 consecutive correct trials, in order to insure that individual pairs would meet that criterion. Seventeen subjects were accepted for the final analysis, after 3 had been rejected for cheating or failure to meet the criterion. Other aspects of the experiment were similar to those of the previous latency experiment.

The solid line of Fig. 7.7 shows the traditional recall measure rising before the last error. The free recall means, indicated by the dashed line, also show such a rise, but it is more gradual. The free recall measures, like latencies in the earlier experiment, show improved performance after the last error.

There were some problems raised by the free recall data. A gradually improving measure continuing uninterrupted through the trial of the last error was not found. Performance in free recall, on the last error trial of traditional recall, showed a drop to near the zero of traditional recall. Some free recall responses were correct on that trial, but the number was not great. Further, the largest increase for free recall occurred on the trial following the last error. As in the previous experiments there is evidence of a discontinuity in performance in the neighborhood of the last error. It may be, of course, that the free recall measure is not a completely satisfactory measure of unedited response strength. Subjects undoubtedly varied in their interpretations of the instruction to guess.

There is fairly good agreement between the studies using free recall measures of two different kinds in the attempt to get a continuing measure of response strength. In both cases there was some increase in probability of occurrence of the correct response as the last error was approached, and there

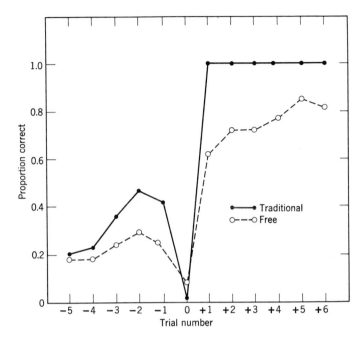

Fig. 7.7 Modified free recall versus traditional recall in the
neighborhood of the last error.

was a marked regression at the point of the last error. In both
cases the greatest increase in likelihood of occurrence came
with the first trial after the last error. This seemed to be true
even though the trial of the last error on the traditional recall
measure is discounted on the ground that it was a selected
trial. In both cases there was improvement after errors on
traditional recall stopped. Thus, there is some indication that
both measures reflected the same phenomenon.

COMPUTER SIMULATION

The view of memory as a process of search ending in a
judgment seems well suited to simulation on a computer. By
testing the effects of building various assumptions into the
computer program some understanding of the limits on ways in
which the process could occur in humans may be achieved.
An attempt was made to simulate the chief characteristics of

human frequency and latency data in the neighborhood of the last error of a paired-associate learning task.

Figure 7.8 diagrams the general model which was investigated. The cue acts on a storage which produces an implicit

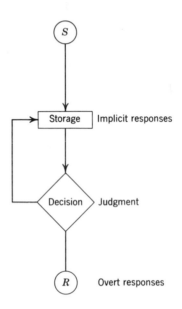

Fig. 7.8   A   model   of   retrieval.

response with a certain probability. This implicit event is subjected to a decision process which either terminates in an overt response or waits for another implicit response to be produced. The process is repeated until an overt response occurs. The number of implicit responses which are tested before the overt response occurs gives a measure of the latency of the overt response. No assumption is made that the subject can describe the implicit events as they occur.

In learning over trials the characteristics of the storage are assumed to change gradually. Probabilities of responses in the hierarchy of possible alternatives are considered to change from trial to trial in the manner described by a linear learning model. Probability of the correct response, the one being paired with the cue, increases, while the alternatives, being considered equally likely, decrease uniformly.

The judgmental factor, the ability to recognize the correct

response given that it did occur, was examined under several alternate assumptions. First, the assumption was tested that the decision is based on a gradually improving ability to recognize the right response. A growth function was also assumed to respresent the increasingly available implicit response. However, the learning parameter for recognition was assumed to reflect faster learning than the occurrence factor. When these assumptions were made explicit in the model, the computer did not behave entirely as did the human. The data generated by the computer were analyzed backward and forward from the trial of the last error. A dropping latency curve after errors had stopped was found just as in the case of humans. However, the backward learning curve tended to be considerably higher for the computer than had been the case with the humans. This tendency persisted in spite of changes in parameters. There was something of a discontinuity at the neighborhood of the trial of the last error, but it was not as marked as in the human data. What there was could be attributed to the criterion artifact.

At this point the assumption was introduced that the ability to recognize the correct response changed in an all-or-none fashion. Occurrence of the implicit responses was again assumed to change according to a linear learning model. Implicit responses were drawn from storage as before. The likelihood of their being recognized and vocalized was assumed to be $1/N$, the chance level, until some trial when this likelihood became 1.0. The probability that this recognition occurred on any one given trial was a parameter of the model. At the same time, if erroneous implicit responses occurred up to the time when the recognition probability reached 1.0, they might also be judged to be correct and vocalized with probability $1/N$. After the recognition probability reached 1.0, the probability of judging an erroneous response to be correct was assumed to be 0.

Figure 7.9 presents a backward learning curve obtained by computer simulation under these assumptions. It can be seen that it resembles data obtained from human subjects before the last error. There is an upward trend, which does not go above fifty per cent, so that the discontinuity characteristic of human curves in the neighborhood of the last error was simulated. Figure 7.10 presents a latency curve for the same simulated subjects for 10 trials after the last error.

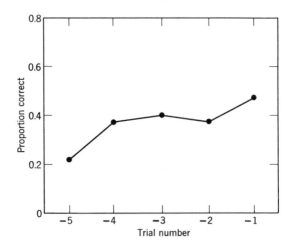

Fig. 7.9 A backward learning curve of frequency correct based
on simulated retrieval.

The units along the ordinate are the mean numbers of
implicit events occurring before an overt response. It can be
seen that the curve is not unlike the analagous curve obtained
on human subjects. The biggest drop occurred from the first
to second trials after the last error, just as with the human
subjects. The improvement tended to asympotote at about the
same rate as was the case with the human data. From one
point of view it is not unusual that these curves resemble the
human data, since we tried out various parameters and selected the data that looked best. However, note that it was impossible to do this when we started with the other assumptions.

There is at least one characteristic of the computer
simulation that does not adequately represent what seems to be
true of humans, that is the confidence rating that was measured
in one of the human experiments. Presumably this is related
to the subject's judgment, and since the confidence level was
higher with humans for right responses as compared with
wrong responses, it suggests that his judgment does improve
before the last error. This was not an assumption of the
computer model that fit the frequency and latency data. So,
like all models, it represents a simplification of the true
state of affairs, and is not to be taken as a finished product.

Related to this point is the consideration of individual

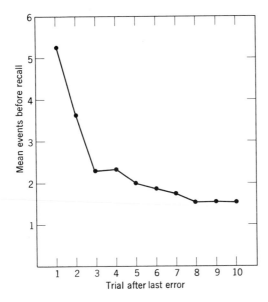

Fig. 7.10   Latencies after the last error in simulated retrieval.

differences among subjects and pairs which are admittedly present when humans learn. The computer data represents curves for 201 pairs with identical parameters (the linear learning parameter being .05 and the all-or-none parameter being .15). In the human case some subjects learn faster than others. Within the individual subject some pairs are learned more quickly than others. Subjects may report after the experiment that for some pairs they were able to discover mnemonic devices that aided learning, others may have been learned more laboriously. Some of the characteristics of the curve averaged over human subjects may be the result of the averaging. The change in confidence with right as opposed to wrong responses before the last error may be the result of some pairs acquiring recognition features in a gradual manner. There may be a mixture of pairs whose recognition occurred in an all-or-none fashion and pairs whose recognition was acquired more slowly. The simulation data suggests that a goodly portion of the recognition probably occurred suddenly, but there is no necessity for denying that partial recognition for some pairs may have occurred before the last error.

The use of mnemonic devices by human subjects has long been known to investigators of verbal learning. The discontinuity resulting from the assumed discovery of a mediating element which ties two members together is not a novel possibility. However, from the point of view of this paper, there is a point to be made which is somewhat at variance with many contemporary accounts of the role of mediating responses in verbal learning. It seems to be generally assumed that the role of the mediator is to provide a link in a chain whereby the response is made available to the subject. We suggest that a more important role of mediating events is to provide a means of recognizing that two members of a pair belong together. The mediating events do not necessarily affect the availability of the response in question. Rather, they may provide a means of testing whether a response which has occurred by some means or other is the correct response or whether it is an error.

The present view considers that there are gradual growth processes in learning as well as discovery-type learning. The earliest learning of an individual organism seems likely to have been of a slow gradual nature; a good deal of human adult learning is abrupt in nature, but not all. The rapid kind of responding that is characteristic of the skilled adult in many situations seems to be an automatic, as opposed to reflective, responding that is acquired gradually through repeated exposure to the same stimulating circumstances.

The approach outlined in this paper has much in common with various information processing models (Miller, Galanter, and Pribram, 1960; Hunt, 1962; Norman and Wickelgren, 1965). One of its aims has been to suggest that there is considerable evidence from the long history of verbal learning research to support such an approach. Indeed, much of the discussion among verbal learning experimenters concerning various aspects of competition and the occurrence of intrusions seems to implicitly assume processes similar to those explained in this paper. It is not overly optimistic to expect that new modifications of already existent techniques in the field of verbal learning can further explore the nature of the retrieval process. This may lead to a clearer picture of the structure of memory as a process of search and judgment. To the extent that memory is involved, the nature of concept attainment should also be clarified.

CHAPTER 8

Charles N. Cofer

The Pennsylvania State University

DOES CONCEPTUAL ORGANIZATION INFLUENCE THE AMOUNT RETAINED IN IMMEDIATE FREE RECALL?*

Knowing that the title of this conference is "Concept Attainment and the Structure of Memory," I have focussed my paper on questions which I feel seek an answer in concept-like processes in the case of immediate free recall. In this method for studying memory, the data, in the first instance, provide two major features for analysis, the number of items recalled and the way in which the items recalled are organized. If organization, as in category clustering, for example, is evidence for the role of concepts in free recall, we may question the relationship between organization and the number of items produced. It is widely observed, however, that in free recall, whatever its degree of organization, the number of items produced is less than the number of items presented. It is of considerable interest to examine, from the point of view of concept-like processes, what factors are associated with the number of items recalled and, further, to use techniques designed to indicate whether the loss of items observed at recall is due to their failure to enter memory at all or to their failure to be retrieved from memory at recall. In considering this storage-retrieval question, I shall describe experiments

Much of the research reported in this paper was supported by the Office of Naval Research under contracts with the University of Maryland, New York University, and the Pennsylvania State University. It has been described in technical reports prepared under the contracts. Several of these reports, as indicated in other footnotes, are being published (in part) here for the first time. This paper was presented at the Conference on Concept Attainment and the Structure of Memory, Carnegie Institute of Technology, April 7 - 8, 1966.

using a recognition procedure and experiments employing a method I have termed "forced recall."

Although the method of free recall has a long history (Tulving, 1966), its significance as a technique for the investigation of processes in human memory has had a marked increment since the publication of Bousfield's paper on clustering in free recall (1953).[1] Bousfield's concern was to study the reorganization in recall of items which fell into mutually exclusive categories but which were presented in a scrambled sequence. He analyzed sequences of items from the same category as they appeared in recall and observed that these clusters did occur to an extent much greater than was true in the original presentation or that might be attributed to chance expectancy. So far as I know, however, Bousfield did not use a control list of unrelated items by which he could estimate whether clustering was associated with an augmentation of the number of items recalled.

However, evidence from two old and unpublished studies from my laboratory and from one by Underwood, (1964, pp. 63-65) suggests that clustering and categorization are associated with augmented recall. In the first of these experiments I employed a list of 60 unrelated words, there being 15 at each of 4 Thorndike-Lorge (1944) frequency levels (AA, 30-49, 14-18, and 8-9). These items were randomized and presented a single time for free recall. The mean number of words recalled for the 4 frequency levels was, from high to low, 4.00, 2.9, 2.48, and 2.23. In the second experiment, the list was 40 items long, with 10 items each from the frequency levels 47-39, 37-39, 27-29, and 17-19. Mean recalls in order were 2.56, 3.60, 2.10, and 2.70. For 60 word lists (composed of items classifiable in 4 categories) whose T-L frequencies averaged

---

[1] Bousfield actually presented the first account of his technique (to my knowledge) in a symposium at the APA meetings in Chicago in 1951, the title of which was Analysis of language behavior in personality and social studies. I was privileged to be present at an informal dinner following this symposium, at which Bousfield discussed his method with J. J. Jenkins and W. A. Russell. The latter then carried out their experiment on associative clustering, which reached publication earlier (Jenkins and Russell, 1952) than Bousfield's first paper.

7.33, Bousfield (1953) found mean recall scores of 24.97, which, divided by 4, yielded 6.25, a value which can be compared directly to the mean of 2.48 for a 15-item set of T-L frequency 8-9, reported above. Bousfield & Cohen (1955) reported recalls for 60-item lists of low T-L frequency (2.60) of 22.18 (which divided by 4 yields 5.54) and of high T-L frequency (23.87) of 25.55 (which, divided by 4 yields 6.38). These scores from Bousfield's studies are much higher than those from my work with 60-item lists of unrelated words. The inference is that the interrelations among the categorized items in Bousfield's case augmented his recall scores. Similar comparisons could be made with my data for 40-item lists of unrelated words with the same inference permissible.

Underwood's data led to a similar conclusion. He compared recalls after a single presentation of lists of 16 unrelated words with recalls for lists in which the 16 items could be classified into 4 categories. The former lists yielded mean recalls of 11.21 and the latter 14.71. Underwood interprets the superior recall for the categorized lists to the use of the category name.

This evidence is representative of a good deal that has been collected, and the opinion is widespread that recall and organization are closely related, with the former dependent on the latter (Tulving, 1962). I would not wish to question this opinion in all cases, but I do think there are data which are not entirely consistent with it. It is important, at least, to attempt to describe the circumstances under which the assumption seems to be tenable and those under which it is questionable.

To begin with, augmented recall can probably occur for other reasons than organization, especially the kind of organization that involves coding by means of the category name. One alternative basis is inter-item associative relationships. Certain items, such as *north, east, south* and *west* (Cohen, 1963) represent the category, points of the compass, and are also highly inter-associated. That is, given the stimulus *north*, many people would think at once of *south*, and, given *east*, would probably think of *west*. Given any one of these items, a subject might run off the other three as a sort of chain, for example, north → south → east → west, without ever thinking that the items are instances of the more general notion, points of the compass.

That this kind of process can augment free recall is indicated in Deese's (1959) work. I shall have more to say about this later, but, briefly, Deese found that the number of items produced in free recall is a function of the inter-item associations the list members possess, that is, the extent to which in free association the items tend to elicit each other as responses. Now it is often true, as indicated in the example of the points of the compass, that items belonging to a common category are also inter-associated. However, it is also true that items can be inter-associated without belonging to a common category. The two factors are, in perhaps the typical case, confounded.

Let me return to the experiments mentioned earlier. Among the items I used, inter-item associations and common category membership were minimal, if they were present at all. In Bousfield's categorized lists, some inter-item associations surely existed among the items within the categories, and I suspect that this is also true for Underwood's categorized lists. Hence, the category name may not be involved in recall in either of their experiments, despite the augmentation of recall they obtained as contrasted with the unrelated word lists.

My purpose in this paper will be to review my work which has been devoted to the role of category membership and association in organizational characteristics of free recall and to the relation of organization and amount recalled.

Tulving (1966) has observed that, in the present state of the art, it is premature to attempt to separate associative and conceptual factors so far as free recall is concerned. He may well be right, but we have to start some place in order to achieve maturity. He also argues that multitrial-free-recall learning is a better method than the single presentation-immediate-free-recall method I have used. In his own work, however, Tulving (1962) has mainly used lists of unrelated words and has observed the development of subjective organization rather than the effects of experimenter-controlled variables, as I have done. Seibel (1964, 1965) and Mandler (1966) have also stressed subjective groupings. These are valuable approaches, but I think progress can be made by using E-controlled variables. Further, I think that the single-presentation situation is more likely to represent free recall as it appears in daily life than the multi-presentation condition. That is, we are exposed to a list of conferees or to the names of cities we have visited on a trip once or twice but we may recall them many times. If I am right, perhaps we should use single or double presentations but multiple recalls.

STUDIES WITH LISTS VARYING IN INTER-ITEM ASSOCIATIVE STRENGTH

I have observed that in immediate free recall, in the typical case, we do not get back all the items that were presented. This is true even when the items are presented under the most favorable conditions. It is of interest to determine what happens when special techniques are employed to maximize the retrieval obtained. Three such techniques may be discussed—forced recall, recognition, and the use of cue stimuli. I have made extensive use of the first of these techniques, some use of the second, and almost no use of the third.

The "forced recall" technique that I have used is as follows. First, a list is presented under the instruction that a free recall will be obtained on signal immediately after list presentation. Ample time is given for free recall. Following this phase, the subjects are then told how many items the list contained, asked to count the items they have recalled, and, finally to write as many additional items as are needed to match list length. It is this procedure, that of producing items to match list length, which I refer to as forced recall. In it, the subjects are assured, by various techniques, that any items they produce will be acceptable.

I first used this procedure in 1960 because of some notions about free recall advanced by Deese in 1959 (Deese 1961). Deese (1959a, 1959b) had found that the number of words recalled from 15-item lists presented a single time was closely associated with the inter-item associative strength of the lists employed. He had further shown that intrusions, and agreement among subjects in the intrusion errors they made, were fairly well predicted by the same measure. In view of these findings, he argued as follows (Deese, 1961, p. 19):

> If we assume that the obtained relationship between inter-item strength and recall demonstrates that individuals do make use of their latent associative repertoires to increase output in recall,

the question then arises whether or not there is a selective process involved. Do individuals *edit* their associations before emitting them in recall? Such editing would make the output in recall conform more to some memory trace of the list. The data on intrusions make this an unnecessary assumption. The appropriateness or inappropriateness of recall for a particular set of words is determined by the associative structure of the words themselves, not by any selection on the part of the individual doing the recalling. If the list is an organized one, the associations between the words in the list tend to dominate and restrict the range of outside intrusions. If the words on the list serve as associative stimuli for particular intrusions in recall, these appear in recall and thus systematically alter memory for the material. If the list is chosen from unrelated words, there is usually no convergence upon items in the list; thus correct recall is somewhat reduced, the reduction probably depending in absolute amount upon the number of words presented. In addition, it is unlikely that the unrelated words on such a list will converge upon any particular extra-list intrusions; thus the intrusions that do occur are scattered and idiosyncratic. Rather than being systematically altered, the memory for such a collection of words would disintegrate statistically.

My concern was with this interpretation. My point was that if subjects do not edit their recalls it is difficult to see why so many of them fail to approximate list length in their recalls. Most subjects have some knowledge of list length—some actually count the words as they are presented. On the assumption that subjects would want to perform as well as possible in this situation, it might be expected that they would at least approximate list length in their recalls; it should be easy for them to do so if what they mainly do in recall is to give unedited associations to the items they do in fact remember, since all the list members employed are common words with easy and obvious associations. Failure to match list length, then, seemed to me to be compatible with the notion that subjects do edit their recalls. And it led me to investigate the character of the responses subjects add when they are required to match list length.

Before describing these studies of forced recall, it is well to be a little more specific about Deese's lists and his procedure. He used 18 lists, each 15 items in length and having a name. The name was a word taken from the stimulus set of the Kent-Rosanoff Word Association Test (Russell and Jenkins, 1954). Six lists were composed of high frequency associates to the list names (High frequency or *HF* lists), 6 were composed of low frequency associates of the same names (*LF*), and 6 were composed of words not given as associates to these names (zero frequency or *ZF*). The lists were presented with their list names, but for half the subjects Deese changed the list name for the lists from the appropriate *K-R* stimulus to an unrelated word (Deese, 1959, pp. 306-307).

In a sense, the use of list names is a device which might provide *S* with a concept for the list, although the coherence of the concept for a group of associates to the list name may not be very great. To indicate what is meant here, the 15 *HF* items for the *Butterfly* list are *moth, insect, wing, bird, fly, yellow, net, pretty, flower, bug, cocoon, color, stomach, blue, bees,* and the 15 *LF* items for the same name are *garden, sky, flutter, sunshine, nature, chase, spring, collection, beautiful, caterpillar, summer, light, wasp, colorful, grace.* It is noteworthy that recall scores for lists like these did not differ when the list name was the *K-R* stimulus (*Butterfly*) from those for the same lists with the unrelated name (*Deliberate*). This was true at each frequency level (Deese, 1959, p. 308, Table 2) and, so far as it goes, suggests no influence of a "concept" on the number of items recalled.

However, Deese did find a correlation (r) of .88 between his measure of inter-item associative strength (Deese, 1961, p. 18, Table 2-1 for the method of computation) and amount recalled. In the experiment to be reported next, I have replicated this finding using only lists with the appropriate, that is, the *K-R* stimulus, name, and have added the forced recall procedure to it.

Experiment 1[2]

Materials and Procedures. There were three groups of student *Ss*, 17 in one, 22 in another, and 23 in the third. They

---

[2] The description of Experiment 1 is abridged from Inter-item associative strength and immediate free and forced recall, Technical Report No. 1 under contract Nonr 285(47) between the Office of Naval Research and New York University, 1961.

were registered in psychology courses. As in Deese's experiment, there were 18 lists to be learned, all taken from Deese's paper (Deese, 1959, Table 1, p. 307). Each S in each group learned, successively, 2 high-frequency, 2 low-frequency, and 2 zero-frequency lists, there being a different set of 6 lists for each group. Each list was read aloud once, slowly and monotonously, and S gave his recall immediately after presentation. Prior to a list presentation, S was told the "name" of the list, and he was instructed to write this name on his recall sheet before the list was read. The name was actually the Kent-Rosanoff stimulus word to which the responses in the high- and low-frequency lists were associates; the same name was used for the zero-frequency list in that set.

When all Ss had completed their free recalls of a list, E said, "draw a line below the last word you have written. There were 15 words on the list. Count the number you have written. If you have not already written 15 words, I want you to write additional words, below the line you have drawn, until the total is 15. Write any additional words that occur to you, even though you are not sure they were on the original list I read or even though you are sure they were not on the list. Write words until the total number, that is those above the line together with those below the line, comes to 15." During this "forced recall," E said, from time to time, "Any words will do, any words you think of, just so the total is 15."

Data Analysis. Each free recall protocol was scored for correct responses and for intrusions. Minor variations in spelling were counted as correct. Each item given in a forced recall period for a list was scored correct or incorrect. If it was incorrect, it was determined how often it had been given in the group of Ss for that list. Further, free association norms made available by Deese (personal communication) were examined for the frequency of occurrence of any incorrect forced response as an associate to any list member. Forced responses which were additional associates to the list name were checked for associative frequency by means of the Russell-Jenkins (1954) norms.

Results for the Period of Free Recall. The results for
free recall parallel those reported by Deese. Table 8.1 gives

TABLE 8.1   Mean Number of Correct Responses in Free
and Forced Recall and of Intrusions in Free Recall

List*	Free Recall Correct	Intrusions	Forced Recall Correct	%Associates
High Frequency (1)	11.06	0.71	0.53	40
High Frequency (4)	9.76	1.35	0.41	32
High Frequency (7)	9.50	0.45	0.59	42
High Frequency (10)	9.48	0.74	0.57	41
High Frequency (13)	9.09	0.23	0.73	30
High Frequency (16)	10.09	0.45	1.00	54
Mean High Frequency	9.830	0.655	0.638	40
Low Frequency (17)	8.82	2.00	0.41	62
Low Frequency (14)	7.76	1.76	0.18	42
Low Frequency (5)	7.78	1.17	0.43	36
Low Frequency (2)	9.87	0.65	0.39	40
Low Frequency (11)	8.14	1.50	0.50	42
Low Frequency (8)	9.32	0.73	0.27	41
Mean Low Frequency	8.615	1.301	0.363	42
Zero Frequency (9)	8.06	0.94	0.06	42
Zero Frequency (12)	7.65	1.00	0.18	30
Zero Frequency (18)	7.70	0.96	0.22	33
Zero Frequency (15)	7.00	1.09	0.13	27
Zero Frequency (3)	9.04	0.59	0.23	42
Zero Frequency (6)	9.00	0.82	0.045	26
Mean Zero Frequency	8.075	0.900	0.144	33

*The number in parentheses refers to the list number as shown in
Deese's (1959) Tables 1 and 3.

the mean free recall scores for each list and for the 3 frequency categories, as well as the mean number of intrusions
in free recall and the mean number of correct responses
given in forced recall. The free recall scores are higher than
those Deese reported, but the order of the mean values for the
high, low, and zero-frequency lists is the same in the two
experiments. The r between mean free recall score and
inter-item associative strength by list was 0.77 (rho was

0.833). An r of -0.40 was obtained between mean number of intrusions and inter-item associative strength. These values are comparable to those found by Deese.

Results for the Period of Forced Recall. The r between inter-item associative strength and mean number of correct responses in forced recall was 0.73. However, the number of such responses, as Table 8.1 shows, was small, never exceeding a mean of one. This would suggest that the failure of Ss to match list length is probably not due to their inability to recognize correct responses if they occur.

The last column in Table 8.1 indicates for each list the percentage of responses produced in forced recall which were associates of either a list member or of the list name. On the average, for each list frequency, these percentages vary from 33 to 42. Thus, over all, less than half of these forced responses appear to be associates. A tabulation was made of the number of times Ss produced the same response during forced recall. From 2 to 8 Ss did give the same forced responses, but the total number of words on which such agreement occurred constituted only 11% of all the responses given during forced recall of the high-frequency lists, 16% for the low-frequency lists, and 9% for the zero frequency lists. Clearly, the responses which occurred in forced recall were idiosyncratic, even when they were associates of the list member or the list name.

A further analysis of the erroneous forced recall responses was made. In this analysis, the free associations to each list member which occurred in Deese's norms with a frequency of 10 per cent or greater were listed. A tabulation was then made of the frequency of occurrence of each response in the forced recalls. If the subjects were associating to the list members in their efforts to match list length during the forced recall period, one would expect that these words would occur in the forced recalls at about the same frequency levels they display in the free association situation.

Reference to Table 8.2 will clarify the procedure and indicate the nature of the results obtained. In the first column of Table 8.2 the members of the low-frequency list *Butterfly* are given in alphabetical order. In the second column the responses and their associative frequencies which occurred with a frequency of 10% or greater in Deese's free associative sample of 50 Ss are given for each list member. The number in parentheses following a word gives its associative frequency. The third column for each list member

TABLE 8.2 Free Association Responses with Frequency of 10% or Greater to List Members of the Low-Frequency Butterfly List and Their Frequencies of Occurrence in Forced Recall. List Members Presented in Alphabetical Order in Table.

List Member	Associative Response Frequency (N = 50)	Forced Recall Frequency (N = 23)	Free Recall Frequency of List Member
Beautiful:	girl(18), woman, lovely(5)	0, 0, 0	19
Caterpillar:	tractor, bug(8), crawl(s)(7)	0, 1, 1	19
Chase:	run(15)	0	9
Collection:	stamp(s)(16)	0	11
Colorful:	gay(8), red(6)	0, 0	20
Flutter:	fly(11), butterfly(7), bird(6)	6, -, 0	17
Garden:	flower(s)(10), hose, plant(s)(5)	8, 0, 0	23
Grace:	God(5)	0	18
Light:	dark(29), bulb(8)	0, 0	7
Nature:	tree(s)(6)	4	7
Sky:	blue(40)	1	20
Spring:	summer(12), fall(10)	-, 0	12
Summer:	winter(21), hot(7)	0, 1	21
Sunshine:	warm(th)(8)	2	6
Wasp:	sting(16), bee(14), fly, bug(7)	0, 0, 6, 1	19

gives for each of its associates (Column 2) its frequency of occurrence in the forced recall of 23 Ss. If the associate is a list member, this fact is indicated by a dash rather than by a number. The final column gives the frequency of occurrence in free recall of the list member for the 23 Ss.

For example, the list member *beautiful* occurrs 19 times in free recall; its high-frequency associates are *girl, woman,* and *lovely.* None of these three associates occurs in forced recall. The list member *flutter* occurs 17 times in free recall, and its associates are *fly, butterfly,* and *bird. Fly,* occurs in 6 of the forced recalls, representing one-third of the times *flutter* is recalled. *Butterfly* is the list name, and *bird* does not occur in forced recall.

The data displayed in Table 8.2 are representative of those found in the 17 tables constructed for the other 17 lists. The relations seen in Table 8.2 are harder to see in the lists composed of high-frequency associates, because so many of the associates of list members are also list members. Table 8.3, however, displays parallel data for the high-frequency *Butterfly* list. Table 8.4 gives parallel data for the

TABLE 8.3   Free Association Responses with Frequency of 10% or Greater to List Members of the High-Frequency Butterfly List and Their Frequencies of Occurrence in Forced Recall. List Members Presented in Alphabetical Order in Table.

List Member	Associative Response Frequency (N= 50)	Forced Recall Frequency (N = 17)	Free Recall Frequency of List Member
Bees:	sting, honey(10), birds(9), buzz(6)	0, 1, -, 0	11
Bird:	fly(15), dog(5)	-, 0	11
Blue:	red(13), sky, color(6)	0, 1, -	14
Bug:	insect(18), ant(5)	-, 0	7
Cocoon:	moth, butterfly(8), bug(5)	-, -, -	16
Color:	red(16), black, white(8), blue(5)	0, 1, 0, -	9
Flower:	garden, smell(6)	1, 0	9
Fly:	bug(19), insect(5)	-, -	10
Insect:	bug(24), fly(9)	-, -	16
Moth:	fly(10), ball(s)(6), cloth(es), bug(5)	-, 0, 0, -	16
Net:	fish(ing)(17)	0	10
Pretty:	girl(18), ugly(15), nice(6)	0, 0, 0	14
Stomach:	ache(16), food(12)	0, 1	13
Sing:	bird(25), fly(12)	-, -	17
Yellow:	red(6), color, green(5)	0, -, 3	15

zero-frequency *Butterfly* list.[3]

Returning to Table 8.2, we may describe some of its important features. Some of the high-frequency responses given in free association to the list members simply do not occur in forced recall; examples are response of *girl, tractor,*

[3] It should be remembered that each list was presented in a single serial (unalphabetized) order to all Ss. Recalls for all lists showed marked curves of serial position. Variations in the recall frequencies of list members may be due to this serial position factor. See Fig. 8.1.

TABLE 8.4   Free Association Responses with Frequency of 10% or Greater to List Members of the Zero-Frequency Butterfly List and Their Frequencies of Occurrence in ForcedRecall. List Members Presented in Alphabetical Order in Table.

List Member	Associative Response Frequency (N = 50)	Forced Recall Frequency (N = 22)	Free Recall Frequency of List Member
Arithmetic:	math(17), add(10)	1, 0	21
Arrow:	straight(9), bow(8), head(5)	0, 0, 0	10
Book:	read(13)	0	21
Early:	late(24), morning(16)	0, 1	11
Government:	people(5)	0	17
Help:	aid, me(8)	3, 0	12
Line:	straight(18), up(7)	0, 0	9
Payroll:	money(42)	2	7
Spray:	paint(12), water(11)	0, 0	13
Study:	hard, book(s) (8), learn, (home) work(6)	3, 0, 2, 3	10
Tutor:	teach(er) (27)	2	18
Typical:	usual(7), same(6)	0, 0	11
Velvet:	soft(15), smooth(8), cloth(7)	0, 0, 0	10
Winter:	summer(15), snow(13), cold(9)	1, 1, 2	10
Zebra:	stripe(s) (ed) (25), animal(10)	0, 1	19

run, *stamp*(*s*), *gay* to the first five list members listed. Others occur with a frequency in forced recall the same as, or greater than, that expected from the associative norms; examples are responses of *fly*, *flower*(*s*), *tree*(*s*), and *fly* (again) to the stimuli *flutter*, *garden*, *nature*, and *wasp*, respectively. *Girl*, *tractor*, *run*, *stamp*(*s*), and *gay* probably do not fit into the general context of the list, whereas *fly*, *flower*(*s*), and *tree*(*s*) perhaps do. Thus it is possible that some kind of contextual or conceptual feature of the list determines the under- or over-utilization of associations to list members in forced recall. However, associative convergence, or its absence, might account for these results. *Fly* is an associative response to two list members as well as to *butterfly*; *flower*(*s*) is an associative response to one list member as well as to *butterfly*. *Tree*(*s*), however, occurs to only one list member. In addition, there are cases of convergence in which forced recall frequency is low. *Bug* occurs to two list members and to *butterfly*, but it is infrequent in forced recall. *Blue* occurs with a frequency of 80% to *sky*, a list member, and also to *butterfly*; it occurs but once in forced recall. *Bird* also occurs both to *butterfly* and to a list member, but not in forced recall.

It appears that a contextual factor established by the list, or by the members of it *S* recalls, is responsible for the suppression of some and the facilitation of other associations to list members during forced recall. The nature of these suppressing and facilitating effects remains to be understood and the parameters of which they are a function remain to be specified. However, it would seem as though such contextual effects must modulate the influence of direct associative relationships in the process of free recall.

Several additional control experiments were run to determine whether this conclusion can be regarded as established. It may be that more specific instructions to associate to list members or to the list name and instructions designed to reduce any set for accuracy would significantly alter the results obtained.[4] Further, the separation of forced recall from free recall may have introduced problems of set which have complicated the results. The control experiments are presented below.

Another way of examining the response pool provided by the free and forced recall of a list is to take all of the responses obtained and to attempt to identify their sources. I will do this for 3 lists, *HF* Butterfly, *LF* Butterfly and *ZF* Butterfly. In this analysis, I have included all associates of list name or list member, without applying a frequency cutoff.

In the case of *LF* Butterfly, there were 23 *S*s, and we should have a total of 345 items (23 × 15) to work with. However, 3 *S*s provided 4 responses too few, leaving 341. There are 228 responses correct in free recall and 9 correct responses added in forced recall, so, assuming that these responses arise from list presentation, we can deduct them

---

[4] Deese (personal communication) has reported that instructions that the list members were associates to the name and that *S* could increase his score by associating to the name did not alter the results of the original experiment.

from the total, leaving 104 to be traced to other sources. These 104 responses are distributed as follows:

Free Recall
  Intrusions   15

Forced Recall
  List name and list member
    associates   37
  List member associates only   7
  List name associates only   5
  Other   40

Total   104

In a moment, let us consider the "Other" responses, which constitute 11% of the total of 341 responses, and examine the other categories first.

The 15 intrusions during free recall occur over 8 words and of these all but one (*case*, which occurs once) are found as associates in the free association norms for either the list name (*flight*, *air*, once each), a list member (*night*, *butterfly*, once each) or both the list name and a list member (*tree*, *flower*, and *fly*, occurring twice, once, and seven times respectively). Thirty-seven responses in forced recall can be found as associates of both the list name and a list member: *bug*, *blue*, *catch*, *flower* (again), *fly* (again), *insect*, *moth*, *sun*, *tree*, *wings*, *warm*, *yellow*, at frequencies varying from 1 to 8. Only 5 responses in forced recall are associates of the list name only (*cocoon*, *silk*, *tiger*) and seven occur as associates to a list member only: *color*, *crawl*, *green*, *high*, *lovely*, *graceful*, *time* (at frequencies of 1). These 22 different words which appear in forced recall provide 49 responses.

The 40 responses in the "Other" category are provided by 35 different words. Except for *antennae*, *cool*, and *change*, each of which occurs more than once, the other 32 words occur once each. None of these 35 words is an associate (in the norms) of the list name or of any list member. To show the kinds of responses involved, here are 10 of them: *below*, *cool*, *dotted*, *from*, *hurry*, *in*, *movement*, *pace*, *smoothly*, *tomorrow*.

It may help here to list again the list members and the responses obtained as intrusions and in forced recall (associates only):

List Members	Associates to Name & Members		Associates to Name Only		Associates to List Member Only		Intrusions	
(*Butterfly*)								
Beautiful	Bug*	1	Cocoon*	2	Color*	1	Air	1
Caterpillar	Blue*	1	Silk	2	Crawl	1	Butter- fly	1
Chase	Catch	1	Tiger- Swallow-		Green	1	Case	1
Collection	Flower*	8	Tail	1	High	1	Flight	1
Colorful	Fly*	6			Lovely	1	Flower*	1
Flutter	Insect*	1			Graceful	1	Fly*	7
Garden	Moth*	2			Time	1	Night	1
Grace	Sun	3					Tree	2
Light	Tree	4						
Nature	Wings*	6						
Sky	Warm	2						
Spring	Yellow*	2						
Summer		37		5		1		15
Sunshine								
Wasp								

I have starred the 10 items (*flower* and *fly* occur in two columns each) which are members of the *HF* Butterfly list and which are, therefore, high-frequency associates to the list name. The five other words in this list, however, occur neither as intrusions nor as items in forced recall. They are *bees, bird, net, pretty, stomach.*

This analysis permits, perhaps, a little more precision in our analysis of the processes involved in recall and forced recall of this list which I referred to earlier as context. The associative responses found in forced recall are mainly those (37 of 49) which are associates of both the list name and of one or more list members; this is also true of 10 (*flower, fly,* and *tree*) of the 15 intrusions in free recall. Perhaps these converging associations represent a list "concept." The concept then permits the selection of certain kinds of responses to be given as intrusions in free recall and as additions in the course of matching list length, but it excludes other relatively strong associates which do not fit well conceptually: Items like the 5 *HF* Butterfly list members given above or the high-frequency list member associates such *as girl, tractor, run, stamp*(s), *God, dark, winter, and sting.*

Now it is also noteworthy that this concept in the case of this list does relatively little so far as the addition of correct responses is concerned (only 9) and, further, it does not seem to mediate the production of enough responses to match list length. I say this because of the 40 "Other" responses most of which, I would judge, are provided on idiosyncratic bases. For example, one subject, needing 7 items to get a total of 15, wrote "tomorrow creeps in this petty pace from."

My impression is that free recall largely, if not entirely, exhausts the "storage," and I think our data on forced recall are consistent with this interpretation. I suspect also that subjects are well aware, at least at immediate recall, of what items were not on the list. An experiment to be reported a little later will, I think, support this statement. Before proceeding to that experiment, I will make a detailed analysis of the *HF* and *ZF* Butterfly lists comparable to the one just presented.

Free Recall	
Correct	188
Intrusions	12
Forced Recall	
Correct	9
List name and list member associates	8
List member associates only	12
List name associates only	1
Other	24
Total	254

In the case of the *HF* Butterfly list, there were 17 *Ss* which, with 15 items each, gives 255 responses. One *S* gave only 14 responses, however, reducing the pool to 254.

Nine per cent of all responses are classified as "Other." Most of the intrusions are associates neither of the list name nor of list member, as far as available norms go (*beads, beast* (twice), *beat, mouth, neck, nest* (twice) *pink*), but *tree, catch* and *bud* are. Responses added which are list name associates only are infrequent (*beautiful*, occurring once), but associates to both the list name and list members and to list members only combine to provide 20 responses (16 different words).

The responses not identifiable as associates are as follows: *antenna, beak, building, chrysalis, clumsy, food, gull, hand, heavy, larva, leaf* (twice), *meadows, mountains, open, pink, run, sail, sign, stamen, stare, stern, the, vulture.* Several of these responses look appropriate to the list concept, but others do not. Again, several strong associates to list names are missing from forced recall. These include *sting, red,* (a primary response to 3 list members), *fish, girl, ugly, ache,* The list context or concept evidently prevented these responses from being used to match list length and the 24 "Other" responses were employed instead.

The 22 Ss who recalled the *ZF* Butterfly list provided 328 responses in free and forced recall (rather than 330). The distribution of these responses is as follows:

Free Recall	
Correct	199
Intrusions	13
Forced Recall	
Correct	5
List name and list member associates	6
List member associates only	38
List name associates only	10
Other	57
Total	328

Seventeen per cent of the responses may be classed as in the "Other" category, as compared with 9 and 11 per cent for the *HF* and *LF* lists respectively. Other comparisons among these distributions will be made shortly.

It is noteworthy that, among the intrusions, only *stripe,* an associate of zebra, occurs in the associative norms for either the list name or list members. In forced recall, the items that appear which are associates of the list name only are *chase, spring,* and *caterpillar* (each once only) from the *LF* list and only *net, wing, fly, flower, pretty,* and *color* (once each) from the *HF* list. The list member associates are largely specific to the specific list member, and very few occur jointly as associates to both the list name and a list member. The 57 "Other" responses cover a wide range, representing 55 different words. Ten illustrative responses are: *board*, *travel*, *corduroy*, *around*, *marriage*, *bright*, *glass*, *smash*, *philosophy*, *year*.

In the following tabulation I have brought together for the 3 butterfly lists the total number of forced recall responses in the categories indicated in the tabulation and the proportion each category contributes to the total.

	HF	LF	ZF
Total	44	89	111
% List name associates	1	5	10
% List member associates	27	8	34
% List name and list member associates	18	42	5
% Other	54	45	51

The *LF* list is differentiated from the others by the fact that 42% of its responses in forced recall are associates jointly of the list name and one or more list members; the comparable values for the *HF* and *ZF* lists are 18% and 5%. On the other hand, responses which are list member associates only are prominent in the forced recalls of list *HF* (27%) and list *ZF* (34%), as contrasted with only 8% for list *LF*.

It is noteworthy that the proportion of "Other" responses varies within a small range for the 3 lists. This suggests to me that after virtually exhausting his "storage" during his free recall S, at forced recall, uses sources of association which provide responses that "fit" with the conception he has of the list; however, he is unable to match list length from these sources and resorts to a variety of other responses, the sources of which are not easily specified, after the fact.

Experiment 2[5]

Method. Four small classes of psychology students were

[5] The description of Experiment 2 is much abridged from Further experiments on immediate recall of word lists with the requirement to match list length in recall, Technical Report No. 7 under contract Nonr 285(47) between the Office of Naval Research and New York University, 1961.

used, one for each experiment. Only 6 of the original lists constructed by Deese were employed in these experiments, and the same 6 lists were used for each group. The lists were number 1, 4, 14, 17, 9, and 12 (Deese, 1959a, Table 1, p. 307), presented in that order. List 1 and 4 were composed of the high-frequency associates of *Butterfly*, and of *Slow*, respectively; 14 and 17 of the low-frequency associates of *Command* and *Chair*, respectively; and 9 and 12 of the zero-frequency associates of *Music* and *Whistle*, respectively.

E gave the general instructions and presented each list and its name as he had done in the prior experiment. *S* wrote down the list name, listened to the list presentation, and then wrote his recall. Where forced recall was used, it was carried out as described in the report of the previous experiment. The variations introduced were as follows:

Group IC. Deese's instructions were used (Deese, 1959a, 306-307) but both before and after they were presented and before and after each list was read *E* said that there would be 15 items on the list and that *S* was to produce 15 words, whether or not he was sure that the words he put down were on the list. He was told that he could use any cues at all in helping him think of words to make his total of 15. No separation of free and forced recall was introduced here.

Group IIC. Here free and forced recall periods were used. At the beginning of forced recall *S* was told to add items until his total was 15 and to use the list name as a stimulus for associations in doing so. He was told the original lists were composed of associates to the list name.

Group IIIC. The same procedure was used in Group *IIIC* as in *IIC*, except that *S* was told to use the words he had written down already (in free recall) as stimuli for associations (during forced recall).

Group IVC. This group like Group *IC* was told to produce 15 words in the recall of the list, there being no break in the recall period. Instructions, further, were to use the list name and the items already written as stimuli for associates. *S* was further told to mark each word he had written down by a code *E* provided to indicate that he was sure it had been on the list, he was uncertain whether it was on the list, or that he was sure it was not on the list.

A total of 40 subjects were run, 11 in *IC*, 8 in *IIC*, 9 in *IIIC*, and 12 in *IVC*. The lists used for these four groups were the same as those used for Group I (N of 17) in experiment one.

Results. The results of these instructional manipulations showed no essential differences from the data already summarized for Experiment 1, so far as the content of the responses produced in forced recall is concerned. However, I want to mention the results from Group *IVC* which was told to recall 15 items and to mark the items produced to indicate whether the Ss were sure the items were on the list, uncertain about the list membership, or sure the items were not on the list. These data are shown in the following tabulation.

Accuracy of Identification of Words as List members

List	% Correct identification when word was right	% Correct identification when word was wrong
HF (1)	91	77
HF (4)	90	64
LF (14)	92	70
LF (17)	92	60
ZF (9)	96	76
ZF (12)	99	65
Mean	93.33	68.67

Clearly, the Ss are able, at a high level of accuracy, to identify list membership when the words they produce were in fact on the list; they are somewhat less accurate in correctly identifying words they produce as not being on the list. Their judgments of being uncertain were chiefly made on this latter type of word. Overall, the accuracy of judgments, not including those of being uncertain, is at 81%.

We now have several sets of facts. One is that free recall approximately exhausts the list items that are in storage, since few new ones are added when list length is to be matched. A second is that Ss have reasonably accurate knowledge of list membership. A third is that the generation of items to match list length does, apparently, make use of list-name and list-member associates, but that these sources are not used without some respect for the appropriateness of the items generated to the overall context or concept of the list. Fourth, for approximately half the items he generates to match list length, S resorts to odd and idiosyncratic responses.

It is of some interest to discover factors which limit the number of items recalled. Two attempts may be mentioned. One is to plot the recall curves as a function of serial position. Figure 8.1 shows such a plot for the 3 frequency levels of the lists used in Experiment 1, averaged across 6 lists at each frequency level. Figure 8.2 shows plots for the 3 lists I

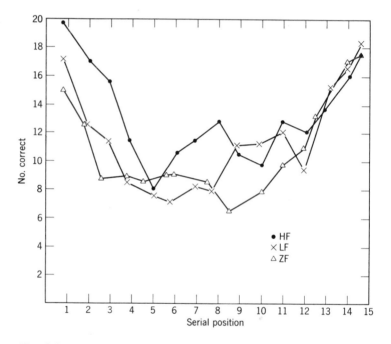

Fig. 8.1   Mean number of correct responses at immediate free recall as a function of serial positions of items in the list. Each of the 3 curves (HF, LF, and ZF) is based on data from 6 lists. The data are those discussed in conjunction with Experiment 1.

have discussed here, *HF*, *LF*, and *ZF* Butterfly. All the curves agree in showing low points for recall for the mid-list items, although they are somewhat irregular. Position at presentation then appears to be a factor associated with poor recall.

We have been interested in whether a recognition procedure would reveal that all the items are still available or not, despite the considerably less than perfect scores on recall.

The next experiment, conducted by Howard Walker, was directed to this question.

Experiment 3

Method. Lists 1, 4, 14, 17, 9, and 12 were used again. They were presented once each to 25 Ss in a group situation, as they were in the previous experiments. In this case, however, after each list was presented, S received a recognition sheet on which he was instructed to identify the 15 items he had just heard. This sheet contained the 15 list items intermixed among 15 distractors. The distractors used were items given in forced recall by the subjects in previous experiments and included all of the items given at the higher frequencies. S knew at the time of list presentation that he would be asked to find the 15 items presented in a larger set.

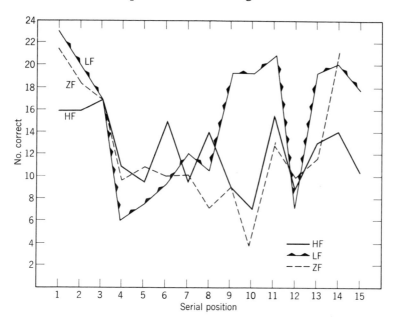

Fig. 8.2   Mean number of correct responses at immediate free recall as a function of serial positions of items in the list. The 3 curves (HF, LF, and ZF) are for the three "Butterfly" lists discussed in the report of Experiment 1.

Results. The following table gives the proportion of items identified correctly for each list (the differences between these proportions and 100 are made up of incorrect identifications).

TABLE 8.5   Accuracy of Recognition (in per cent) for
Items in 6 Lists

List	% Right
1 Butterfly (*HF*)	87.20
4 Slow (*HF*)	87.47
14 Command (*LF*)	82.40
17 Chair (*LF*)	83.43
9 Music (*ZF*)	86.93
12 Whistle (*ZF*)	85.87

It may be seen that there is little variation among the lists (range of 5.07 percentage points) and that from 12.5 to 17.6 per cent of the responses are incorrect; this amounts to from 1.88 to 2.64 items per subject.

In recognition, as in recall, we find some evidence for a serial position effect. Table 8.6 shows mean items correctly

TABLE 8.6   Serial Position for Recognition Scores for Two
Lists Each at *HF*, *LF*, and *ZF*, Averaged Together. Number
Correct Responses.   Perfect Performance would Yield a
Score of 75 in Each Cell.

	Positions				
	1 - 3	4 - 6	7 - 9	10 - 12	13 - 15
HF	69.0	65.0	58.5	65.0	71.0
LF	63.5	63.0	54.0	67.5	67.0
ZF	64.0	61.0	57.5	69.5	70.5

recognized for the 2 lists at each frequency level combined with the serial positions grouped into 5 blocks of 3 each. Positions 7-9 yield the fewest correct responses for all the frequency levels, and this is true for 5 of the 6 individual lists.

I am well aware of the difficulties of comparing recognition scores with recall scores and of the fact that recognition scores will vary with the number of distractors and their similarity to the correct items (Bahrick, 1964, 1965; Bahrick and Bahrick, 1964; Bruce and Cofer, 1967). Nevertheless, it is clear that substantially more items can be recognized than can be recalled, that recognition does not seem to be a function of the inter-item associative strengths of the lists, and that there is evidence for serial position effects in the recognition data.

A STUDY WITH FREE AND FORCED RECALL
OF A CATEGORIZED LIST

Before making further comments about what these data may mean, I should like to report a further experiment. In this one, conducted by Miss Bonnie Travelet, we used two 40-item word lists the items belonging to 4 mutually exclusive categories. The lists were presented a single time, and *Ss* gave immediate free recall. Then, they were asked to match list length in forced recall. We also presented the items randomly in two groups and by block presentation in two other groups. Clearly, these lists are conceptually or categorically organized, and the results with them should give us a good deal of insight into how conceptualization relates to recall.

Experiment 4

Method. The items used were drawn from the Connecticut Cultural Norms (Cohen, Bousfield, and Whitmarsh, 1957) for the categories 4-legged animals, occupations, articles of clothing, and weapons. Ten high-frequency associates were chosen from each category to make up the high frequency (HF) list of 40 items, and 10 were drawn from each category to make up the low-frequency (LF) list of the same length. At presentation one version of each of these lists involved random sequences of the items (HFR, LFR) and the other version involved block presentation, that is, all the items from a given category were presented one after another before items from another category were given. These lists will be referred to as HFB and LFB. The items were presented at a 4-second rate on a Stowe memory drum, and the *Ss*, who were tested individually, were asked, following presentation, to write as many items as they could in any order. Following this free recall, they were asked to match list length by generating the number of items needed to do so in view of the number they had written already. There were 20 Ss in each of the 4 groups.

In addition to scoring for number correct in free recall (*n*), the data were scored for clustering (ratio of repetition - *RR*), for relevant intrusions (non-list items that fit into a list-category) and irrelevant intrusions. Forced recall was scored for number of correct items added, relevant intrusions, and irrelevant intrusions.

Results. The data are shown in Table 8.7. As expected from prior work (Cofer, Bruce, and Reicher, 1966) number of

TABLE 8.7   Mean and Total Recall and Clustering Scores
for Experiment with *HF* and *LF* Categorized Word Lists

List	Regular Recall					Forced Recall			
	Mean No. Items	Mean No. Correct	No. Intrusions Rel.	No. Intrusions Irrel.	RR	No. Items	Mean % Correct	Mean % Relevant	Mean % Irrelevant
HFB	26.10	26.00	2	0	.772	273	26.0	48.0	26.0
HFR	23.60	23.55	1	0	.694	314	29.0	42.0	29.0
LFB	20.45	19.80	13	0	.695	386	8.5	71.0	20.5
LFR	19.15	18.10	18	3	.583	415	7.5	56.5	36.0

correct items in free recall is greatest for *HFB*, next in *HFR*, next in *LFB*, and least in *LFR*. Clustering scores are highest for *HFB*, next and equal for *HFR* and *LFB*, and least in *LFR*. I will devote most of my attention to the forced recall data.

In Table 8.7 I have shown the proportion of the items produced in forced recall which have been allocated to each of the 3 categories. The total number of items in forced recall is also shown.

There is evidence (Cofer, Bruce, and Reicher, 1966) that block presentation of items in these lists permits Ss to be aware of the categories the lists contain. They are also aware of the categories in *HFR* but less so in *LFR*. It is interesting to note, then, that correct responses added in forced recall are almost identical for *LFB* and *LFR*; however, the number of relevant intrusions added by Group *LFB* exceeds those added by Group *LFR* by almost 15%. Knowledge of the conceptual character of the list does not aid *LFB* to generate more correct items than *LFR* provides. Rather, the major difference lies in the relevance of the intrusions that are added. It is also noteworthy that, in free recall, *LFB* shows clustering at the same magnitude as *HFR*; yet the recall score of *LFB* is considerably below that of *HFR*.

These facts suggest two things. One is that organization does not necessarily augment accurate recall following a single presentation of a list. The second is more indirect. It is that the inter-associations among items may be more important than the conceptual category so far as list recall is concerned. We may reasonably believe that inter-item association is greater for *HF* than for *LF* sets. The failure of *LFB* to show substantially more correct items in either free or forced recall than *LFR* suggests to me that it is inter-item association, rather than organization, which is the critical variable for item recall in this situation.

Before concluding, let me mention two things: One concerns the relation of organization to recall; the other concerns the use of cues as a means of retrieving material from storage.

Organization and Recall

The evidence presented from Travelet's experiment suggests that clustering can be independent of number of items (*n*) recalled; the best evidence is in the relevant scores for the *LFB* and *LFR* groups. Using the same lists, Cofer, Bruce, and Reicher (1966) found the same thing; their *LFB* groups clustered much more than their *LFR* groups, yet the recall scores for these groups were almost identical. This led me to survey a number of our past experiments for evidence pertinent to this issue (Cofer, Bruce, and Reicher, 1966, footnote 2). One source of evidence comes from studies in which, after a single list presentation, we have obtained 2 recalls, one immediately, the other after a filled interval of 5 minutes from the same *S*s. The experiments have employed a variety of procedures and materials, but I will ignore them here. Table 8.8 shows the data from our series of studies at

TABLE 8.8   Evidence Concerning RR and n (Number of Items Recalled) at 2 Recalls Obtained in a Number of Experiments

Reference	Immediate Recall RR*	Immediate Recall n	Delayed Recall RR	Delayed Recall n	Direction of Change RR	Direction of Change n
Gonzalez & Cofer (1959, p. 316)						
Control group	42.69	21.00	45.58	19.10	+	−
Experimental group	38.17	20.24	45.32	15.05	+	−
Gonzalez & Cofer (1959, Table 1)						
Group V	40.57	18.04	43.49	17.65	+	−
II	38.52	16.96	48.60	17.33	+	+
IV	36.44	13.39	40.59	13.71	+	+
I	31.67	11.58	34.79	12.33	+	+
III	21.47	6.22	22.58	5.94	+	−
Gonzalez & Cofer (1959, Tables 3 and 4) Specificity						
Control	32.07	15.35	38.85	14.73	+	−
Experimental	26.70	9.63	26.89	9.33	+	−
Conflict group 1	46.62	19.63	52.87	18.87	+	−
2	40.60	16.29	45.94	16.00	+	−
3	34.80	13.26	39.15	13.81	+	+
4	29.17	10.04	34.80	10.28	+	+
Facilitation 5	45.66	17.26	47.96	17.30	+	+
6	36.50	11.72	44.40	12.04	+	+
Gonzalez & Cofer (1959, Tables 5 and 6) Experiment I						
Group I	38.95	13.67	40.45	12.46	+	−
II	35.22	11.76	36.79	10.68	+	−
III	37.26	9.21	42.02	8.25	+	−
IV	31.46	7.36	35.96	7.64	+	+
Experiment II						
Group I	33.98	6.16	34.95	5.92	+	−
II	35.08	9.45	41.86	10.27	+	+
III	39.54	10.71	41.40	10.91	+	+
IV	25.90	5.88	24.46	5.63	−	−

TABLE 8.8 (Continued)

Reference	Immediate Recall		Delayed Recall		Direction of Change	
	RR*	n	RR	n	RR	n
Gonzalez & Cofer (1959, Table 7)						
Group I	27.67	10.61	28.88	9.50	+	-
II	30.24	11.07	30.53	10.81	+	-
III	24.96	9.34	33.17	9.45	+	+
IV	28.15	8.59	29.18	9.30	+	+
Cofer & Segal (TR 27) †						
Group S	.366	11.93	.430	11.80	+	-
SO	.458	16.25	.528	15.80	+	-
RO	.485	14.58	.572	14.05	+	-
Cofer & Segal (TR 28) †						
Experimental	.374	10.11	.450	8.78	+	-
Control	.546	18.11	.589	17.83	+	-
Cofer & Segal (TR 29) † Experiment I						
Group HC	.529	21.35	.631	20.40	+	-
IHC	.411	15.26	.498	14.32	+	-
WC	.283	12.90	.358	11.60	+	-
IWC	.307	7.85	.328	7.20	+	-
Experiment II						
Group SHC	.448	16.21	.525	15.89	+	-
SWC	.306	10.90	.409	9.85	+	-

*RR values in the Gonzalez & Cofer studies were transformed by means of the arcsine transformation. The values in the Cofer & Segal studies are means of raw scores.

†These data are taken from unpublished technical reports by C. N. Cofer and E. Segal under contract Nonr 595(04) between the Office of Naval Research and the University of Maryland as follows:

#27. An exploration of clustering in the recall of nouns embedded during presentation in sentences.

#28. Inappropriate modification of nouns in a facilitation design.

#29. Certain modifier effects with nouns varying in degree of clustering tendency.

the University of Maryland.

Let us look simply at the double column headed "Direction of Change." If RR at second recall is greater or less than that at first recall I have entered a+ or a-, irrespective of the size or the significance of the difference. I have done the same thing for n. Of the 38 instances for RR, 37 are positive and one negative. For n, the corresponding values are 12 and 26. We have a good many other data which would show the same directional differences. These comparisons clearly suggest that recall (n) may change in a direction different from organization (RR).

I have made only one analysis in terms of fate of items on second recall as a function of their being recalled in clusters or as single items on first recall. The data were obtained in an RI experiment[6] and data from the control group are shown in Table 8.9. This table shows that 15% - 18% of the words

TABLE 8.9   Fate on Second Recall of Items Recalled Singly or in Clusters on First Recall (Control Group in Cofer, see footnote 6)

First Recall	Single Words	Clustered Words
N	136	306
Second Recall		
As single words	47 (35%)	46 (15%)
In clusters	64 (47%)	215 (70%)
Dropped	25 (18%)	45 (15%)

recalled on first recall, whether as single words or in clusters, are dropped in second recall. Appearing in a cluster at first recall, then, does little to maintain an item's place in second recall. About half the single words from first recall do enter clusters at second recall, and this probably accounts for the general increase in clustering at second recall as shown in Table 8.8. But this reorganization is not necessarily associated with an increment in recall, as I have shown. Whether the items that enter into clusters at second recall are "protected" from being forgotten by being clustered is a possibility which only further research can evaluate.

[6] These data are taken from Retroactive interference, retention and clustering in free recall, Technical Report No. 3 under contract Nonr 595(04) between the Office of Naval Research and the University of Maryland.

Use of Cues in Retrieval

Some writers (Tulving, 1966; Bilodeau, 1966) have suggested that in free recall items may well be in storage but that the retrieval process is at fault when they do not appear overtly in recall. It has been suggested that use of appropriate cues (e.g., category names) may permit retrieval of items which otherwise would not appear. This is an interesting and useful suggestion. It does, however, run into some methodological problems, mainly the control condition against which such cued retrieval is to be compared. I have run one experiment which illustrates the difficulties.

Experiment 5 [7]

Method. Six lists were chosen from Deese's set (*HF* Butterfly and Slow, *LF* Music and Whistle, and *ZF* Command and Chair). They were not presented to *S*s, instead for each list *S* was told the list name (which he wrote down) and then was told to write down 5 additional items from dictation. These were the first, fourth, sixth, ninth, and twelfth members of the list in terms of their serial positions as listed by Deese. Then *S* was told that the name and the 5 items were from a list which consisted of 15 items and that he was to add 10 items which, with the ones given, could be list members. Twenty-eight *S*s performed this task on the 6 lists in turn, and the items were scored correct if they were among the 10 list members that were not presented.

Results. "Correct" responses were added as shown in Table 8.10.
Clearly the number of "correct" responses achieved is related to the inter-item associative strength of the list. The point is that for inter-associated and probably categorized items the presentation of cues to recall may activate items whether they were presented or not. It is difficult to know,

---

[7] The description of Experiment 5 is much abridged from Generation of list items without list presentation as a function of inter-item associative strength, Technical Report No. 9 under contract Nonr 285(47) between the office of Naval Research and New York University, 1962.

therefore, whether the items are being retrieved from a memory store or from a verbal hierarchy which exists independently of the presentation of a particular list.

TABLE 8.10   Mean Number of "Correct" Responses Added in Presence of List Name and Five List Members

Frequency Level	List	Mean Correct
High	Butterfly	2.60
High	Slow	1.80
Low	Music	1.00
Low	Whistle	0.35
Zero	Command	0.00
Zero	Chair	0.00

We have also examined the items produced by the Ss in this experiment to comply with the task imposed upon them. Associates to the 5 sample list members were used with some frequency, especially in the HF lists and the ZF lists, and in both cases this occurred more often than it did for the same lists following their actual presentation. This lends some support to the assertion made earlier that, after list presentation, there appears to be a hesitation to employ list member associates freely, presumably because they do not, in some sense, fit in with the general character of the list which the presentation of the list establishes.

CONCLUDING COMMENTS

The evidence I have presented seems to me to be consistent with three assertions so far as the situations I have described are concerned:

1. Inter-item associations provide the major basis for variations in amount recalled, for lists composed of categorized items as well as those composed of sets of associates to the list name.

2. A major factor associated with the failure of recall to approximate list length is the serial position effect. The presence of this effect in the recognition data, as well as in the recall data, may be compatible with an interpretation that mid-list items fail to some extent to enter storage,

although other interpretations are certainly possible. I am sure that one could find, by judicious selection of distractors, perfect recognition scores for lists presented under circumstances like those I have described.

3. Contextual or conceptual factors do not seem to be involved in recall of correct items. Rather, they impose a restriction on the kinds of responses S will generate in attempting to match list length, such that the responses added are relevant to, but not members of, the pool of items presented.

I would like to make a few further comments pertinent to these points. First, I wish to clarify that the three assertions I have made may not apply to all free recall situations. Elsewhere (Cofer, 1966) I have presented data indicating that pairs of words the members of which are easily categorized together (e.g., *crow*, *eagle*) are better recalled and cluster more than pairs of words of equal associative overlap which are not easily categorized together (e.g., *soft silk*). Here a conceptual factor clearly operates, and its nature may well be that categorized words are easy to link together by a code name as compared with the non-categorized words.

Second, in the multitrial free recall learning situation it may well be that the formation of subjective units, to use Tulving's (1962) term, may function to overcome the deleterious effects of serial position. The units developed may be well-integrated, through the practice that a number of trials provide; there is some evidence, in Fig. 8.1 especially, that the serial position curves for *HF* lists are distorted chiefly in the middle positions, showing higher scores for these lists there than is the case for the *LF* and *ZF* lists. Perhaps organization, whether associative, conceptual, or subjective, operates in such a way as to circumvent the effects of serial position and thus to permit more items to enter storage or to be retrieved than would otherwise be the case. I have a hypothesis, which cannot be explored further here, that the role of grammar may be to group the items in sentences so as to permit the information-carrying words to be stored despite the effects of serial position.

Finally, it seems important to mention that interference is likely to be a potent reason for the failure of recall to represent list length or of forced recall to provide many correct responses. When subjects are required to match list length, it is clear, as we have seen, that they do use associates and high-frequency associates of the category name (in Travelet's experiment), even though they do so with some selectivity. It is perhaps not too much to postulate that these responses "get in the way," either at list presentation (cf. Underwood, 1965) or at recall, of the correct items which are not found in recall. There is an interesting possibility that such interference may be greater for mid-list than for end-of-the list items, but whether this is a fact and, if it is a fact, why it should be so are problems that remain to be explored.

That this kind of interference may be important is indicated by the results of a recent experiment reported by Blick (1965). Blick selected sets of K-R stimulus words and then exposed his Ss to 2 lists of 5 words each. The first list was composed of high-frequency associates to the stimulus words and the second list of less frequent associates to the same stimuli. After study of these lists and a 2-minute filled interval following the study of the second list, S was asked to recall the second list in the presence of the appropriate K-R stimuli. First-list responses intruded into this recall and did so as a function of the free-association frequency of the first list members. In some Ss, Blick (1965, p. 249) says, "intrusions of primaries were total (100%)." Blick's procedure is one which probably maximizes the appearance of overt intrusions in the recall of List 2, but it seems likely that this is just an extreme case of what may go on under other circumstances.

An interesting possibility for the study of conceptual processes in recall would be to repeat Blick's experiment in such a way that the List 2 members were conceptually related but so that the List 1 primaries were not. It might indicate the power of the influence of the concept or context on response selection if under this arrangement intrusions of List 1 responses did not occur or were much diminished in frequency. But the association variable might be seen to operate anyway if, under these conditions, omissions or response failures were prominent features of List 2 "recall."

CHAPTER 9

Arthur W. Melton
University of Michigan

DECISION PROCESSES IN RETRIEVAL
FROM MEMORY: Comment on
the Contributions of
Lloyd R. Peterson and Charles N. Cofer

There is much in the papers by Professors Cofer and Peterson that deserves favorable comment, but in the interests of brevity I will concentrate of Professor Peterson's model of the process of recall in studies of verbal learning and memory. Professor Cofer's contribution will enter this discussion as important supporting evidence on some issues I detect in the model for retrieval from memory as presented by Peterson. Those who are familiar with my S-R associationistic biases will, of course, recognize that I am quite sympathetic with his modified-modified stone-age approach to memory and the data Cofer brings to its support. On the other hand, Peterson's notion that there is an "editor" inserted between the implicit response to a stimulus and the overt response to it is an alerting stimulus to a stone-age memory theorist, whether modified, or modified-modified.

Peterson is concerned with the processes that occur between the presentation of a stimulus and the overt occurrence of a response, right or wrong, in a subject's attempt to recall a response previously paired one or more times with the stimulus. His first concern is to show that implicit responses to stimuli in this testing for memory by a recall procedure are not necessarily expressed in overt vocal or written responses, that is, there is a lack of one-to-one correspondence between implicit and overt responses to a stimulus. This leads to the notion that overt responses are the outcome of an "editing" process, and this is further specified as a decision process in which the criterion is "judged correctness of the response to that stimulus." This criterion is said to be based on a recognition memory process.

A necessary feature of this model is that there is more

than one implicit response to the stimulus, which enables the decision mechanisms to draw again from the memory store whenever an implicit response does not satisfy the subject's criterion of recognized correctness. Therefore, the overt response is an end-product of the sequential sampling of the store of available implicit responses. The latency of the overt response is taken as a simple linear function of the number of implicit responses which are tested before the overt response is made; overt errors are implicit responses which are accepted as "correct" for some reason that relates to their discriminability from the correct responses. However, both correct and incorrect responses are emitted with varying degrees of confidence in correctness, and this confidence can be assessed by direct questioning of the subject.

This is an attractive conceptualization of the processes involved in the voluntary recall of a response term in a paired-associate learning task following the presentation of the stimulus. We are indebted to Peterson for his sketch of the model as well as for his emphasis on a relatively neglected aspect of the functioning of memory. I suspect that the refinement of this or some other model of the process of retrieval from memory that results in overt oral or written responses will be one of the main foci of research on long-term and short-term memory during the next few years. Peterson has also sketched the methods and results of several ingenious efforts to obtain independent measures of the pre-decision array of implicit responses and the post-decision assessment of the correctness of the emitted response. As with some other methodological inventions that can be traced to him (e.g., Peterson and Peterson, 1959; Peterson, Saltzman, Hillner and Land, 1962), I suspect that these new methods will either be adopted and refined or encourage the invention of other methods to achieve the same kind of input-output analysis with respect to the editing or decision function.

It seems to me that some decision process which might be called "editing" surely occurs in the recall of partially learned associations between stimulus objects and verbal responses, just as it occurs in the utilization of previously learned categories, concepts, relations, or specific responses in new higher-order learning such as concept attainment and problem-solving. Unless this were so, there would be no proper basis for distinguishing between thought and action, nor perhaps even between implicit and overt responses. Our civilization could never have developed if man always automatically said what he thought, never reserved judgment and action until alternatives had been examined, nor experienced uncertainty about the appropriateness of any overt response. One may even maintain that if there were a one-to-one relationship between implicit verbal responses and overt verbal responses, the adaptive utility of language would be so slight that man might have failed to develop this important mechanism for thought and a variety of intellectual skills.

The idea that our theory of verbal learning and remembering should encompass hypothetical process components—or "sub-phenomena" as Underwood (1964) calls them—should also elicit little resistance among neobehavioristic S-R associationists. This is the age of analysis in the study of human verbal learning and performance, and the analysis takes the form of inferring that apparently unitary processes are in fact composed of sub-processes. This kind of thinking about verbal learning and memory has been going on quite explicitly ever since McGeoch and McKinney (1937) hypothesized that retroactive inhibition was interpretable as reproductive inhibition (competition of responses at the time of attempted recall). It was furthered by the hypothesis that "unlearning" was involved differentially in retroactive and proactive inhibition (Melton and Irwin, 1940; Melton and VonLackum, 1941), by the hypothesis that conditioning processes were involved as sub-processes in paired-associate learning (Gibson, 1940), and by the distinction between stimulus processes and response processes in the analysis of transfer paradigms (Osgood, 1949). Most recently this analysis of component processes is well represented in the widely accepted multiprocess model of paired-associate learning (Mandler, 1954; McGuire, 1961; Underwood and Schulz, 1960) which requires separate consideration of stimulus learning, response learning, and S-R "hook-up" in any predictions about learning and retention of paired associates. Recent applications of signal-detection theory to recognition memory also imply sub-processes (e.g., Parks, 1966).

Contemporary association theory accepts the need for sub-process analysis. Therefore, Peterson's model, which inserts a decision process between elicited implicit responses and emitted overt responses, may be thought of as a further extension of this analytic approach. At the level of theory, it may or may not be consistent with basic tenets of S-R association theory. Our response to his model should be directed toward its refinement in the customary give-and-take that scientists engage in when they recognize that an important concept has been identified, but they are uncertain about the details of its operation and application.

It is in this spirit that I wish to make two points that relate in one way or another to the deceptive simplicity of Peterson's model, as sketched in his Fig. 7.8 and as discussed in the associated text. This deceptive simplicity derives from the fact that he has a great deal to say about the way in which the decision process operates on the store of available responses in memory, and very little to say about either (a) what determines whether the stimuli are distinctively coded or the responses are available in the memory store, or (b) how the variations in stimulus coding and response availability affect the outcome of the decision process. One is left, therefore, with the implication that the principal selective factor in paired-associate learning is the decision process based on recognition of the belongingness [I use the term advisedly, in order to elicit associations with Thorndike's (1932) concept] of a discriminated stimulus term and the set of available responses that may be scanned until the correct "match" is obtained.

My first point is that it seems highly likely that the characteristics of the decision process involved in emission of overt responses may be quite different in various associative learning tasks that differ with respect to the requirements for stimulus coding, response integration, and "hook-up" of the coded stimulus and integrated response terms. The multiprocess model of paired-associate learning that most S-R associationists now accept may be symbolized as follows:

$$S_a \qquad\qquad S_a$$
$$r_1(s_1) \ ----\!\!\!> \ r_a(s_a) \ ----\!\!\!> R_a$$

where S_1 is the nominal stimulus object, r_1 is the relatively invariant implicit coding or identifying response to it, s_1 is the stimulus function of this coding response, $r_a(s_a)$ is the implicit coding or identifying response that must become associated with s_1 through contiguous occurrence of S_1 and S_a, and R_a is the overt expression of r_a vocally, in writing, or by some other differentiated response. The point of the multiprocess model is that there are at least 4 learning processes potentially involved in the elicitation of R_a by S_1: (1) coding of S_1 by a relatively invariant response (r_1) and functional stimulus (s_1), (2) the integration and coding of the implicit response term (r_a) through its elicitation by S_a, (3) the association between r_a (s_a) and the appropriate overt response (R_a), and (4) the "hook-up" of r_1 (s_1) and r_a (s_a).

It should be noted that, in this multiprocess model of S-R associative learning, the integration of a novel complex response term into a unitary response term (r_a) is a serial-learning process embedded within the overall paired-associate learning process. This response learning sub-process is directly studied in the case of sub-memory-span units (e.g., TKR) of the kind frequently employed in paired-associate lists, either by the short-term recall method Peterson refers to (Peterson and Gentile, 1965; Wickens, Born and Allen, 1963), or by the method of free recall following free learning (of the kind described in Cofer's paper) or paired-associate learning (e.g., Ekstrand, 1966). In all such methods, the recall is made without benefit of the presentation of an appropriate unique nominal stimulus term, and is presumed to be based on associations between contextual stimuli and the implicit response (r_a). There is, of course, other functional evidence for the existence of such contextual associations (Barnes and Underwood, 1959; McGovern, 1964). Peterson's reference to short-term memory studies implies that his model is appropriate to response learning to contextual cues in the free recall situation.

The point I wish to make from this digression into the multiprocess theory of associative learning (and this digression is an incomplete statement of that theory) is a simple one, but not, in my opinion, a trivial one. It is that the model must be examined in associative learning tasks that involve stimulus learning and/or response learning, as well as in those that involve the association of already well-differentiated and recognized stimulus terms and already well-integrated response terms. Let us not, once again, commit the costly error of assuming the constancy or invariance of a process—in this case, the "editing" process—over a class of learning processes which is known to have marked intraclass hetero-geneity (Carr, 1933; Melton, 1964).

Secondly I wish to question the emphasis Peterson places on the selective function of the decision process that intervenes between the elicited implicit response (r_a) and the emitted overt response (R_a). The operation of a number of selective factors in overt recall is localized in the "editing" process rather than in the elicitation of the "available" set of implicit responses on which the editing process operates by means of a recognition matching process. An alternative view, and one that is implicit in the S-R associationistic theory as repre-sented in the multiprocess model, is that a principal deter-minant of the selection of the overt response (R_a) is the selec-tion of the implicit response (r_a) by the stimulus events that precede it.

This issue is well illustrated by the statements made by Peterson about the Wickens, Born and Allen (1963) experiment in which it was shown that there was almost complete release from proactive inhibition in short-term memory for a sub-span to-be-remembered unit when it was preceded by units of a different class. Of this phenomenon Peterson says: "It does not seem likely that the availability of the previous items de-creased as a result of the new class (of items) being used. Rather, it seems that subjects can remember class member-ship, that letters were used in the most recent test, and they can edit their responses on the basis of the information." The same kind of interpretation is made of the steady state of proactive inhibition in short-term memory for trigrams (Loess, 1964) after the first 3 or 4 such trigrams have been presented and recalled, but here the argument is that those trigrams that are more than 3 or 4 back in the series can be discriminated on the basis of temporal tags or recency, and so do not contribute to overt intrusions. The same kind of interpretation is again applied to the lack of intrusions in recall in the retroactive inhibition experiment in which the response terms in the two paired-associate lists are from different classes (letters and digits), and to the whole concept of list differentiation in the interpretation of retroactive and proactive inhibition. While I do not wish to exaggerate Peterson's posi-tion, to me, his words mean that strong but wrong responses occur in the available memory store, as elicited by antecedent stimulus events, but are rejected by applying the editing process. While an association theorist would grant that some few [or many, depending on the lack of differentiation of the antecedent stimulus coding responses, $r_1(s_1)$]such wrong responses would occur in the available memory store and would need to be examined by the editing process, he would, I think, need to insist that the fundamental selection in such learning and recall is the selection of the pool of implicit responses (r_a) that can be traced to the coding of the antecedent stimulus events $[r_1(s_1)]$. It should, of course, be possible to test these different interpretations, especially if one accepts the Peterson thesis that the latency of the correct or incorrect overt response (R_a) is a linear function of the number of implicit responses that are examined before the overt response is emitted. Unfortunately, we do not have latency of response data under the conditions that are required for testing these notions. One important consequence of Peterson's paper is that henceforward the recording and analysis of latencies of overt responses in memory studies will be as necessary as the recording and analysis of erroneous intrusions.

Another way of describing the problem I see in Peterson's overloading of the "editing" process with selective functions is the location there of all discrimination of differences between available competing responses. Particularly enlightening in this connection are the failures of discrimination which result in the emission of overt erroneous intrusions in short-term memory. In the case of the recall of word triads, Loess (1965) has shown that the release from proactive inhibition that Wickens, Born, and Allen (1963) demonstrated by shifting from trigrams to 3-digit numbers also occurs when there is a shift from one concept category (e.g., metals) to another (e.g., furniture). Further, Noyd (1965) has shown that the recall of a string of 2, 3, or 5 unrelated nouns after short intervals of time reflects (a) the coding of each string in terms of its length, and (b) the coding of each word in a string in terms of its serial position. Thus, there is more proactive interference, as measured either by the number of words correctly recalled or by the number of erroneous intrusions from the preceding stimulus, when a 3-word stimulus is preceded by a 3-word stimulus than when it is preceded by a 2-word or 5-word stimulus. Also, when 2 successive stimuli are the same length, there is a very high correlation between the serial position of occurrence of an intrusion and the serial position that intruding word had when it was a part of the to-be-remembered stimulus element. At the very least, therefore, the data available on determinants of proactive inhibition in short-term memory for verbal units suggest that the list of discriminanda would contain the following: Formal class of material, serial position, length of stimulus, semantic category, acoustic confusability, and perhaps temporal position in the recent experience of the subject. With respect to these discriminanda, Peterson's model raises the question whether they serve as the basis for decision during the editing process or as the basis for coding of the stimulus antecedents of the implicit response (r_a) at the time of storage. My bias is to build such complex multidimensional determination of the implicit response (r_a) into its eliciting antecedents, rather than into a monitoring of the transmission from the implicit response to the overt response. But again, it will be necessary to have latency data, at the very least, if we are to obtain evidence on this point.

An issue of considerable importance relating to the role of intrusions in recall deserves mention here because Peterson appears to gain confidence in his notion of "editing" from data that show a lack of covariation of the frequencies of intrusions and correct responses. In his RI study with variation of the time interval between List 2 and the recall of List 1, he notes that the frequency of overt intrusions (from List 2) increased as the interval increased, but that "there was no significant difference in the number correct." In his experiment in which List 1 and List 2 had response terms from the same or different classes (letters versus digits), there were no intrusions when different classes were used and many intrusions when the same class was used, but again he notes that "there was no significant difference in the number of correct responses."

Unfortunately, Peterson does not examine the implications of his model with respect to the role of overt intrusions in forgetting. The S-R associative interference theory of forgetting would, in the context of his model, place one locus of interference in the elicitation of implicit responses $(r_a \ldots r_z)$ and a second locus in the recognition-decision process that controls the emitted response. The first is a reproductive inhibition process associated with response elicitation, the second a reproductive inhibition process associated with recognition memory. Both imply that the frequency of occurrence of overt intrusions, that is, errors that may be traced to some stimulus similarity factor, covaries negatively with the frequency of overt correct responses. Intrusions displace correct responses. On the other hand, there is currently a theory (Conrad, 1964) which considers such intrusion errors to be epiphenomena; intrusions occur because the correct response is forgotten. In common with Peterson, this theory appeals to a failure of discrimination in the "editing" process to explain why intrusions show similarity relations to the correct response. Instances of intrusions varying in number while correct responses remain constant are, of course, prime support for such an interpretation (e.g., Conrad, 1960).

Peterson seems to be following this latter line of thought about intrusions. If this is his position, I would object on three counts. First, his new evidence should be reported in more detail before acceptance. Acceptance of the null hypothesis about notoriously variable recall scores is especially risky. Second, Peterson's RI experiment with the same or different response classes has been performed by Postman, Keppel and Stark (1965), and the frequencies of intrusions and correct recalls clearly covary negatively in their data. Finally, one may question whether Peterson's model would predict no covariation of number of overt intrusions and number of correct responses. If there is the possibility that incorrect responses can be elicited as members of the set of implicit responses $(r_a \ldots r_Z)$ that is available for scanning, and if there is some fallibility of the recognition process, such that the wrong response may be recognized as "correct" even though the set of available implicit responses contains the truly correct response, it would seem that the occurrence of an overt intrusion necessarily implies the loss of an opportunity to make the correct response. Also, specific testable predictions about the latencies of intrusions, correct responses, and "guessing" responses should be possible. Since Peterson does not consider such implications in depth, no purpose will be served by discussing them here, but I do urge their immediate consideration in both theory and experiment.

Before leaving the Peterson paper, one final comment should be made in further support of the utility of the multiprocess analysis of associative learning, and of the importance of stimulus variables in the selection of responses. The multi-process model assumes a stimulus learning or coding process which becomes involved whenever stimuli are presented that are not yet distinctively coded. Martin (in press) has shown that stimulus recognition is a necessary condition for the elicitation of the paired response term in the learning of CCC-digit pairs. His study involved a study-test method in which the test trials involved the presentation of new CCCs as well as the CCCs to which the responses had been trained on study trials. Recognition of the stimuli of the list as "old" gained over trials, and recognition of high-meaningful CCCs was better than recognition of low-meaningful CCCs, but throughout learning, the emission of the correct response occurred with non-chance frequency only when the stimulus had been recognized as "old." Bernbach (1965) has confirmed this finding in a continuous paired-associate task with the same materials. The involvement of this stimulus recognition or identification process in all learning, and its fallibility, appears to be an important refinement of the component of the multiprocess model of S-R associative learning referred to in the concepts of stimulus selection (Underwood, 1963), stimulus discrimination (McGuire, 1961), and stimulus coding (Lawrence, 1963).

Thus far, nothing has been said about Cofer's paper. This is because Peterson's paper touched a sensitive nerve (some might call it a soft spot) in an old associationist. Cofer's did not; in fact, Cofer's thesis, and his carefully marshalled evidence for it, soothed that nerve. His evidence for the effect of categorization of stimulus input at the time of storage in memory, rather than at the time of retrieval, is quite congruent with the position I have taken regarding the role of the coded stimulus $[r_i(s_i)]$ in the selectivity of retrieval processes. Further, he shows that the effect of categories on storage and retrieval, including the intrusions in the latter process, seem best interpreted in terms of inter-item associations, rather than through some magic of cognitive organization. His thesis and data agree with inferences derived from analyses of short-term memory in which the proactive interference observed can be traced to the categorization of input in terms of the length of the stimulus, the serial position of an element within the stimulus, semantic categories, and acoustic categories.

In conclusion, Peterson and Cofer have brought forcefully

to our attention the need for focussing research and theory on the processes involved in retrieval from memory. Parallel studies of recall and recognition will certainly play an important role in this analysis, as will judgments of confidence and measurements of latencies of response. It is to be hoped that these efforts to "unpack" the retrieval process will make full use of the insights and technology that have developed over the last ten years as we unpacked the paired-associate learning process and arrived at the multiprocess model of it. A rapprochement of S-R association and cognitive theories is, it seems to me, a likely outcome of this focus of our efforts.

CHAPTER **10**   *Calvin F. Nodine*

Carnegie Institute of Technology

THE ROLE OF TEMPORAL VARIABLES IN THE ACQUISITION OF CONCEPTS*

Certain similarities, from a methodological viewpoint, exist between verbal and concept-learning tasks when presentation of stimuli is controlled by the experimenter. The purpose of this paper is to consider the role of two classes of temporal variables of presentation common to both these tasks. One class of intratrial temporal variables is referred to as stimulus durations and the other as stimulus intervals. Until recently intratrial temporal variables have received little attention in verbal learning tasks, and have been largely neglected in concept-learning tasks (e.g., Bourne and Restle, 1959; Bower and Trabasso, 1964).

In verbal learning, stimulus durations and stimulus intervals, more generally referred to as "rate of presentation," have been shown to influence the acquisition of paired-associates over a wide range of time values (e.g., Nodine, 1963; Nodine and Nodine, 1966; Nodine, Nodine, and Thomas, in press). The generality of these findings extends to acquisition and recall in other verbal learning situations such as serial learning (e.g., Keppel and Rehula, 1965) and connected meaningful learning (e.g., King, Cole, Kinsey, and Sheffers, 1966; Rothkopf and Coke, 1966). Performance in each of these situations has been found to improve as rate of presentation decreases when conventional dependent measures are used (e.g., trials to criterion, number of correct responses, and number of errors). Total learning time, however, has frequently been found invariant with respect to presentation rate (e.g., Bugelski, 1962; Nodine, 1965; Keppel and Rehula, 1965).

Preparation of this paper was facilitated by Public Health Service Research Grants MH 11974-02 *and MH* 07722 *from the National Institute of Mental Health.*

Experimenter-controlled paradigms have been widely used in concept-learning tasks.[1] Certain of these have been borrowed directly or with minor modifications from paired-associates learning and have involved the anticipation format (e.g., Oseas and Underwood, 1952; Underwood and Richardson, 1956; Lloyd, 1960; Richardson, 1960). The major advantage of using paired-associates procedures in concept learning is that the experimenter is able to exercise precise control over temporal and sequential aspects of stimulus presentation which have been demonstrated to be important factors determining rate of acquisition of concepts. Goss (1966) has elaborated, the advantages of using the paired-associates situation for the study of verbal learning phenomena.

Despite certain methodological similarities between paired-associates learning and concept learning, there are important differences in what is learned in the two situations. In both cases, the subject's assignment is to learn how stimuli are related. But, as Goss (1961) pointed out, one-to-one stimulus-response relationships are learned in the paired-associates task, whereas n-to-one relationships are learned in conceptual tasks. He and other investigators have labeled this latter situation as acquired equivalence (Goss, 1955), convergent, or S_1-R, S_2-R (Wittlinger and Voss, 1964).

Musgrave, Cohen, and Stewart (1966) have further extended the n-to-one notion by distinguishing between superordinate labels (response items common to m subsets of n stimulus items) and subordinate labels (response items unique to single subsets of n stimulus items). Musgrave, et al., using a paired-associates procedure, showed that subjects can simultaneously acquire both superordinate and subordinate labels in a verbal hierarchy. Thus, by experimentally manipulating the ratio of stimulus and response elements using the paired-associates procedure, it is possible to establish in the laboratory n-to-one associations between stimulus and response events which form verbal response hierarchies.

The remainder of this paper will consider in detail the

---

[1]Experiment procedures designed to investigate the acquisition of concepts can be categorized generally as involving the presentation of stimuli which are either primarily experimenter-controlled or subject-controlled (e.g., Bruner, Goodnow, and Austin, 1956). The present paper will deal almost exclusively with experimenter-controlled presentation procedures.

role of intratrial temporal variables by comparing effects of these variables on acquisition and short-term retention in paired-associates and concept-learning situations.

BACKGROUND OF THE PROBLEM

Although some interest has been shown concerning the effects of temporal aspects of presentation of stimuli on acquisition and retention of concepts, it is interesting to note certain basic methodological differences in approach to this problem between investigators of concept learning and those of verbal learning. The basic impetus to research on the effects of temporal variables of presentation in concept learning can be traced to Underwood's (1952) paper in which he advanced the theoretical argument that response contiguity is fundamental to concept learning. Response contiguity refers, according to the theory, to temporal contiguity between the subject's responses to several instances of the same concept. Underwood specifies that response contiguity may be increased by either: (a) decreasing the time between trials in which instances of a given concept are presented (e.g., shortening the intertrial interval as in massed practice) or; (b) decreasing the number of instances of different concepts intervening between a given (same) concept, referred to hereafter as instance contiguity. Increasing time between trials or number of intervening concepts reduces response contiguity. Such reductions in response contiguity result in slower concept acquisition presumably as a consequence of intertrial forgetting in the former case or "interference" in the latter case. Dominowski (1965) has reviewed most of the research which has tested Underwood's theoretical notions. Most studies of massed versus spaced practice involving manipulation of the intertrial interval have failed to find consistent differences favoring massed practice in support of Underwood's predictions. Furthermore, a recent finding by Bourne, Guy, Dodd, and Justesen (1965) suggests optimum intertrial intervals in concept learning increase, rather than decrease, with task difficulty. Interestingly, massed versus distributed practice has also been shown to be ineffective in verbal learning (e.g., Underwood, 1961; Underwood, Ekstrand and Keppel, 1964), although the prediction in verbal learning is opposite (i.e., favors distributed practice over massed practice) that for concept learning.

DESCRIPTION OF TEMPORAL VARIABLES
IN CONCEPT LEARNING

Several variables, besides the intertrial interval, involving temporal relations among stimulus events have been investigated in concept learning. These intratrial temporal parameters are described in Fig. 10.1. Two sequences of concept presentation are illustrated in Fig. 10.1; Homogeneous or unmixed presentation in which instances of the same concept are presented on a single trial (e.g., BEET, CORN, CABBAGE, and BEAN which are all instances of the same concept GAX); and heterogeneous or mixed presentation in which 4 instances of different concepts are presented on a single trial (e.g., BEET which is an instance of the concept GAX, GRANITE which is an instance of the concept ROQ, POODLE which is an instance of the concept DAG, and ROSE which is an instance of the concept ZEL). The heterogeneous presentation is shown in parentheses.

Intratrial temporal variables in Fig. 10.1 are designated a-d and include (a) exposure duration of a stimulus representing a concept instance (stimulus duration), (b) interval separating presentation of concept instance from joint presentation of concept instance and stimulus representing concept response or label (interstimulus interval), (c) exposure duration of joint presentation of concept instance and concept label (pair duration), and (d) interval separating joint presentation of concept instance and concept label from succeeding stimulus representing same (or different) concept instance (interunit interval). The intertrial temporal variable is designated (e) interval separating joint presentation of concept instance and concept label on trial n from different (or same) concept instance on trial $n + 1$ (intertrial interval). Note that under homogeneous presentation response contiguity is determined primarily by the interunit interval. On the other hand, under heterogeneous presentation response contiguity is primarily determined by the number of different concept instances intervening between a given concept. In this latter case, the interunit interval decreases as a factor as the number of

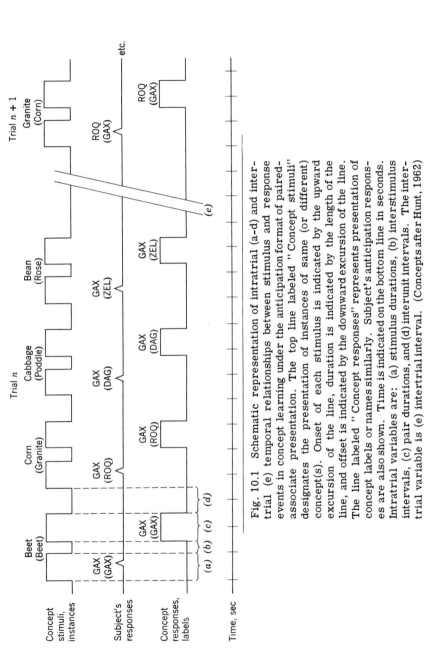

Fig. 10.1 Schematic representation of intratrial (a–d) and inter-trial (e) temporal relationships between stimulus and response events in concept learning under the anticipation format of paired-associate presentation. The top line labeled "Concept stimuli" designates the presentation of instances of same (or different) concept(s). Onset of each stimulus is indicated by the upward excursion of the line, duration is indicated by the length of the line, and offset is indicated by the downward excursion of the line. The line labeled "Concept responses" represents presentation of concept labels or names similarly. Subject's anticipation responses are also shown. Time is indicated on the bottom line in seconds. Intratrial variables are: (a) stimulus durations, (b) interstimulus intervals, (c) pair durations, and (d) interunit intervals. The inter-trial variable is (e) intertrial interval. (Concepts after Hunt, 1962)

intervening concept instances increases.

Other intratrial and intertrial temporal variables are derivable from Fig. 10.1 (e.g., total trial time, total learning time, etc.) and distinctions can be made among the intratrial temporal relationships under anticipation and recall formats of presentation. These temporal relationships are considered in detail elsewhere (Nodine, 1966). It would be premature, at this point, to speculate on the specific roles of each of the intratrial temporal variables in concept learning. It can be generally assumed, however, based on effects of stimulus durations and stimulus intervals in paired-associates learning, that pair durations and interunit intervals are particularly critical for learning. It is during these periods that subjects are able to compare the relationship between a present concept instance and concept label and relate this to past information about other instances of the same concept. Limiting stimulus durations and/or interstimulus intervals imposes restrictions on the amount of time given to the subject to anticipate the correct concept label which should influence performance but not necessarily learning.

In Fig. 10.1, the terms concept stimuli and concept responses are used to denote the fact that these stimuli are manipulatively separable into initiating stimuli and stimuli for responses without specifying their function. In the paired-associates situation, however, such stimuli are regarded as functional in that each stimulus term functions as an initiating stimulus to a (stimulus for) response term.

The outline of temporal parameters of presentation in concept learning is an extension of an earlier analysis by the author of temporal parameters of presentation in paired-associates learning (Nodine and Nodine, 1966). It should be noted that the paired-associates paradigm does not have to be limited to experimenter-supplied responses, but can also include subject-supplied responses which may or may not be designated correct or incorrect by the experimenter (e.g., Bourne, 1966). In Bourne's analysis of concept learning the stimulus-response elements and temporal relationships remain essentially unchanged, except for the Informative-Feedback (I-F) interval, which is defined by the subject's response rather than manipulated by the experimenter. Such a definition precludes its usefulness under the experimenter-controlled paradigm. For example, Bourne refers to three intratrial events; stimulus, response, and informative feedback in concept-learning tasks. Three basic temporal variables are derived from his analysis: (1) Stimulus interval which is equivalent to stimulus duration in Fig. 10.1; (2) Informative-Feedback or I-F interval which is measured from the subject's response to presentation of feedback and is equivalent to interstimulus interval plus some portion of the stimulus duration remaining after the subject's response; and (3) Post Informative-Feedback or Post I-F interval which is equivalent to the interunit interval.

Temporal Variables and Instance Contiguity

It is interesting to note that most tests of Underwood's response contiguity notions, other than those already mentioned involving the intertrial interval, have manipulated time between responses to instances of a given concept by inserting instances of other concepts, (e.g., Newman, 1956), rather than by manipulating time between presentations of instances of the same or different concepts by varying intratrial temporal variables outlined in Fig. 10.1. Notable exceptions to this statement are experiments by Peterson (1962), Bourne (1957), and Bourne and Bunderson (1963) which will be considered below.

Studies involving effects of instance contiguity (e.g., Richardson, 1962) have been reviewed in detail by Dominowski. In general, Underwood's prediction of faster concept learning under conditions of greater instance contiguity have been supported. The question of whether facilitation in concept learning due to instance contiguity is the result of shorter temporal intervals between instances of the same concept, or fewer instances of different intervening concepts have been explored by Peterson (1962). Her findings suggest that slower concept learning associated with lengthening of the interval between instances of a concept under heterogeneous or mixed presentation is due to interference from the presentation of instances of other concepts or the introduction of an interpolated task rather than a decrease in temporal contiguity per se.

Effects of Intratrial Temporal Variables in Concept Learning

Bourne (1957), and Bourne and Bunderson (1963) have investigated intratrial temporal variables in order to understand their role in concept learning. Bourne's earlier study manipulated the I-F interval over values of 0, .5, 1, 2, 4, and 8 seconds. He found that as the I-F interval increased, performance decreased, and that this effect became more pronounced as task complexity increased. Because of a confounding of I-F interval and Post I-F interval in this experiment, Bourne and Bunderson undertook a second experiment in which they combined 3 I-F intervals; 0, 4, and 8 seconds with 3 Post I-F intervals; 1, 5, and 9 seconds in a 3 x 3 x 2 factorial design which also included 2 levels of task complexity. The results of this study indicated that the effects of I-F interval on performance in the earlier study could be largely attributed to failure to control Post I-F interval since performance was found to increase directly with Post I-F interval and interact as in the earlier study with task complexity, but no systematic effects on performance were found as a function of I-F interval.

The failure of I-F intervals to influence performance and the direct relationship between Post I-F intervals and performance is in direct contradiction to Underwood's predictions since lengthening either interval decreases response contiguity. The data are also at variance with the instance contiguity data. These data show that shortening intervals between instances of the same concept by decreasing the number of intervening concepts is associated with faster acquisition than lengthening such intervals by increasing the number of intervening concepts between instances of the same concept. It is apparent that lengthening intervals between stimulus-response events by filling them with additional stimulus-response events, particularly when these intervening events are also relevant to the task, is quite different from lengthening intervals which remain unfilled or contain interpolated events not relevant to the task (e.g., color naming, digit cancellation, number tracking, etc.).

Effects of Temporal Variables in Paired-Associates Learning

One obvious conclusion which would help to reconcile the

differences between the instance contiguity data and the results of manipulating intratrial temporal variables is that subjects utilize unfilled intervals in the latter case to rehearse. The interunit interval (Post *I-F* interval) would be particularly sensitive to increases in opportunities for rehearsal since subjects can review the present instance-concept relation as well as past relations involving instances of the same concept. A similar conclusion was generated by the author in a recent paired-associates learning study (Nodine, Nodine, and Thomas, in press) in which orthogonal combinations of interstimulus and interunit intervals of 0, 2, and 4 seconds were investigated under three task conditions: Inhibited Rehearsal, in which the intervals were filled with number tracking; Controlled Rehearsal, in which the intervals were filled with overt repetitions of the paired-associate items; and Free Rehearsal, in which the intervals remained unfilled. A mixed listing containing two levels of difficulty, hard and easy, was acquired by all subjects. Performance was found to increase directly with stimulus intervals, particularly interunit intervals. However, interval effects were attenuated in the order Free Rehearsal > Controlled Rehearsal > Inhibited Rehearsal, and more pronounced for hard than easy items in the same direction. These findings are interpreted as supporting the notion that filling stimulus intervals with interpolated activity, particularly when such activity is irrelevant to the task such as number tracking in Inhibited Rehearsal conditions, increased information-processing demands on subjects, thus reducing time utilized for rehearsal which consequently resulted in performance decrements.

If one assumes that increased rehearsal opportunities are primarily responsible for the facilitation which accompanies lengthening interunit (Post *I-F*) intervals in concept learning, this still does not account for the facilitative effects due to instance contiguity. As noted above, instance contiguity involves the filling of temporal intervals with task-relevant events whereas manipulating intratrial temporal variables has conventionally involved either unfilled intervals or intervals filled with non-relevant task events.

Again, let me cite an experiment involving paired-associates learning which bears on this point. Jones and Bourne (1964) report several experiments which have investigated effects of *I-F* intervals and Post *I-F* intervals on paired-associates learning. Experiments 1 and 2 report no effects of unfilled I-F intervals on verbal maze performance. In Experiment 3, the authors combined orthogonal combinations of 0-, 3-, and 6-second I-F and Post I-F intervals using the anticipation format much like the Nodine et al. experiment reported earlier. Both I-F and Post I-F intervals were unfilled. Trials to criterion were found inversely related to both I-F and Post I-F intervals, the effects being additive. Of particular interest are Experiments 4 and 5 in which task-relevant activities filled I-F intervals. This was accomplished by using what Jones and Bourne refer to as a trials-delay technique. Under this procedure, subjects were required to respond (anticipation format) to 2, 4, or 8 successive stimulus terms before receiving informative feedback in the form of either stimulus-response pairs (Experiment 5) or response terms alone (Experiment 6). The results indicated no effect on paired-associates performance due to I-F intervals in Experiment 5, but decreases in performance, in terms of increases in errors, were obtained as I-F intervals increased in Experiment 6.

There is a close resemblance between the method of manipulating I-F intervals in Jones and Bourne's Experiments 5 and 6 and the method of manipulating such intervals by instance contiguity. It is therefore not surprising that the Jones and Bourne data are in agreement with the instance contiguity data from concept learning where increasing the number of instances of different intervening concepts also results in decreasing performance (Cahill and Hovland, 1960; Hunt, 1961). The Jones and Bourne data are, however, in conflict with the Nodine, Nodine, and Thomas data in which paired-associates performance was found directly related to interstimulus (I-F) intervals. This relationship was consistent regardless of whether interstimulus intervals were filled with interpolated activities or remained unfilled in the Nodine et al. study.

Jones and Bourne's trials-delay procedure is most likely responsible for the conflict with the Nodine et al. data. It is only when partial information is removed during presentation by eliminating the stimulus terms and presenting only response terms as informative feedback (Experiment 6), that decrements in paired-associates performance occur as I-F intervals lengthen. Such a procedure decreases contiguity between stimulus term and response term by filling the inter-stimulus or *I-F* interval with task-relevant activity. The main finding from Experiment 6 was that errors increased as a function of the number of successive stimulus items presented prior to informative feedback. Considering the increased information-processing requirements on the part of subjects as the number of successive stimulus items increased in this task, one would expect large performance decrements. Under the trials-delay technique, subjects are not only required to make successive anticipation responses during stimulus-term presentation, but must remember the order of occurrence of each stimulus item in order to utilize the information in the form which follows. Subjects must retain order information about the sequence of stimulus items because informative feedback, which follows stimulus-term presentation, consists of only the presentation of response items rather than stimulus-response pairs. The short-term memory load, under these conditions, should increase directly with the number of successive stimulus items prior to informative feedback.

SHORT-TERM MEMORY AND CONCEPT LEARNING

The type of increased information-processing demands on subjects described in the Jones and Bourne experiment is similar to that encountered in concept learning as the result of decreasing instance contiguity. In concept learning, it is assumed that upon presentation of each concept instance, the subject must remember past instances of the same concept and compare them with the present instance in order to attain the correct concept. Memory load is reduced proportionally by the number of concept instances which intervene between instances of a given concept. Recent evidence by Restle and Emmerich (1966) indicates that subjects can process concurrently up to 2 problems, each consisting of 8 instance-concept pairs involving 3 dimensions, before short-term memory limitations influence performance. Unfortunately, the *I-F* interval (2 sec) was defined by the authors from the last response made by a group of subjects to onset of feedback rather than experimenter controlled. Such a definition precludes generalizations with reference to the *I-F* interval in concept-learning tasks.

I would now like to turn to investigations of short-term retention of paired associates, which have information-processing requirements similar to those found in concept learning. Murdock (1963), for example, found an orderly decrease in the proportion of responses correctly recalled as a function of the number of paired-associates units intervening between the presentation and recall of a critical pair. Peterson (1966) proposes that interference in the form of competition at recall is produced when temporal intervals are manipulated by the insertion of intervening task-relevant events such as additional paired-associate items. Such competition increases the probability of errors through changes in the subject's guessing probabilities.

Peterson has also shown that short-term retention improves as the spacing interval between repetitions of a paired-associate unit is lengthened from 0-16 seconds, and decreases from 16-32 seconds. Increasing the spacing interval between repetitions of a paired-associate unit could be considered analogous to decreasing instance contiguity in concept learning since, in both cases, presentation and test of other pairs fill the intervals. The Peterson data would suggest an optimum time interval of approximately 16 seconds between instances of the same concept under heterogeneous presentation before decreases in performance due to short-term memory occur. Increases in error probabilities due to competition plus temporal limitations on short-term memory may be able to account, in part, for the Jones and Bourne data and also the instance contiguity data although information on specific types of errors made in these situations is lacking. Together, these findings bring into focus the importance of short-term memory since increasing temporal intervals under instance contiguity conditions requires subjects to retain concept-relevant dimensions of each concept in order to achieve a discrimination among the several concepts in the face of increasing competition from intervening concepts.

Let me suggest that one way to reduce response competition is to increase exposure duration of the concept pair (Item c in Fig. 10.1) which should, as a consequence, increase opportunities for discrimination and rehearsal of the concept-relevant features of each instance of a concept stimulus. Increasing exposure durations of both stimulus terms and stimulus-response pairs have been shown to produce better performance in paired-associates learning (e.g., Nodine, 1963; Nodine, 1965), and, if one assumes that increasing exposure durations of stimulus-response events is equivalent to increasing the number of repetitions of these events, it would be expected that short-term memory should also improve as exposure durations increase. This relationship has been confirmed in several studies (e.g., Peterson, 1963; Jahnke and Davidson, 1966). Thus, I view concept learning as a combination of successive acquisitions during the pairing of concept stimuli and concept responses, and short-term retention between instances of a given concept. Accordingly, information derived from the paired-associates situation should be of considerable value in the specification of temporal parameters which influence the acquisition of conceptual behaviors.

CONCLUSION

Data from paired-associates learning and short-term memory experiments point to the importance of the role of temporal variables of presentation in concept learning. It is perhaps significant to note that mathematical models of concept learning (e.g., Bourne and Restle, 1959; Restle, 1962; Bower and Trabasso, 1964) have ignored both temporal variables of presentation and short-term memory aspects of the problem in considering concept learning. It is the view of the present paper that only models which incorporate such temporal variables can hope to explain human conceptual behavior. This statement should not be construed to imply that temporal variables per se are the important factors, rather, it is how these temporal intervals are filled by the subject that determines rates of acquisition in conceptual tasks.

CHAPTER 11   *Allen Newell and Herbert A. Simon*

Carnegie Institute of Technology

OVERVIEW: MEMORY AND PROCESS
IN CONCEPT FORMATION*

In the history of psychology, the topics of concept formation and memory have generally occupied separate chapters.
The case is easily made, however, that this separation could
not endure — that an adequate account of concept formation
and concept attainment must rest on an understanding of the
structure of both long-term and short-term memory.

Long-term memory is implicated because the subject
comes to the laboratory with a host of elementary and complex
concepts stored in memory, which he brings to bear on the task
posed for him by the experimenter. His behavior in the experiment is influenced by the repertory stored in memory as
significantly as it is by the experimental stimuli. In Bartlett's
Remembering (1932), the role of stored concepts is abundantly
clear; and Heidbredder's main experimental results were to
show that in our culture definite regularities exist in the relative availabilities in memory of different attribute dimensions.

Short-term memory is implicated because the subject is
called upon to extract and retain information from a series of
instances in order to determine the concept the experimenter
has chosen. As Bruner, Goodnow, and Austin (1956) demonstrated, the short-term memory load ("cognitive strain") has
important effects on the strategies that subjects choose in
performing concept-attainment tasks. Again, as Feldman
(1963) showed, limits on short-term memory enable subjects
to detect patterns in "noisy" sequences of stimuli where none
exist, that is, only the forgetting of earlier exceptions allows
a subject to infer simple patterns in a random sequence.

*This investigation was supported in part by the Public Health Service
Research Grant MH-0722 from the National Institute of Mental Health.*

241

This symposium was intended to provide additional evidence on the close connections between concept attainment and the structure of memory. Indeed, the papers of this volume do provide a fine collection of such evidence. A close perusal of the studies shows, however, that the role of the conceptual task is gradually retreating from the center of the stage, and is becoming chiefly a means for revealing underlying processes. It is the purpose of this final essay to show this — and to illustrate the continued dependence of concept formation on the structure and content of memory.

ON PROCESSING

The strongest theme common to the papers in this symposium is concern for the processing that occurs in a subject's central nervous system when he performs intellective tasks. It is striking that all of the papers make explicit and extensive reference to the process. The whole raison d'etre of Hunt's analysis is to explore the behaviorial consequences of different formally specified processing systems, testing, as it were, the range of possibilities within which one might search to discover the characteristics of the human processing system.

Professor Martin takes as his central theme the hypothesis that the process of inhibition is an essential component of all concept learning. Professor Peterson undertakes to explain some phenomena of free recall in paired-associate learning — a "classical" experimental task – by hypothesizing a response-generating process followed by a response-recognition process. Professor Cofer, in examining behavior on a forced recall task, likewise considers a total process composed of a generator and a recognizer.

The two papers in which interest in process is most elaborately developed are those of Professors Bourne and Gregg. An important reason for using relatively complex tasks, such as the ones employed in their experiments, is to get a better view of the sequential dependencies in behavior — that is, of the organization of processes. In Gregg's experiment, a single task may occupy the subject for 3 hours, with the result that a mass of detail can be recorded about his sequences of behavior. Bourne studies changes in the subject's behavior — that is, learning processes — under repeated exposure to the same task.

The strong interest of all the experimenters in the organization of process would have been startling a decade ago. To be sure, *S-R* psychology contained rudimentary theories of process. These were pretty much limited, however, to the notion that simple associations could be formed, broken, strengthened, and weakened. The structure of associations required to account for behavior was worked out only for extremely simple tasks. The then prevailing methodology of explaining responses as simple functions of stimuli encouraged the experimenter to abjure from describing the processes that intervened.

The papers in this volume testify to the radical change in the *Zeitgeist* that has occurred since World War II. Both necessity and possibility have prompted the change. It has gradually become apparent that to try to formulate stimulus-response regularities for complex behavior was about as feasible as constructing a theory of stethoscope noises without mention of the heart's pumping activity. Discussion of process was mothered by necessity.

At the same time, psychologists have discovered that there are ways of talking about process clearly, operationally, and without cloudiness or metaphysics. Hebb's (1949) neurological metaphors, combined with his careful analysis of the evidence in terms of process, contributed much to this development. What contributed especially was the gradual realization that one could reject or qualify Hebb's neurology without entirely destroying the content of his theory. Finally, the emergence of computer simulation languages has provided assurance — even to those who do not themselves use them — that formal process theories can describe the behavior of complex information processing systems. We are still so close to these developments that it is safest to leave their interpretation to future historians of science. What seems certain, and what is clearly illustrated by this symposium, is that many experimental psychologists today consider their task to include a discovery of the processes that provide the basis for the relation of response to stimulus.

Let us return to Hunt's paper to make a point about the concern with process. The belief that an organization of processes underlies a particular exhibited behavior entails the attempt to discover this organization. But the scientist's ability to propose candidate processes rests strongly on his understanding of what possible processes can perform the experimental task. Especially within the domain of intellectual tasks, such as concept attainment, processes which could produce the observed behavior are often unknown. Thus efforts aimed at the pure understanding of complex processes, such as Hunt's work on his concept-learning system, become an essential part of the scientific enterprise. As his paper testifies, there is much to be found out. Murdoch notes in his discussion that Hunt's work is not as pure an example of exploration of process as Hunt himself pretends, since it includes some systematic comparison of the behavior of *CLS* with the behavior of humans. Nevertheless, the main thing we take away from the work on *CLS* is an increased repetoire of processes from which to propose systems that fit human performance.

It is true, of course, that one cannot deduce structure unambiguously from function. Knowing that a given process can produce the behavior in question does not prove that it, rather than some functionally equivalent alternative, actually does produce it. However, the lesson to be drawn is that one must have an ever deepening understanding of processes so that alternatives can be enunciated and explored. We will encounter this point again in the examination of some of the papers below.

ON MEMORY

In information-processing systems, what processes can perform a given task depends critically on the structure and amount of memory available. Let us review briefly a few very general characteristics of human memory. These points are not novel, but appear to be shared, if not by all psychologists, at least by most of those who are willing to consider what goes on "between the ears."

Memory hierarchy. Information is stored in the central nervous system in a variety of forms, but in at least two different kinds of memories having quite different capacities, storage times, and access times. (There is evidence for additional forms, but we will need only the two discussed below.)

The *long-term memory* is essentially unlimited in size — it does not get "filled up." Its contents are as varied as human knowledge, employing an unknown variety of representations. A considerable part of its contents seem to be isomorphic with verbal symbols and associatively organized structures of verbal symbols, for example, binary relations (black-white) and ternary relations (color of apple is red). The *short-term memory* is very small indeed. Under some conditions, especially, it seems, when the contents are not being processed in any complex way, it appears to hold the famous seven chunks. Where the contents are undergoing active processing, its capacity seems closer to two. By recoding input material from many "small" chunks to fewer "large" chunks, its apparent capacity can be increased almost indefinitely. However, a symbol structure only becomes a chunk by being fixated in long-term memory (a process called in some contexts "familiarization").

Information can be stored and retrieved in short-term memory in a matter of a few hundred milliseconds. In long-term memory, although the retrieval process is of the same order as for short-term memory (a few hundred milliseconds), the storage process is more than an order of magnitude slower. It takes about 5 to 10 seconds for a normal young adult to form a new association between a pair of symbols that are already in associative store. While such figures hardly yet approach the status of universal constants, the large disparity in speed between long-term read and write processes is beyond doubt.

Serial processing. Anything that is being attended to must be held in short-term memory. Moreover, symbols must be held in short-term memory while they are being fixated, that is, transferred to long-term memory. Since the short-term memory has small capacity, this implies that the human is a serial processor as far as his deliberate mental behavior is concerned. However, this restriction does not bear on the question of parallelism in recognition — of the effect of being set to react to multiple alternatives.

Program memory. The long-term memory contains not only associative structures of symbols, but also structures that have the characteristics of programs - that is, enable the organization to do certain things. Note that a program is not simply a list of responses, but rather given additional data, is a schema for response. It is not the same thing to be able to respond with the number that is the average of several specific numbers (e.g., 7 is the average of 6 and 8) and to be able to respond to the average of any set of numbers when given (e.g., to have the program for summing, counting the number of items in the sum and dividing by that number). Psychology has never found it appropriate to provide formal empirical verification of the existence of programs (see Miller, Galanter, and Pribram, 1960) but almost every use of linguistic instructions in experimentation depends upon in their existence. These characterizations are seen to be quite compatible with the scheme proposed by Waugh and Norman (1965) who did not, however, elaborate long-term memory as much as we have here.

These specifications have strong consequences for the study of human behavior in general, and of concept formation and attainment which are the particular foci of this volume. First, the total amount of material in the long-term memory is very much greater than the amount that can be accessed or processed during the time of performance of any limited task. Even at 5 a second, less than five thousand retrievals can be made from long-term memory in a 15-minute experiment. Thus, although the whole content of the memory is potentially implicated in any given cognitive performance, only a minuscule fraction of the total is *actually* implicated, that is, exerts any influence on the performance.

Second, that long-term memory contains programs as well as "facts" means that the processes used in a task are not fixed. The methods, strategies, plans, etc. will not stay put, but vary from person to person and from occasion to occasion, depending on the content of long-term memory, and the fragment of it that is evoked. What does stay fixed, apparently, are processing rates and memory sizes. These certainly exert significant, and predictable, biases in the methods a subject can utilize to accomplish a task. In limiting situations, as in many short-term memory experiments, these features can be the most important, experimentally. But in more complex activity, such as concept formation, the subject has great scope for maneuvering and his behavior becomes acutely dependent on the particular programs evoked - that is, on the content of long-term memory.

In short, a processing system with the characteristics listed will strikingly exhibit the blind-men-and-elephant phenomenon. Different experimental tasks and experimental paradigms will "touch" different parts of the mechanism, and none of them will reflect the combined properties of the whole system. Furthermore, unless some care is taken to identify and label the various parts touched, the conclusion will be that of the blind men — that they are not talking about the same beast at all.

ON CONCEPTS

There is real diversity in the notions of concept used by the participants in this symposium. Almost any inferred use of organized information would seem to qualify. Bourne and Hunt are most in accord with the traditional research on concept identification and attainment: Subjects (human or program) are to classify objects as belonging or not belonging to the class defined by the concept. Gregg's experiment requires a somewhat broader notion, for while the class of objects is the class of members of the sequence, each object belongs not merely to the sequence but to a particular position in the sequence, defined by its relation to the preceding and following items. Cofer asks whether the concept of his lists are used by the subjects in their forced responses, and is able to pose this question experimentally without defining in detail how his subjects would represent the "concept of a list."

This diversity coupled, as Martin notes, with the fact that external operations, rather than internal processes, are used to define a particular variety of behavior, would seem to give free play to the blind-man-and-elephant spectre raised above. And so it does, unless one goes behind the external situation into the process that permits the organized information to be used. Since, however, these processes are inferred, one must pay special attention to the external signatures, exhibited in behavior, of different possible processes.

Thus, the outcome of a set of studies such as we have before us is not simply an additional set of empirical assertions about the forms of concept behavior. Rather, it consists of a number of distinct pieces:

1. Possible mechanisms that can produce the particular forms of conceptual behavior under question.
2. Empirical verification that these mechanisms are consistent with the behavior exhibited.
3. Discovery of unique behavioral consequences of the mechanisms, that permit their detection and identification (distinguishing them from other mechanisms known to be sufficient also for the task at hand).
4. Background verification of what is believed to be invariant - rate and capacity limits on both memory and processing.

With the freedoms mentioned in our discussion of memory, we must expect something akin to a catalog of mechanisms and identifying marks, instead of a few simple laws of uniform applicability. Keeping this view in mind, let us return to the studies at hand.

Generators and Tests

Given a system capable of associating a relatively arbitrary response with a relatively arbitrary stimulus, the simplest mechanism for any new task is a direct S-R evocation, either learned during the experimental session or evoked from past learning. This is the minimal processing assumption. There have been repeated attempts in the literature on concept formation and attainment to compare rote learning and concept learning in situations where the paired associate experimental paradigm can be made to apply (see, for example, Goldiamond, 1966). In this volume Gregg spends some time in such comparisons.

The next least complicated processing structure is "generate-and-test". That is, three processes are posited: a generator, which produces a sequence or set of candidates; a test, which determines whether a given candidate will be accepted or rejected; and a response process, which produces the actual response from the candidate. It is clear, in all events, that the generator does not produce the response itself, since the test must be able to intervene. Beyond that, however, the generator may produce more complex structures, such as hypotheses or rules. These themselves are, at least, generators of responses, and are evaluated by the test on the basis of feedback from the responses produced. In these cases, considerable processing may be required to generate an actual response.

Despite the difference in complexity between generators of responses (i.e., representations of single responses) and generators of response rules, there is much similarity in the organization of the two processing schemes. Peterson depends on this to tie his work in with concept formation:

> This view of concept learning as a search through hypotheses that become available to the subject will be applied in this paper to retrieval processes in general.

Our earlier remarks about the existence of programs in long term memory implies that from a processing point of view the generator is delivering associational structures, or access thereto, to immediate memory in either case.

Three papers, by Peterson, Martin, and Cofer, are concerned almost exclusively with generate-test processing organizations. The emphasis is either on the problem of identifying such an organization, which we noted was a key issue, or on establishing some properties of the component processes.

Professor Peterson's paper is devoted to exploring the possibility of a generate-test processing organization in the recall of verbal material. Although he considers a number of different aspects, the main event in his paper is the isolation and explanation of a particular observed feature of behavior. Its explanation is in terms of a generator with continuous learning combined with a test with all-or-none learning. This feature in the data is a discontinuity in probability of error prior to the last error, coupled with a continuous decrease in latency after the last error, that is, when the list has already been learned, as far as the error criterion is concerned. Gross aspects of the observed behavior rule out various standard explanations: The discontinuities give trouble to continuous learning assumptions; the decrease in errors before the last error as well as the continued decrease in latencies give trouble to all-or-none learning assumptions.

To support the generate-test model, Professor Peterson constructs a simulation. It is noteworthy that a critical part of his argument is provided by the failure of the simulation model when different, but also plausible, assumptions are substituted in it. Without this, the argument that the observed feature is an identifying signature of a generate-test organization would be much less strong.

The simulation is, however, incomplete. That is, what was provided in the simulation were laws that governed measurable properties of the various learning processes. No mechanisms were provided that would actually learn to recognize the correct items in a discontinuous fashion, nor was a mechanism suggested for the continuous shaping of the generator, although we have come to be relatively unquestioning about how probabilistic learning would in fact be carried out. The former poses the more intriguing question, since the obvious model of a discontinuous learning process is the generate-test model, but here we are concerned with the internal structure of the test phase alone.

That inference from performance to process is indeed a hazardous game (but no less worth playing for that), can be seen in Peterson's discussion of the effect class membership, digits versus letters, has on the interference during sequences of recall experiments. The effect is clear and eminently plausible - "the switch provides a change of context." But assigning the effect to the test or to the generator seems quite arbitrary. Humans appear to have direct generating processes available for either letters or digits, as well as recognizers for them. One might almost argue that if editing takes time, then the modification is most likely in the generator, not the editor. But this use of latencies to identify the process organization is really the central concern of Martin's paper.

We will largely ignore the assertions that Martin makes concerning the universality of the particular mechanisms that he proposes for conceptual behavior. It is clear from our initial comments that we expect a great pluralism of mechanisms, limited only by basic memory and processing constraints, the logic of the task, and the content of the subject's long-term memory. Since we view long-term memory as capable of holding programs, there is no necessity for physiological mechanisms, such as inhibition, to "show through" in behavior, although, equally, no reason why they should not show in appropriately designed tasks.

For us, then, the central core of Martin's paper is the proposal of a generate-test mechanism for producing conceptual behavior and the attempt to develop some signatures for it, so that one can identify when the proposed mechanism is operating. The generator is not one that produces candidate responses (Martin calls them response tendencies) sequentially, but one that activates simultaneously an entire set of response tendencies. Which set is activated is governed by the dimensions to which the organism is attending. The test phase involves the mutual inhibition of these responses so that, at least when all goes well, one and only one eventuates in overt behavior.

Separation of the process into a generation (or excitation) phase and a test (or inhibition) phase is part, it seems to us, of the assertion that the more alternatives evoked, the longer it takes the inhibitory processes to work. This argument underlies the use of lengthened RT as a signature of the conceptual behavior: Namely, the subject has a concept only if he has mutually induced response tendencies. These lead to more inhibition, hence longer RTs, than would singly-induced responses.

Alternative mechanisms are available for discrimination that do not imply inhibition, nor any version of the generate-and-test organization we have been discussing in this section. In particular, the sorting net schemes, as described in this symposium by Hunt and developed also in a program called EPAM by Feigenbaum and Simon (1963, 1964), involve not only selection without inhibition, but also predict that RT will increase with the number of alternatives. In fact, sorting nets, generally, predict the appropriate quantitative relationship as well; namely, that it is logarithmic in the number of alternatives.

Consider, for example, how EPAM[1] would operate in the experiment associated with Martin's Table 2.1. In Group I, the response does not require any discrimination process. In Groups II and III, it requires a net with a single node, sorting "circular shapes" from "square shapes" (number is irrelevant). The discrimination time in both cases is 325 msec. Group IV must make two discriminations - shape and number - and has an average discrimination time of 690 - 135 = 555 msec. The difference between 555/2 = 277.5 msec and 325 msec is only about 15%, in agreement with the hypothesis of a

---

[1] We use EPAM here, rather than *CLS*, because it is constructed to handle the experimental paradigms.

net with constant test times.

In the EPAM process, retrieval of the response to an associated pair involves discriminating the stimulus to retrieve cues identifying its associate, then discriminating the associate to make the response - two discriminations are involved. Thus in Martin's Fig. 2.3, conditions Compatible-C and Compatible-B require only a single discrimination (since the response is identical with the stimulus, hence retrieved as soon as the stimulus is discriminated). The Incompatible-B condition requires one discrimination plus production of a different, but constant, response, while the Incompatible-B condition requires two discriminations. The difference between C-B and I-B, 160 msec, is smaller than the time required for a discrimination in the experiment previously described but of course the stimuli are also quite different in the two experiments - visual in one and auditory in the other - and we should not expect quantitative agreement.

Our aim here is not to urge the validity of the discrimination net theory, but only to emphasize that the larder of possible mechanisms should be well stocked before we consider which one or ones are supported by the data. In fact, with Martin's data, we cannot find any reason for preferring a process involving inhibition to a process incorporating a discrimination net mechanism. Indeed, we have seen that the latter makes some substantiated quantitative predictions not provided by the former.

Cofer is also concerned with whether recall involves a generate-test organization or simply operates directly on the associational structure. The starting point, which Cofer quotes, is Deese's conclusion that no editing seems to be required to explain free recall of lists of verbal material. At least as far as number of items produced in recall and the nature of intrusions are concerned, Deese found they were functions of associational structure, hence appeared not to require a more complicated processing structure. But, to quote Cofer:

> My concern was with this interpretation. My point was that if subjects do not edit their recalls it is difficult to see why so many of them fail to approximate list length in their recall. Most subjects have some knowledge of list length — some actually count the words as they are presented. On the assumption that subjects would

want to perform as well as possible in this situation it might be expected that they would at least approximate list length in their recalls; it should be easy for them to do so if what they mainly do in recall is to give unedited associations to the items they do in fact remember, since all the list members employed are common words with easy and obvious associations. Failure to match list length, then seemed to me to be compatible with the notion that subjects do edit their recalls, and it led me to investigate the character of the responses subjects add when they are required to match list length.

Thus, the truncation of response becomes a possible signature of a generate-and-test process, and it seems to us that Cofer's investigation into what does govern forced recall can be viewed as an attempt to establish this signature, even though he does not return to the issue directly in his own conclusions.

Representation of Concepts in Memory

The experiments of Bourne and Gregg illustrate that as we turn toward more complex tasks, the range of possible mechanisms for performing the task increases. In analysing these works in detail, our underlying aim is to emphasize that such richness of mechanism is to be expected in general - not just in these particular experiments.

Bourne's experiments evoke the subject's ability to detect the presence or absence of simple properties (color, shape) in stimulus objects, and his prior understanding of relations like "and," "or," "if-then," and "if-and-only-if." In these experiments, the defining properties of a class may combine not only conjunctively (the narrowest notion of concept), but also disjunctively, conditionally, or bi-conditionally. The experiments focus on why, and whether, some of these relations are easier for subjects than others.

In these experiments the stimulus has 4 dimensions (not all relevant), with three values on each dimension.[2] Ignoring irrelevant dimensions, for a 2-dimensional conjunctive con-

---

[2] In his paper, Bourne uses the term "attribute" in reference to the value on a dimension, not the dimension itself. Because many writers use the pair attribute—value where Bourne used dimension—attribute, we shall avoid ambiguity by using dimension—value. Thus, color is a dimension; red, blue, green are its values.

cept 1 of the 9 possible stimulus classes would constitute positive instances, the remaining 8 classes, negative instances.
Bourne shows that the subjects behave as though the world
were even simpler - as though there were only 2 values on
each relevant dimension, and hence 4 classes of stimuli, 1
positive and 3 negative. Thus, if the concept is "red square,"
the subjects appear to handle a red triangle as though it were
"red non-square," and hence, as equivalent to a red circle.

The evidence that subjects treat the space of possible
classes as 2 × 2 rather than 3 × 3 is that they learn most of
the concepts by the time an example of each of the 2 × 2 classes
has been presented, and long before an example of each of the
3 × 3 classes has been presented. On the basis of this evidence,
Bourne concludes that "most subjects learn and use a strategy
which simplifies and facilitates this attainment process...
simplication of the problem seems to result from collapsing
...a 3 × 3 ...matrix of stimulus combination...to a four-fold
table."

The evidence certainly supports the hypothesis that subjects distinguish only 4 classes of stimuli, not 9, but not
necessarily that they represent the situation by a 4-fold
table, nor that they *learn* the representation in the course of
the experiment. Let us consider an alternative interpretation.

In the instructions, the subject is told which values are
relevant -- e.g., that the concept has to do with "red" and with
"square." [3] This suggests to him directly that the appropriate
perceptions are to determine whether a particular stimulus is
red (or not), and whether it is square (or not). Hence, the
subject may not need to learn to use the 2 × 2 classification,
by abstracting from the 3 × 3, but may be led directly to it by
the form of the instructions.

The 4-fold table is certainly one possible way in which
concepts of this kind could be represented in a subject's memory. The subject detects the presence or absence of each of 2
values in the object, and associates with each of the 4 possible

[3] It is not clear, incidentally, how the experimenter avoids suggesting
that the concept is conjunctive, and hence suggesting to the subject that he
try a conjunctive relation before any other. If, to most naive subjects,
"concept" means "conjunctive concept," the observation that conjunctive
concepts are easier than others (and that the advantage gradually dis-
appears) is immediately explained. However, this would not explain why
conditional and biconditional concepts are initially so much harder than disjunctive concepts.

outcomes of the pair of tests the appropriate response — positive or negative. Thus, for the disjunction, he would store: ++ = P, +- = P, -+ = P, -- = N. With this representation, concept learning becomes simply paired-associate learning. Bourne describes the process thus:

> The (subject's) routine is to observe the assignment of one example of each of the stimulus classes and then to classify all subsequent instances in accord with these examples. The plan reduces the potentially unlimited stimulus population to four classes, then merely maps these four onto a binary response system. While we have no reason to believe that the algorithm is carried out formally — attempts by subjects to tell us in post-experimental interviews about their own problem solving behavior are often rather unintelligible — our measures and analyses of category responses do strongly suggest the utilization of some such routine on an informal or intuitive level.
>
> Learning to use nominal, deterministic rules of the type considered in this research may be conceived as a two-phased process involving (a) reductive coding of a stimulus population to a small number of classes and (b) acquisition of the associations between classes and response categories.

Now in the last three experiments described by Bourne (III, IV, and V), the experimenter took explicit pains to induce subjects to behave in the way described by this algorithm. In these three experiments, the subject was supplied with 4 sample patterns, one representing each of the 4 stimulus classes; and these patterns were displayed, along with the response appropriate to each of the problems.

> Each group of four patterns was selected so that subjects could determine the relevant attributes and/or rule without responding to any of the stimuli presented in the problem. The fact that sample patterns provided sufficient information to solve the problem was indicated without explanation to all subjects.

In other words, in these experiments a subject could make the correct response on all trials, without fixating any of the concepts whatsoever (as paired associates or otherwise), by adopting the following algorithm, or its equivalent: Classify the stimulus on the two relevant values; find the sample pattern that belongs to the same class; observe the (displayed) response for that pattern; make the response.

In Experiment V, half the subjects were specifically trained to use the sample patterns in this way. Hence, that experiment, and to a lesser extent Experiments III and IV, must be regarded as a study of subjects' abilities to follow directions rather than a study of concept formation. This interpretation is supported by the finding that the pretrained subjects in Experiment V had little more difficulty with biconditional and conditional than with disjunctive and conjunctive concepts. That there were any differences at all between the different concepts is perhaps evidence that not all the subjects could follow directions or listened carefully to the instructions.

We must therefore regard the provision of sample patterns in these experiments as a fundamental change in the task — perhaps even taking it out of the realm of concept formation — and not as evidence that, in the absence of such information the subject represents the concept as a quartet of paired associates. In what other ways could he represent it?

Suppose, in analogy with the serial pattern representation discussed by Gregg, the subject acquired a process or "program" with the characteristics of the stimulus as inputs, and the response as output. The programs are built from a small set of elementary processes that the subject already has available:

TEST ( ), SET CONTENTS OF X = Y (symbolized by X ← Y), REPORT ( ),

and a few others that will be mentioned in a moment. Then, the program for a conjunction $(A. B)$, might go like this:

Test for A; if the test for A is positive, test for B. Report the outcome of the last test performed (i.e., "Negative" if A was negative; otherwise the outcome of B).

Assuming that the subject has associated the verbal response "Positive" with passing a test and "Negative" with failing it, we can write this program in a more or less formal language thus (where M means "short-term" memory)

Conjunction: M ← TEST(A)*
                IF (M) = +, THEN M ← TEST(B)
                M ← ASSOC((M))†
                REPORT(M)

* (Set contents of M to outcome of test for A)
† (Replace contents of M with associate of contents of M; i.e., "+" with "Positive" and "-" with "Negative")

Similarly, for the other concepts, we write

    Disjunction: M ← TEST(A)
                  IF (M) = -, THEN M ← TEST(B)
                  M ← ASSOC((M))
                  REPORT(M)

    Joint Denial: M ← TEST(A)
                  IF (M) = -, THEN M ← TEST (B)
                  M ← REVERSE(M)
                  M ← ASSOC((M))
                  REPORT(M)

    Conditional: M ← TEST(A)
                  IF (M) = -, THEN REVERSE (M), GO TO 1.
                  ELSE, M ← TEST((B))
                1 M ← ASSOC((M))
                  REPORT(M)

    Biconditional: M ← TEST(A)
                  IF (M) = +, THEN M ← TEST(B), GO TO 1.
                  ELSE, M ← TEST(B), REVERSE(M)
                1 M ← ASSOC((M))
                  REPORT(M)

The interpretation of the conditional instructions, "IF...
THEN....ELSE" is clear from standard programming usage; if
the condition is not satisfied, the instruction is simply skipped.
"REVERSE" means replace the test outcome with its opposite
(+ for - and - for +), and hence is identical with NEXT (on the
alphabet +, -) in the serial tasks. There is no guarantee that
if subjects stored concepts as programs, the programs would
be identical with the ones we have just written down. We have
simply written them in a way that a computer programmer
would regard as natural and intuitive.

If we think of the program steps as a list that the subject
must fixate in order to learn the concept, then we see that the
numbers of elements in the list for the conjunction (5), disjunction (5), and joint denial (6), are smaller than the numbers
for the conditional (8) and biconditional (9). Thus, the programs arrange the concepts in the same order of difficulty as do
the experimental data. The two conditional concepts have a

"GO TO" step not involved in the others (although they can be rewritten to avoid it). In a similar vein, neither conjunction nor disjunction require a "REVERSE" operation, while the three others do. As studies of language show, humans notoriously have difficulties with negations. In a way, these differences among the programs provide us with an embarrassment of riches, for they suggest a number of alternative reasons why some of the concepts might be more difficult then others.

In the paired-associate representation proposed by Bourne, there is no such asymmetry among the concepts; each requires the subject to learn precisely four pairs. Hence the present approach offers a more parsimonious route to the interpretation of the data. We will carry our speculations just a step further, not to argue that this particular representation is the one actually used by all or some of the subjects, but to show some of the implications that hypotheses about representation have for the data, and hence how we can go about testing process models that incorporate such hypotheses.

In Bourne's rule identification problems, the subject must acquire the concept, and then apply it. If the concept has the form of a program, there are still several possible means of acquisition. Programs for the conjunction, disjunction, conditional, and biconditional (or some of these) may already be stored in the memories of subjects in our culture; alternatively, the programs may be "assembled" from their elements when required for a task. Consider the former alternative. The subject can then generate the concepts from a stored list until he finds one that fits. It is plausible to assume that the concepts that have been used most frequently in the past will be generated first. Suppose the order is as given above. Now, for the conditional, the correct response agrees with the correct response for the conjunction in the cases TT and TF; it agrees with the correct response for the disjunction in the cases RR and FT; with neither in the case FF. The correct response for the biconditional agrees with conjunction in cases TT, TF, and FT; with disjunction, in case TT; with neither, in case FF. In Bourne's Tables 1.5 and 1.6, we see that few errors are made in TT, where conditional and biconditional agree with the easier concepts, and that many errors are made in the cases where the more difficult concepts disagree with disjunction. These data are consistent with the hypothesis that subjects first try conjunction, which is soon disconfirmed; then disjunction, but persist somewhat longer (for lack of a readily available alternative?) when it is disconfirmed.

This explanation only holds water if there is some kind of "discontinuity" between conjunction and disjunction, on the one hand, and the conditional concepts on the other - if the former are already available in memory, say, but the latter must be composed. Bourne reports additional data that make this hypothesis plausible. In his Experiment IV, subjects were pretrained on a concept, then switched to a new one. Bourne's Table 1.7 shows that subjects pretrained on the conditional learned the biconditional much faster than subjects trained on conjunction or disjunction. In fact, Bourne observes that: "All 9 subjects who solved the first biconditional in minimal trials were trained on the conditional rule."

Turning to Gregg's experiments, he presented his subjects with the task of reproducing 16 switch settings in a specified sequence. Formally, the task is identical with running a maze by the correction method; and also with learning a serial list of 16 nonsense syllables (although in this latter, the non-correction method is almost always employed). Gregg's data show clearly that when the stimulus (the sequence of correct settings) was constructed so as to allow subjects to detect and use "patterns," their performance was very different from the performance of subjects who had to learn a "random" sequence (one with no obvious sequential pattern). Subjects in the un-patterned condition took two or three times as many trials as subjects in the patterned conditions.

Such a shift is indicative of a shift in method - that is, in processing organization. In the one case, all the separate items are fixated, the strategy both of learning and responding corresponding to that used in a paired-associate task. In the other case, the pattern is discovered (at least by most of the subjects), only the pattern is fixated, and responding requires a process that takes pattern and current state as input and produces the next switch setting as response. Learning the pattern calls for fixating fewer symbols than does memorizing the entire sequence. It is this shrinking of the learning task, according to the theory, that accounts for the faster learning. The underlying fixation processes (e.g., 10 seconds per chunk) do not proceed faster in the patterned than in the random case; it is simply that fewer fixations are required.

For this explanation to hold, it must also be, that either both variations evoke the same discovery processes, although successful in one case and not in the other, or that these discovery processes take appreciably less time than the fixation processes. Likewise, responding, which involves more complex processes in the patterned than in the unpatterned case, must not account for a significant amount of time.

Thus, what we have here with a change in experimental conditions is not just a shift in a parameter, but two quite different organizations of processes. Both strategies reflect the structure of memory with its relative processing costs, as well as the structure of the task. The real thing we want is not to know, as an empirical fact, that patterned sequences take less time than random ones. Given that we knew the organization of processing and some rough measures of memory times, we could calculate the effect in the manner of an industrial time and motion study. It takes more detail than we have reviewed here, but not more detail than Gregg has given. Rather, what we do need to know is the organizations that subjects do have and when they are evoked or, as we have now said several times, by what clues they make their presence known.

The Content of Long-Term Memory

Our discussion of Bourne pointed up the strong effects of the content of long-term memory on behavior; how performance might depend on what concepts the subject already had available. This same phenomenon can be seen in several of the other papers. In Cofer's work, what associations the subject has to the stimulus words form a prime basis for responding to match list length. Certainly none of these associations are learned by the subject during the course of the single exposure, indeed, we get to know about them precisely because the words do not occur in the experimenter's list. Likewise, none of these associations "come" with the organism. They are contingent content, as contingent as a piece of gossip. Witness the quoted completion, "tomorrow creeps in the petty pace from."

In Gregg's experiment, too, content of long-term memory

is crucial. The subjects fashion their concepts in the patterned case from some familiar alphabets (the two symbols "left" and "right"), and familiar process-concepts ("same," "next," etc.). Those few subjects who had access to the concept of "binary alphabet" (and also evoked it in the experimental situation), proceeded with different processes and solved the problem very quickly.

The experimenter's natural reaction, perhaps, to the dependence of most experimental results on the contents of the memories that happen to come into the laboratory is either despair or the feeling that psychology should concentrate on the "basic mechanisms" that remain invariant under differences in memory content. As we have indicated, these invariant mechanisms, although crucial, may form only a very small part of the sum of mechanisms that control behavior.

However, we think the work in this volume is not reason for despair. Rather it teaches a different lesson: By relying on cultural regularities, one can find stable modes of behavior that will appear dependably. The variety in behavior, although unlimited in principle, can in reality be catalogued and made explicit.

Thus, to return to Cofer once more, it is possible to make strong predictions, based on cultural uniformities, about what words the subjects will write down in forced recall. Nearly half of these words will appear in the Russell-Jenkins association norm list for associates of the list name or list members. (Cofer states that "*less* than half of these forced responses appear to be associates," but, of course, given the total size of a subject's vocabulary, the fact that *nearly* half were associates is highly significant.) And Gregg is able to draw the basic conceptual apparatus ("same," "next," etc.) he posits of his subjects from the cultural norm, and not derive it specifically from his data. Exactly the same processing apparatus is posited by Feldman (1963) and by Simon and Kotovsky (1963) to explain other tasks involving behavior with sequential patterns of relatively well-educated American college youth.

CONCLUSION

We have reiterated two basic themes throughout the essay: (1) That there are a very few basic features of the processing system, among them memory size and accessing characteristics, which are very important and affect everything the organism does; and (2) that much of what passes for process and mechanism in complex behavior is either specified by long-term memory content, or depends on mechanisms so specified.

Thus the study of complex behavior, such as concept formation and attainment, involves the discovery of possible information processes for accomplishing various tasks within the constraints imposed by memory and processing limitations, and the behavioral cues to tell us when the different mechanism are being evoked. This leads to a science that is much more analogous to a highly elaborated physiology based on a rich biochemistry, than to a sparse mechanics based on a small finite axiom set. We think we see in the papers of this volume a number of contributions to this physiology.

REFERENCES

Archer, E. J. A re-evaluation of the meaningfulness of all possible CVC trigrams. Psychological Monographs, 1960, **74** (Whole No. 497).

Archer, E. J. On verbalizations and concepts: Comments on Professor Kendler's paper. In A. W. Melton (Ed.) Categories of Human Learning. New York: Academic Press, 1964.

Archer, E. J., Bourne, L. E., Jr., & Brown, F. G. Concept identification as a function of irrelevant information and instructions. Journal of Experimental Psychology, 1955, **49**, 153-164.

Ashby, W. R. Introduction to Cybernetics. New York: John Wiley & Sons, 1956.

Ashby, W. R. Design for a Brain (2nd Ed.). New York: John Wiley & Sons, 1960.

Bahrick, H. P. Retention curves - facts or artifacts? Psychological Bulletin, 1964, 1, 188-194.

Bahrick, H. P. The ebb of retention. Psychological Review, 1965, **72**, 60-73.

Bahrick, H. P., & Bahrick, P. O. A re-examination of the interrelations among measures of retention. Quarterly Journal of Experimental Psychology, 1964, **16**, 318-324.

Bandura, A. Psychotherapy as a learning process. Psychological Bulletin, 1961, **58**, 143-159.

Barnes, J. M., & Underwood, B. M. "Fate" of first-list associations in transfer theory. Journal of Experimental Psychology, 1959, **58**, 97-105.

Bartlett, F. C. Remembering. Cambridge: Cambridge University Press, 1932.

Bernbach, H. A. Stimulus learning and recognition in paired-associate learning. Unpublished Ph.D. thesis, University of Michigan, 1965.

Bertelson, P. Sequential redundancy and speed in a serial two-choice responding task. Quarterly Journal of Experimental Psychology, 1961, **12**, 90-102.

Bertelson, P. S-R relationships and reaction times to new versus repeated signals in a serial task. Journal of Experimental Psychology, 1963, **65**, 478-484.

Bilodeau, E. A. Retention. In E. A. Bilodeau (Ed.), Acquisition of Skill. New York: Academic Press, 1966.

Blick, K. A. Cultural primaries as a source of interference in short-term verbal retention. Journal of Experimental Psychology, 1965, **69**, 246-250.

263

Bourne, L. E., Jr.   Effects of delay of information feedback and task complexity of the identification of concepts. Journal of Experimental Psychology, 1957, 54, 201-207.

Bourne, L. E., Jr.   Human Conceptual Behavior. Boston: Allyn and Bacon, 1966.

Bourne, L. E. Jr.   Learning and utilization of conceptual rules. In Kleinmuntz, B. (Ed.). Concepts and the Structure of Memory. New York: John Wiley & Sons, 1967.

Bourne, L. E., Jr. & Bunderson, C. V.   Effects of delay of informative feedback and length of post feedback interval on concept identification. Journal of Experimental Psychology, 1963, 65, 1-5.

Bourne, L. E., Jr., Guy, D. E., Dodd, D. H., & Justesen, D. R.   Concept identification: The effects of varying length and informational components of the intertrial interval. Journal of Experimental Psychology, 1965, 69, 624-629.

Bourne, L. E., Jr., & Restle, F.   Mathematical theory of concept identification. Psychological Review, 1959, 66, 278-296.

Bousfield, W. A.   The occurrence of clustering in the recall of randomly arranged associates. Journal of General Psychology, 1953, 49, 229-240.

Bousfield, W. A., & Cohen, B. H.   The occurrence of clustering in the recall of randomly arranged words of different frequencies-of-usage. Journal of General Psychology, 1955, 52, 83-95.

Bower, G., & Trabasso, T.   Concept identification. In R. C. Atkinson (Ed.), Studies in Mathematical Psychology. Stanford: Stanford University Press, 1964, 32-94.

Briggs, G. E.   Acquisition, extinction and recovery functions in retroactive inhibition. Journal of Experimental Psychology, 1954, 47, 285-293.

Broadbent, D. E., & Gregory, M.   Donders b- and c-reaction and S-R compatibility. Journal of Experimental Psychology, 1962, 63, 575-578.

Bruce, D. R., & Cofer, C. N.   An examination of recognition in free recall as measures of acquisition and long-term retention. Journal of Experimental Psychology, 1967 (In press).

Bruner, J. S., Goodnow, J. J., & Austin, G. A.   A Study of Thinking. New York: John Wiley & Sons, 1956.

Bugelski, B. R.   Presentation time, total time, and mediation in paired-associate learning. Journal of Experimental Psychology, 1962, 63, 409-412.

Cahill, H. E., & Hovland, C. I.   The role of memory in the acquisition of concepts. Journal of Experimental Psychology, 1960, 59, 137-144.

Carr, H. A.   The quest for constants. Psychological Review, 1933, 40, 514-532.

Cofer, C. N.   Some evidence for coding processes derived from clustering in free recall. Journal of Verbal Learning and Verbal Behavior, 1966 (In press).

Cofer, C. N., Bruce, D. R., & Reicher, G. M.   Clustering in free recall as a function of certain methodological variations. Journal of Experimental Psychology, 1966, 71, 858-866.

Cofer, C. N., & Musgrave, B. S. (Eds).   Verbal Behavior and Learning. New York: McGraw-Hill, 1963.

Cohen, B. H.   Recall of categorized word lists. Journal of Experimental Psychology, 1963, **66**, 227-234.

Cohen, B. H., Bousfield, W. A., & Whitmarsh, G. A.   Cultural norms for verbal items in 43 categories. Technical Report No. 22, 1957, University of Connecticut, Contract Nonr 631(00), Office of Naval Research.

Conrad, R.   Serial order intrusions in immediate memory. British Journal of Psychology, 1960, **51**, 45-48.

Conrad, R.   Acoustic confusions in immediate memory. British Journal of Psychology, 1964, **55**, 75-84.

Deese, J.   Influence of inter-item associative strength upon immediate free recall. Psychological Reports, 1959 (a), **5**, 305-312.

Deese, J.   On the prediction of occurrence of particular verbal intrusions in immediate free recall. Journal of Experimental Psychology, 1959 (b), **58**, 17-22.

Deese, J.   From the isolated verbal unit to connected discourse. In C. N. Cofer (Ed.). Verbal Learning and Verbal Behavior. New York: McGraw-Hill, 1961, Pp. 11-31.

Diamond, S., Balvin, R. S., & Diamond, F. R.   Inhibition and Choice. New York: Harper & Row, 1963.

Dollard, J., & Miller, N. E.   Personality and Psychotherapy. New York: McGraw-Hill, 1950.

Dominowski, R. L.   Role of memory in concept learning. Psychological Bulletin, 1965, **63**, 271-280.

Ekstrand, B. R.   A note on measuring response learning during paired-associate learning. Journal of Verbal Learning and Verbal Behavior, 1966, **5**, 344-347.

Estes, W. K., & Taylor, H. A.   A detection method and probabilistic models for assessing information processing from brief visual displays. Proceedings of the National Academy of Science, 1964, **52**, 446-454.

Favreau, O.   Proactive decremental effects on response speed in a continuous DRT task. Psychonomic Science, 1964, **1**, 319-320.

Feigenbaum, E. A.   The simulation of verbal learning behavior, Proceedings of Western Joint Computer Conference, 1961, 121-132 (Also reprinted in Feigenbaum, E. A., & Feldman, J. (Eds.). Computers and Thought. New York: McGraw-Hill, 1963).

Feigenbaum, E. A.   The simulation of verbal learning behavior. In Feigenbaum, E. A., & Feldman, J. (Eds.). Computers and Thought. New York: McGraw-Hill, 1963.

Feigenbaum, E. A., & Simon, H. A.   An information-processing theory of some effects of similarity, familiarization, and meaningfulness in verbal learning. Journal of Verbal Learning and Verbal Behavior, 1964, **3**, 385-396.

Feldman, J.   Simulation of behavior in the binary choice experiment. In Feigenbaum, E. A., and Feldman, J. (Eds). Computers and Thought. New York: McGraw-Hill, 1963.

Ferrier, D.   The Function of the Brain. London: Smith Elder, 1876.

Fitts, P. M., Peterson, J. R., & Wolpe, G.   Cognitive aspects of information processing: II. Adjustments to stimulus redundancy. Journal of Experimental Psychology, 1963, **65**, 423-432.

Fitts, P. M., & Switzer, G.   Cognitive aspects of information processing:
    I. The familiarity of S-R sets and subsets.   Journal of Experimental Psy-
    chology, 1962, 63, 321-329.
Forrin, B., & Morin, R. E.   Effect of contextual associations upon selective
    reaction time in a numeral-naming task.   Journal of Experimental Psy-
    chology, 1966, 71, 40-46.
Garner, W. R.   Uncertainty and Structure as Psychological Concepts.   New
    York: John Wiley & Sons, 1962.
Garner, W. R., & Whitman, J. R.   Form and amount of internal structure as
    factors in free-recall learning of nonsense words.   Journal of Verbal
    Learning and Verbal Behavior, 1965, 4, 257-266.
Gibson, E. J.   Sensory generalization with voluntary reactions.   Journal of
    Experimental Psychology, 1939, 24, 237-253.
Gibson, E. J.   A systematic application of the concepts of generalization
    and differentiation to verbal learning.   Psychological Review, 1940, 47,
    196-229.
Goldiamond, I.   Perception, language and conceptualization rules.   In B.
    Kleinmuntz (Ed.).   Problem Solving: Research, Method and Theory.   New
    York: John Wiley & Sons, 1966.
Gonzales, R. C., & Cofer, C. N.   Exploratory studies of verbal context by
    means of clustering in free recall.   Journal of Genetic Psychology, 1959,
    95, 293-320.
Goss, A. E.   A stimulus-response analysis of the interaction of cue-produc-
    ing and instrumental responses.   Psychological Review, 1955, 62, 20-31.
Goss, A. E.   Verbal mediating responses and concept formation.   Psycho-
    logical Review, 1961, 68, 248-274.
Goss, A. E.   Paired-associates and connected discourse in the acquisition
    of knowledge.   Paper presented at Symposium on Verbal Learning Re-
    search and the Technology of Written Instruction sponsored by the Office
    of Naval Research through the Bell Telephone Laboratories, March, 1966.
Green, E. J.   Concept formation: A problem in human operant condition-
    ing.   Journal of Experimental Psychology, 1955, 49, 175-180.
Gregg, L. W., & Olshavsky, R.   Latency Measures of Implicit Information
    Processes as a Function of Task Complexity, Complex Information
    Processing Working Paper No. 89, Carnegie Institute of Technology,
    Pittsburgh, Pa., May 31, 1966.
Guthrie, E. R.   The Psychology of Learning.   (Rev. Ed.)   New York:
    Harper, 1952.
Guttman, R., & Kalish, H. J.   Discriminability and stimulus generalization.
    Journal of Experimental Psychology, 1956, 51, 79-88.
Gynther, M. D.   Differential eyelid conditioning as a function of stimulus
    similarity and strength of response to the CS.   Journal of Experimental
    Psychology, 1957, 53, 408-416.
Haygood, R. C., & Bourne, L. E., Jr.   Attribute- and rule-learning aspects
    of conceptual behavior.   Psychological Review, 1965, 72, 175-195.
Haygood, R. C., & Kiehlbauch, J. B.   Effects of logical pre-training on con-
    cept rule-learning performance.   Kansas State University: Dittoed, 1965.
Hebb, D. O.   The Organization of Behavior.   New York: John Wiley & Sons,
    1949.

Herrnstein, R. J., & Loveland, D. H.   Complex visual concept in the pigeon. Science, 1964, **146**, 549-551.

Hilgard, E. R.   The relationship between the conditioned response and conventional learning experiments. Psychological Bulletin, 1937, **34**, 61-102.

Holland, J. G.   Teaching machines: An application of principles from the laboratory. Journal of Experimental Analysis of Behavior, 1960, **3**, 275-287.

Holland, J. G.   New directions in teaching-machine research. In J. E. Coulson (Ed.). Programmed Learning and Computer-based Instruction, New York: John Wiley & Sons, 1962.

Hovland, C. I.   A "Communication Analysis" of concept learning. Psychological Review, 1952, **59**, 461-472.

Hovland, C. I., & Weiss, W.   Transmission of information concerning concepts through positive and negative instances. Journal of Experimental Psychology, 1953, **45**, 175-182.

Hull, C. L.   A functional interpretation of the conditioned response. Psychological Review, 1929, **36**, 498-511.

Hull, C. L.   Simple trial and error learning: A study in psychological theory. Psychological Review, 1930 (a), **37**, 241-256.

Hull, C. L.   Knowledge and purpose as habit mechanisms. Psychological Review, 1930 (b), **37**, 511-525.

Hull, C. L.   Principles of Behavior. New York: Appleton-Century-Crofts, 1943.

Hunt, E. B.   Memory effects in concept learning. Journal of Experimental Psychology, 1961, **62**, 598-604.

Hunt, E. B.   Concept Learning: An Information Processing Problem New York: John Wiley & Sons, 1962.

Hunt, E. B.   Criteria for establishing locally optimal diagnostic test sequences. Working paper 88, Western Management Science Institute, University of California, Los Angeles. 1965.

Hunt, E. B., & Kreuter, J. M.   The Development of Decision Trees in Concept Learning: III. Learning the Connectives. Los Angeles, Western Management Sciences Institute, 1962.

Hunt, E. B., Marin, Janet, & Stone, P. J.   Experiments in Induction. New York: Academic Press, 1966.

Hyman, R.   Stimulus information as a determinant of reaction time. Journal of Experimental Psychology, 1953, **45**, 188-196.

Jahnke, J. C., & Davidson, W. R.   The effects of three temporal variables on short-term memory for paired associates. Paper read at Midwestern Psychological Association meetings, Chicago, May, 1966.

James, William.   Principles of Psychology: Vol. I. Holt, New York, 1890.

Jaynes, J.   The routes of science. American Scientist, 1966, **54**, 94-102.

Jenkins, J. J., & Russell, W. A.   Associative clustering during recall. Journal of Abnormal and Social Psychology, 1952, **47**, 818-821.

Jones, R. E., & Bourne, L. E., Jr.   Delay of informative feedback in verbal learning. Canadian Journal of Psychology, 1964, **18**(4), 266-280.

Kemeny, J. G., Snell, J. L., & Thompson, G. L.   Introduction to Finite Mathematics. New York: Prentice-Hall, 1956.

Kendler, H. H.   The concept of the concept. In A. W. Melton (Ed.). Categories of Human Learning. New York: Academic Press, 1964, 211-236.

Kendler, H. H., & Kendler, T. S.   Vertical and horizontal process in problem solving. Psychological Review, 1962, 69, 1-16.

Kendler, T. S.   Concept formation. Annual Review of Psychology, 1961, 12, 447-472.

Keppel, G., & Rehula, R. J.   Rate of presentation in serial learning. Journal of Experimental Psychology, 1965, 69, 121-126.

Keppel, G., & Underwood, B. J.   Proactive inhibition in short-term retention of single items. Journal of Verbal Learning and Verbal Behavior. 1962, 1, 153-161.

King, D. J., Cole, N., Kinsey, D., & Sheffers, J.   The influence of inter-item interval on the learning of connected meaningful material. (Personal communication, 1966).

King, W.   A developmental study of rule learning. Ph.D. Dissertation, University of Colorado, 1964.

Koffka, K.   The Growth of Mind. (Transl. R. M. Ogden). New York: Harcourt, Brace, 1925.

Konorski, J.   The physiological approach to the problem of recent memory. In J. F. Delafresnaye (Ed.). Brain Mechanisms and Learning. Oxford: 1961, 115-132.

Krechevsky, I.   "Hypotheses" in rats. Psychological Review, 1932, 39, 516-532.

Lashley, K. S.   The problem of serial order in behavior. In L. A. Jeffress (Ed.). Cerebral Mechanisms in Behavior. New York: John Wiley & Sons, 1951, 112-136.

Laughery, K. R., & Gregg, L. W.   Simulation of human problem-solving behavior. Psychometrika, 1962, 27, 265-282.

Lawrence, D. H.   The nature of a stimulus: Some relationships between learning and perception. In S. Koch (Ed.). Psychology: A Study of a Science. New York: McGraw-Hill, 1963. 5, 179-212.

Levine, M.   The assumption concerning "wrongs" in Restle's model of strategies in cue learning. Psychological Review, 1963, 70, 559-564.

Lloyd, K. E.   Retention of responses to stimulus classes and to specific stimuli. Journal of Experimental Psychology, 1960, 59, 54-59.

Lloyd, K. E., Reid, L. S., & Feallock, J. B.   Short-term retention as a function of the average number of items presented. Journal of Experimental Psychology, 1960, 60, 201-207.

Loess, H.   Proactive inhibition in short-term memory. Journal of Verbal Learning and Verbal Behavior, 1964, 3, 362-368.

Loess, H.   Proactive inhibition and word category in short-term memory. Paper presented at meetings of the Midwestern Psychological Association, St. Louis, Missouri, 1965.

Mandler, G.   Response factors in human learning. Psychological Review, 1954, 61, 235-244.

Mandler, G.   Organization and memory. In K. W. Spence and J. T. Spence (Eds.). The Psychology of Learning and Motivation: Advances in Research and Theory. New York: Academic Press, 1966 (In press).

Marschak, J.   Decision making. Western Management Science Institute Working Paper 93, University of California, Los Angeles, 1965.

Martin, E.   Concept utilization. In R. D. Luce, R. R. Bush, & E. Galanter (Eds.). Handbook of Mathematical Psychology, Vol. III, New York: John Wiley & Sons, 1965, 205-247.

Martin, E. Stimulus recognition in aural paired-associate learning. Journal of Verbal Learning and Verbal Behavior, (In press).

McGeoch, J. A., & McKinney, F. Studies in retroactive inhibition: VIII. The influence of relative order of presentation of original and interpolated paired-associates. Journal of Experimental Psychology, 1937, 20, 60-83.

McGovern, J. B. Extinction of associations in four transfer paradigms. Psychological Monograph, 1964, 78, Whole No. 593.

McGuire, W. J. A multiprocess model for paired-associate learning. Journal of Experimental Psychology, 1961, 62, 335-347.

McKinney, F., & McGeoch, J. A. The character and extent of transfer in retroactive inhibition: Disparate serial lists. American Journal of Psychology, 1935, 47, 409-423.

McLean, R. S., & Gregg, L. W. The effects of induced chunking on temporal aspects of serial recitation. Journal of Experimental Psychology, 1967, (In press).

Melton, A. W. The taxonomy of human learning: Overview. In A. W. Melton (Ed.). Categories of Human Learning. New York: Academic Press, 1964.

Melton, A. W., & Irwin, J. McQ. The influence of degree of interpolated learning on retroactive inhibition and the overt transfer of specific responses. American Journal of Psychology, 1940, 53, 173-203.

Melton, A. W., & VonLackum, W. J. Retroactive and proactive inhibition in retention: Evidence for a two-factor theory of retroactive inhibition. American Journal of Psychology, 1941, 54, 157-173.

Merkel, J. Die zeitlichen Verhältnisse der Willensthätigkeit. Philosophische Studien, 1885,.2, 73-127.

Miller, G. The magic number seven, plus or minus two; some limits on our capacity for processing information. Psychological Review, 1956, 63, 81-97.

Miller, G. A. Language and communication. McGraw-Hill, New York, 1951.

Miller, G. A., Galanter, E., & Pribram, K. Plans and the Structure of Behavior. New York: Holt, 1960.

Morin, R. E., Forrin, B., & Archer, W. Information processing behavior: The role of irrelevant stimulus information. Journal of Experimental Psychology, 1961, 61, 89-96.

Mowbray, G. H. Perception and retention of verbal information presented during auditory shadowing. Journal of the Acoustical Society of America, 1964, 36, 1459-1464.

Murdock, B. B., Jr. Short-term memory and paired-associate learning. Journal of Verbal Learning and Verbal Behavior, 1963, 2, 320-328.

Musgrave, B. S., Cohen, J. C., & Stewart, M. T. Superordination and subordination in verbal hierarchy learning. Paper presented at Eastern Psychological Association meetings, New York, April, 1966.

Neisser, U., & Weene, P. Hierarchies in concept attainment. Journal of Experimental Psychology, 1962, 64, 640-645.

Newell, A. (Ed.). Information Processing Language-V Manual, Second Edition. Englewood Cliffs, New Jersey: Prentice-Hall, 1964.

Newell, A. Limitations of the current stock of ideas about problem solving in Kent, A. (Ed.). Electronic Information Handling, Washington: Spartan, 1965.

Newell, A., Shaw, J. C., & Simon, H. 1957 Empirical explorations of the logic theory machine. Proceedings of Western Joint Computer Conference, 1957, 218-239.

Newell, A., Shaw, J. C., & Simon, H. 1959 Report on a general problem solving program. Proceedings International Conference on Information Processing, Paris: UNESCO House, 1959.

Newman, S. E. Effects of contiguity and similarity on the learning of concepts. Journal of Experimental Psychology, 1956, 52, 349-353.

Nilsson, N. Learning Machines. New York: McGraw-Hill, 1965.

Nodine, C. F. Stimulus durations and stimulus characteristics in paired-associates learning. Journal of Experimental Psychology, 1963, 66, 100-106.

Nodine, C. F. Stimulus durations and total learning time in paired-associates learning. Journal of Experimental Psychology, 1965, 69, 534-536.

Nodine, C. F. Temporal parameters in paired-associates learning. Research Bulletin No. 2, Carnegie Institute of Technology, September, 1966.

Nodine, C. F., & Nodine, B. F. Stimulus intervals, stimulus durations and difficulty level in paired-associates learning. Journal of Experimental Psychology, 1966, 72, 156-158.

Nodine, C. F., & Nodine, B. F., & Thomas, R. C. Temporal variables in paired-associates learning: The roles of repetition and number tracking during stimulus intervals. Journal of Experimental Psychology, (In press).

Norman, D. A., & Wickelgren, W. A. Short-term recognition memory for single digits and pairs of digits. Journal of Experimental Psychology, 1965, 70, 479-489.

Noyd, D. E. Proactive and intrastimulus interference in short-term memory for two-, three-, and five-word stimuli. Paper presented at meetings of the Western Psychological Association, Honolulu, Hawaii, 1965.

Olshavsky, R. W. Reaction time measures of information processing behavior." June, 1965, Unpublished Master's Thesis.

Oseas, L., & Underwood, B. J. Studies of distributed practice: V. Learning and retention of concepts. Journal of Experimental Psychology, 1952, 43, 143-148.

Osgood, C. E. The similarity paradox in human learning: A resolution. Psychological Review, 1949, 56, 132-143.

Parks, T. E. Signal-detectability theory of recognition-memory performance. Psychological Review, 1966, 73, 44-59.

Pavlov, I. P. Conditioned Reflexes. (Transl. G. V. Anrep). Oxford: Oxford University Press, 1927.

Peterson, L. R. Associative memory over brief intervals of time. Journal of Verbal Learning and Verbal Behavior, 1963, 2, 102-106.

Peterson, L. R. Paired-associate latencies after the last error. Psychonomic Science, 1965, 2, 167-168.

Peterson, L. R. Short-term verbal memory and learning. Psychological Review, 1966, 73, 193-207.

Peterson, L. R., Brewer, C. L., & Bertucco, R.   A guessing strategy with the anticipation technique. Journal of Experimental Psychology, 1963, **65**, 258-264.

Peterson, L. R., & Gentile, Antoinette.   Proactive interference as a function of time between tests. Journal of Experimental Psychology, 1965, **70**, 473-478.

Peterson, L. R., & Peterson, M. J.   Short-term retention of individual verbal items. Journal of Experimental Psychology, 1959, **58**, 193-198.

Peterson, L. R., Saltzman, D., Hillner, K., & Land, V.   Recency and frequency in paired-associate learning. Journal of Experimental Psychology, 1962, **63**, 396-403.

Peterson, M. J.   Some effects of the percentage of relevant cues and presentation methods on concept formation. Journal of Experimental Psychology, 1962, **64**, 623-627.

Postman, L.   Short-term memory and incidental learning. In A. W. Melton (Ed.). Categories of Human Learning. New York: Academic Press, 1964, 145-201.

Postman, L., & Kaplan, H. L.   Reaction time as a measure of retroactive inhibition. Journal of Experimental Psychology, 1947, **37**, 136-145.

Postman, L., Keppel, G., & Stark, K.   Unlearning as a function of the relationship between successive response classes. Journal of Experimental Psychology, 1965, **69**, 111-118.

Postman, L., & Page, R.   Retroactive inhibition and psychophysical judgment. American Journal of Psychology, 1947, **60**, 367-377.

Postman, L., & Sassenrath, J.   The automatic action of verbal rewards and punishments. Journal of General Psychology, 1961, **65**, 109-136.

Quillian, R.   Word concepts: A theory and simulation of some basic semantic capabilities. Complex Information Processing Working Paper No. 79, Carnegie Institute of Technology, Pittsburgh, Pa., April 5, 1965.

Restle, F.   The selection of strategies for cue learning. Psychological Review, 1962, **69**, 329-343.

Restle, F., & Emmerich, D.   Memory in concept attainment: Effects of giving several problems concurrently. Journal of Experimental Psychology, 1966, **71**, 794-799.

Richardson, J.   Association among stimuli and the learning of verbal concept lists. Journal of Experimental Psychology, 1960, **60**, 290-298.

Richardson, J.   The learning of concept names mediated by concept examples. Journal of Verbal Learning and Verbal Behavior, 1962, **1**, 281-288.

Rosecrance, R.   Action and Reaction in World Politics   Boston: Little, Brown, 1963.

Rothkopf, E. Z., & Coke, E. U.   Variations in phrasing, repetition intervals, and the recall of sentence material. Journal of Verbal Learning and Verbal Behavior, 1966, **5**, 86-91.

Russell, W. A., & Jenkins, J. J.   The complete Minnesota norms for responses to 100 words from the Kent-Rosanoff Word Association Test. Technical Report No. 11, University of Minnesota, Contract N8/ONR 66216, Office of Naval Research, 1954.

Scheffe, H.   The Analysis of Variance. New York: John Wiley & Sons, 1959.

Seibel, R. An experimental paradigm for studying the organizations and strategies utilized by individual Ss in human learning and an experimental evaluation of it. Paper presented at meetings of Psychonomic Society, Niagara Falls, Ontario, October, 1964.

Seibel, R. Organization in human verbal learning: The study sheet paradigm and experiments one and two. Paper presented at meetings of Psychonomic Society, Chicago, October, 1965.

Shepard, R. N., Hovland, C. I., & Jenkins, H. M. Learning and memorization of classifications. Psychological Monographs, 1961, 75, No. 13.

Shepard, R. N., & Teghtsoonian, M. Retention of information under conditions approaching a steady state. Journal of Experimental Psychology, 1961, 62, 302-309.

Sherrington, C. S. The Integrative Action of the Nervous System. New Haven: Yale University Press, 1906.

Simon, H. A., & Kotovsky, K. Human acquisition of concepts for sequential patterns. Psychological Review, 1963, 70, 534-546.

Skinner, B. F. Two types of conditioned reflex and a pseudo-type. Journal of General Psychology, 1935, 12, 66-77.

Skinner, B. F. Two types of conditioned reflex: A reply to Konorski and Miller. Journal of General Psychology, 1937, 16, 272-279.

Skinner, B. F. Teaching machines. Science, 1958, 128, 969-977.

Slagle, J. A heuristic program that solves symbolic integration problems in Freshman calculus. Journal of the Association for Computing Machinery, 1963, 16, 507-520.

Sokolov, Ye. N. Perception and the Conditioned Reflex. (Transl. S. W. Waydenfeld) New York: Macmillian, 1963.

Spence, K. W. Conceptual models of spatial and non-spatial selective learning. In Behavior Theory and Learning, Selected Papers. Englewood Cliffs: Prentice-Hall, 1960, 366-392.

Steiner, C. M. An investigation of Freud's attention cathexis theory in the context of a concept formation task. Unpublished doctoral dissertation, University of Michigan, 1965.

Suppes, P. Mathematical concept formation in children. American Psychologist, 1966, 21, 139-150.

Terrace, H. S. Errorless discrimination learning in the pigeon: Effects of chlorpromazine and imipramine. Science, 1963, 140, 318-319.

Terrace, H. S. Wavelength generalization after discrimination learning with and without errors. Science, 1964, 144, 78-80.

Thorndike, E. L. Human Learning. New York: Century, 1931.

Thorndike, E. L. The Fundamentals of Learning. New York: Teachers College, Columbia University, 1932.

Thorndike, E. L., & Lorge, I. The Teacher's Wordbook of 30,000 Words. New York: Bureau of Publications, Teachers College, Columbia University, 1944.

Titchener, E. B. A Text-Book of Psychology. New York: Macmillian, 1910.

Tulving, E. Subjective organization in free recall of "unrelated" words. Psychological Review, 1962, 69, 344-354.

Tulving, E. Free recall. In T. R. Dixon & D. L. Horton (Eds.). Verbal Behavior and Its Relation to General S-R Theory. Englewood Cliffs, New Jersey: Prentice-Hall, 1966.

Underwood, B. J. The effect of successive interpolations on retroactive and proactive inhibition. Psychological Monographs, 1945, 59, Whole Number 273.

Underwood, B. J. "Spontaneous" recovery of verbal associations. Journal of Experimental Psychology, 1948, 38, 429-439.

Underwood, B. J. Retroactive inhibition with increased recall-time. American Journal of Psychology, 1950 (a), 63, 67-77.

Underwood, B. J. Proactive inhibition with increased recall-time. American Journal of Psychology, 1950 (b), 63, 594-599.

Underwood, B. J. An orientation for research on thinking. Psychological Review, 1952, 59, 209-220.

Underwood, B. J. Ten years of massed practice on distributed practice. Psychological Review, 1961, 68, 229-247.

Underwood, B. J. Stimulus selection in verbal learning. In C. N. Cofer & B. S. Musgrave (Eds.). Verbal Behavior and Learning: Problems and Processes. New York: McGraw-Hill, 1963, 33-48.

Underwood, B. J. The representativeness of rote verbal learning. In A. W. Melton (Ed.). Categories of Human Learning. New York: Academic Press, 1964, 47-78.

Underwood, B. J. False recognitions produced by implicit verbal responses. Journal of Experimental Psychology, 1965, 70, 122-129.

Underwood, B. J., Ekstrand, B. R., & Keppel, G. Studies of distributed practice: XXIII. Variations in response term interference. Journal of Experimental Psychology, 1964, 68, 201-212.

Underwood, B. J., & Richardson, J. Verbal concept learning as a function of instructions and dominance level. Journal of Experimental Psychology, 1956, 51, 229-238.

Underwood, B. J., & Schulz, R. W. Meaningfulness and Verbal Learning. Chicago: Lippincott, 1960.

Van de Geer, J. P., & Jaspars, J. F. M. Cognitive functions. Annual Review of Psychology, 1966, 17, 145-176.

Vinacke, W. E. The investigation of concept formation. Psychological Bulletin, 1951, 48, 1-31.

Waugh, N. C., & Norman, D. A. Primary memory. Psychological Review, 1965, 72, 89-104.

Wells, H. Effects of transfer and problem structure in disjunctive concept formation. Journal of Experimental Psychology, 1963, 65, 63-69.

Whitman, J. R., & Garner, W. R. Concept learning as a function of form of internal structure. Journal of Verbal Learning and Verbal Behavior, 1963, 2, 195-202.

Wickens, D. D. Stimulus-response theory as applied to perception. Kentucky Symposium on Learning Theory, Personality Theory, and Clinical Research. New York: John A. Wiley & Sons, 1954, 22-35.

Wickens, D. D., Born, D. G., & Allen, C. K. Proactive inhibition and item similarity in short-term memory. Journal of Verbal Learning and Verbal Behavior, 1963, 2, 440-445.

Wilcoxon, F. Some rapid approximate statistical procedures. New York: American Cyanamid Company, 1949.

Winer, B. J. Statistical Principles in Experimental Design. New York: McGraw-Hill, 1962.

Wittlinger, R., & Voss, J. F.   Acquisition of S_1-R, S_2-R paired-associates as a function of S_1-R, S_2-R probability. Journal of Experimental Psychology, 1964, **68**, 407-412.

Wolpe, J., Salter, A., & Reyna, L. J.   The Conditioning Therapies. New York: Holt, Rinehart and Winston, 1964.

Yntema, D. B., & Mueser, G. E.   Remembering the present states of a number of variables. Journal of Experimental Psychology, 1960, **60**, 18-22.

Yntema, D. B., & Mueser, G. E.   Keeping track of variables that have few or many states. Journal of Experimental Psychology, 1962, **63**, 391-395.

Yntema, D. B., & Trask, F. P.   Recall as a search process. Journal of Verbal Learning and Verbal Behavior, 1963, **2**, 65-74.

Author Index

275

Subject Index